J. D.
SALINGER

A Study of the Short Fiction

Also available in Twayne's Studies in Short Fiction Series

Jorge Luis Borges: A Study of the Short Fiction by Naomi Lindstrom
Willa Cather: A Study of the Short Fiction by Loretta Wasserman
John Cheever: A Study of the Short Fiction by James O'Hara
Stephen Crane: A Study of the Short Fiction by Chester Wolford
Andre Dubus: A Study of the Short Fiction by Thomas E. Kennedy
F. Scott Fitzgerald: A Study of the Short Fiction by John Kuehl
John Gardner: A Study of the Short Fiction by Jeff Henderson
William Goyen: A Study of the Short Fiction by Reginald Gibbons
Ernest Hemingway: A Study of the Short Fiction by Joseph M. Flora
Henry James: A Study of the Short Fiction by Richard A. Hocks
Franz Kafka: A Study of the Short Fiction by Allen Thiher
Bernard Malamud: A Study of the Short Fiction by Robert Solotaroff
Katherine Mansfield: A Study of the Short Fiction by J. F. Kobler
Liam O'Flaherty: A Study of the Short Fiction by James M. Cahalan
Flannery O'Connor: A Study of the Short Fiction by Suzanne Morrow Paulson
Gabriel García Márquez: A Study of the Short Fiction by Harley D. Oberhelman
Grace Paley: A Study of the Short Fiction by Neil D. Isaacs
Irwin Shaw: A Study of the Short Fiction by James R. Giles
Isaac Bashevis Singer: A Study of the Short Fiction by Edward Alexander
John Steinbeck: A Study of the Short Fiction by R. S. Hughes
Peter Taylor: A Study of the Short Fiction by James Curry Robison
Tennessee Williams: A Study of the Short Fiction by Dennis Vannatta
William Carlos Williams: A Study of the Short Fiction by Robert Gish
Virginia Woolf: A Study of the Short Fiction by Dean Baldwin

Twayne's Studies in Short Fiction

Gordon Weaver, General Editor
Oklahoma State University

J. D.
SALINGER

—————— *A Study of the Short Fiction* ——

John Wenke
Salisbury State University

TWAYNE PUBLISHERS • *BOSTON*
A Division of G. K. Hall & Co.

Twayne's Studies in Short Fiction No. 25

Copyright 1991 by G. K. Hall & Co.
All rights reserved.
Published by Twayne Publishers
A division of G. K. Hall & Co.
70 Lincoln Street
Boston, Massachusetts 02111

Copyediting supervised by Barbara Sutton.
Book production by Gabrielle B. McDonald.
Book design by Janet Z. Reynolds.
Typeset by Compset, Inc., Beverly, Massachusetts.

10 9 8 7 6 5 4 3 2 1

The paper used in this publication meets the minimum requirements
of American National Standard for Information Sciences—Permanence
of Paper for Printed Library Materials, ANSI Z39.48-1984. ∞™

Printed and bound in the United States of America.

Library of Congress Cataloging-in-Publication Data

Wenke, John Paul.
    J. D. Salinger : a study of the short fiction / John Wenke.
        p.   cm.—(Twayne studies in short fiction ; no. 25)
    Includes bibliographical references and index.
    ISBN 0-8057-8334-2
    1. Salinger, J. D. (Jerome David), 1919–   —Criticism and
interpretation.   2. Short story. I. Title. II. Series.
    PS3537.A426Z97   1991
    813'.54—dc20   91-11574

To my sisters—
Maureen, Bernadette, Bernice, Anne Marie, Kathy, Patty—
with love and gratitude

Contents

Preface   xi
Acknowledgments   xiv

PART 1. THE SHORT FICTION

   The Uncollected Stories   3
   Nine Stories   31
   The Glass Family   63
   The Seymour Narratives   90
   Notes to Part 1   109

PART 2. THE WRITER

   Introduction   119
   Biographical Reflections on J. D. Salinger   121

PART 3. THE CRITICS

   Introduction   133
   Theodore L. Gross   134
   James E. Miller, Jr.   136
   James Lundquist   143
   Bruce Bawer   147
   Edward Stone   149
   Warren French   153
   George Panichas   157
   Bernice and Sanford Goldstein   160

Chronology   163
Selected Bibliography   166
Index   172

Preface

Most famous for *The Catcher in the Rye*, J. D. Salinger has published 22 uncollected stories and three collections: *Nine Stories, Franny and Zooey*, and *Raise High the Roof Beam, Carpenters and Seymour: An Introduction*. Salinger's first published short story, "The Young Folks," appeared in 1940, and his most recent novella, "Hapworth 16, 1924," appeared in 1965. Since then Salinger has not published a single story. He no longer presents himself as a public figure, a posture that, ironically, has given him unwanted notoriety. J. D. Salinger is America's preeminent author-in-absentia. While one might claim that Thomas Pynchon—no known address, no interviews, no photographs—has out-Salingered Salinger, Pynchon still publishes, as the recent appearance of *Vineland* attests. This is a notable distinction: a writer, however elusive in real life, is always best known by his words.

This study explores the public record of Salinger's mind at work. The book offers a developmental, though not strictly chronological, approach. In part 1 my chapter on "The Uncollected Stories" examines most of the 21 tales that were published in the 1940s. It is not accurate to see this material as constituting Salinger's apprenticeship. Indeed, most of the stories were placed in high-profile magazines.

As a self-conscious professional, Salinger adjusted his craft to the varied demands of the literary marketplace. He wrote for *Good Housekeeping* and the *New Yorker, Mademoiselle*, and *Esquire*. He turned out sentimental tearjerkers and composed highly-refined psychological explorations. He wrote to formula and he satirized formula. He experimented with the possibilities of the serial tale. In at least seven stories he tried out the voice and character of Holden Caulfield. He killed Holden off; he brought him back to life.

Significantly, however, the uncollected stories establish Salinger's abiding thematic and artistic preoccupations. Along with exploring hypocritical and vapid social contexts, they examine their counterforce, the lost idyll. Salinger's most sympathetic characters find themselves in lonely exile from childhood innocence, or trying to contend with an absent friend or brother. This complex gives retrospective focus to Salinger's early fiction.

The uncollected stories also provide access to the more widely known tales published in *Nine Stories*. The second chapter of part 1 focuses on each story as a distinctive literary entity and considers attending generic questions. "A Perfect Day for Bananafish," the first story in the volume, presents the suicide of Seymour Glass. The end of his life marks the beginning of the Glass family saga. The third chapter of part 1 initiates an in-depth examination of the Glass stories and the religious issues that dominate the later work. *Franny and Zooey* provides an account of Franny Glass's nervous breakdown and the attempts by her brother, Zooey, to wrestle with related familial, theological, artistic, and psychological issues. The fourth chapter, "The Seymour Narratives," examines the three late pieces that explicitly concern the family's firstborn, Seymour Glass—the poet, mystic, and teacher who most engages Buddy Glass's meditations. It is clear that Buddy Glass, a writer, is an alter ego of Salinger himself. Buddy claims, in fact, to have written "A Perfect Day for Bananafish" and "Teddy"; he implies that he wrote *The Catcher in the Rye*. By assigning his own works to a fictional character, Salinger attempts to efface his authorial identity.

Part 2 would normally reprint selections from literary interviews, letters, memoirs—in fact, any materials that reflected the author's sense of the writer's craft, especially as it relates to short fiction. Salinger does not give interviews; some of his letters can be read but not reprinted; he has not written—nor is it likely that he will write—an autobiography. Consequently, this volume prints for the first time an essay by Joseph Wenke, "Biographical Reflections on J. D. Salinger." This piece considers matters relating to Salinger's life and provides summations of the few insubstantial interviews and an assessment of how Salinger's absence has informed his legend. Curiously, Holden Caulfield articulates (and anticipates) Salinger's obsession with the reclusive life. Toward the conclusion of *The Catcher in the Rye*, Holden fantasizes about dropping out, bumming around, hitchhiking out West, taking a job pumping gas. He imagines playing the role of deaf-mute, thereby reducing conversations to scrawled transactions:

> I thought what I'd do was, I'd pretend I was one of those deaf-mutes. That way I wouldn't have to have any goddam stupid useless conversations with anybody. If anybody wanted to tell me some-

thing, they'd have to write it on a piece of paper and shove it over to me. They'd get bored as hell doing that after a while, and then I'd be through with having conversations for the rest of my life. . . . I'd build me a little cabin somewhere with the dough I made and live there for the rest of my life. I'd build it right near the woods, but not right *in* them, because I'd want it to be sunny as hell all the time. I'd cook all my own food, and later on, if I wanted to get married or something, I'd meet this beautiful girl that was also a deaf-mute and we'd get married. She'd come and live in my cabin with me, and if she wanted to say anything to me, she'd have to write it on a goddam piece of paper, like everybody else.[1]

Holden's carefully scripted fantasy combines escape, silence, sex, control, and isolation. In this formulation the myth of Paradise Gained is balanced upon an unsteady, and chilling, misanthropy.

Part 3 offers excerpts from the extensive body of commentary on Salinger's short fiction. I have chosen what I judge to be excellent discussions. Limitations of space necessitate reprinting selections. In every instance the reader is invited to examine each piece in its entirety and to read the other important materials cited in the Bibliography.

I wish to thank the Salisbury State University Foundation and SSU's Fulton School of Liberal Arts for grants that helped me complete this project. Lori Anne Beste, my research assistant at Salisbury State, was unstinting in her efforts. I am grateful to the staff of the Blackwell Library at SSU for their patient efforts on my behalf. Jack R. Sublette's excellent bibliography was indispensable; his book is a model of organization, scholarship, and thoroughness. My brother, Joseph Wenke, did me a great favor in contributing an original essay to this volume. He was kind enough to steal time from his unenviably frenetic schedule as an executive speech writer at IBM. Milton R. Stern gave me much advice and help. My thanks also go out to my true friend Thomas P. Riggio; our conversations enabled me to float many of the ideas that are in this book. I extend my nonscholarly appreciation to Sheila L. Hughes for many reasons, the best of which are inexpressible.

Note

1. J. D. Salinger, *The Catcher in the Rye* (New York: Bantam, 1964), 198–99.

Acknowledgments

Bruce Bawer's "Salinger's Arrested Development" is reprinted from the *New Criterion* 5 (September 1986): 46–47. © 1986 by Bruce Bawer. Reprinted by permission of the author.

Warren French's "Franny" is reprinted from his *J. D. Salinger Revisited*. © 1988 by G. K. Hall & Co. Reprinted with the permission of Twayne Publishers, a division of G. K. Hall & Co., Boston.

Bernice and Sanford Goldstein's "Zen and Salinger" is reprinted from *Modern Fiction Studies* 12 (Autumn 1966): 313–14. © 1966 by Purdue Research Foundation, West Lafayette, Indiana. Reprinted with permission.

Theodore L. Gross's excerpt from his *The Heroic Ideal in American Literature* is reprinted with permission of the Free Press, a division of Macmillan, Inc. © 1971 by Theodore L. Gross.

James Lundquist's "Zen Art and *Nine Stories*" is reprinted from his *J. D. Salinger*. © 1979 by the Frederick Ungar Publishing Company. Reprinted by permission of the publisher.

James E. Miller, Jr.'s excerpt from his *J. D. Salinger* (University of Minnesota Pamphlets on American Writers, no. 51) is reprinted by permission of the University of Minnesota Press. © 1965 by the University of Minnesota.

George Panichas's "J. D. Salinger and the Russian Pilgrim" is reprinted from *The Reverent Discipline: Essays on Literary Criticism* by George Panichas. © 1974 by the University of Tennessee Press. Reprinted by permission of the University of Tennessee Press.

Edward Stone's essay on art in "De Daumier-Smith's Blue Period" is reprinted from *A Certain Morbidness: A View of American Literature* by Edward Stone. © 1969 by Southern Illinois University Press. Reprinted with permission from Southern Illinois University Press.

Part 1

THE SHORT FICTION

The Uncollected Stories

A story never ends. The narrator is usually provided with a
nice, artistic spot for his voice to stop, but that's about all.

—"Blue Melody"

At one time J. D. Salinger sought visibility. In 1939 he was not the
well-published, almost prolific author of many celebrated stories and
one major novel. He had yet to become overtly irritated with the demands associated with public life—that one be a personality, a cooperative and quotable resource. Nor had Salinger surrendered a writer's
customary practice of writing for readers, those "people," as Richard
Ford remarks, "you don't know or aren't related to."[1] In 1939, at the
age of 20, Salinger had no readers.

Toward the end of acquiring some, he enrolled in Whit Burnett's
creative writing class at Columbia University.[2] He sat in the back and
did not say much. At the time he felt drawn to theater, the most public
arena of literary performance. He was interested in becoming an actor
and a playwright, odd choices for a future recluse litigiously assertive
of his right to retain control over the distribution of his words.[3] An actor
plays to the crowd; a playwright's words inform a cooperative, dynamic
medium. The process of any production creates an inevitable series of
recastings, everything from directorial deletions to revisions on demand
to players flubbing their lines. Curiously, many years later, in the first
epigraph to "Seymour: An Introduction," Salinger cites Kafka and
evokes the playwright's inability to control his creation: "The actors
by their presence always convince me, to my horror, that most of what
I've written about them until now is false."[4] Under Burnett's tutelage,
Salinger did not, it seems, work on plays, though his initial inclination
for the theater is reflected in his aptitude for writing dialogue and for
rendering the nuances of social manner. He spent the semester polish-
ing a short story that is essentially dramatic in focus and execution.
Burnett thought enough of the piece to print it in *Story*. Salinger's first
professional publication offers modest intimations of more successful
work to come.

3

Narrated by a detached, often sardonic third-person voice, "The Young Folks" presents Edna Phillips's experience of isolation. She is attending a collegiate party, at which most of the boys are drawn toward a golden girl, Doris Leggett. Edna's friend, Lucille Henderson, attempts to set Edna up with Bill Jameson, a boorish and bored undergraduate. Bill does not know what he is doing at the party: he should be home writing a paper. After Edna mentions Jack Delroy, a mutual acquaintance, and Bill replies, "I don't know him so good," Edna assures him that Jack is "grand."[5] In the social register of Salinger's lexicon, the word *grand* signifies the speaker's pretension to elegance, a pseudosophistication that is crass, obtuse, smug. The story's center of interest takes place after Edna, on the hunt for romance, steers the reluctant Bill onto the terrace. Here she gushes, "It's so grand out here. Amorous voices and all" ("Young," 28). Edna continues their earlier discussion about a failed relationship. She obsesses over Barry, a boy she dated the previous summer. Apparently he spent a lot of money on their dates and felt she owed him sexual favors. The relationship ended because Barry "just asked too much of me. . . . It's gotta be the real thing with me. Before, you know. I mean love and all" ("Young," 29). Bill has interest neither in these semiarticulate revelations nor in becoming Barry's surrogate. Bill deserts Edna to sit at the feet of Doris Leggett. Edna's only solace is her assumption that her high standards account for her various rejections.

Salinger's first published story strains toward wry social criticism. Warren French notes that it is "scarcely more than an unflattering character sketch." Seeking "to emulate the ironic objective deadpan vignettes of heels found in the popular stories of John O'Hara and Ring Lardner," Salinger presents the dialogue of self-absorbed people who unwittingly reveal their drab personalities.[6] The narrator remains aloof from the action and descends only to make an occasional gibe. When describing the darkened love nest, the narrator is precious rather than piercing: "For reading, sewing, mastering crossword puzzles, the Henderson terrace was inadequately lighted" ("Young," 27). Nonetheless, the story provides glimpses of elements that inform Salinger's subsequent work. "The Young Folks" depicts a sterile world populated by petty people. Edna wants to be part of the "grand" circle. Her exclusion from this world conditions her contempt for it, though her disdain lacks the weight of moral indictment: it merely accentuates her estrangement. In fact her private universe replicates the tawdry contours of flawed grandeur. Significantly, the figure of Barry offers the first instance of Salinger's abiding preoccupation with a lost idyll. Though apparently having betrayed Edna, Barry still lives in her memory. As an "artist" in an unspecified medium, Barry embodies a saving grace that the present scene lacks. However crudely handled, Barry is the first of many characters who represent a past and seemingly lost greatness. These figures include Joe Varioni, the Holden Caulfield of the Babe Gladwaller–Vincent Caulfield serial tales, Walt Glass, Allie Caulfield, the ducks in central park, and, most importantly, Seymour Glass.

In the 1940s Salinger went on to publish 20 stories that remain legally uncollected. Two editions of a two-volume pirated collection are in private hands.[7] What Salinger has labeled "the gaucheries of my youth" have elicited sometimes snide, but always brief, remarks.[8] For example, Arthur Mizener writes, "His first published stories . . . will quickly destroy any romantic notions one may have had about the unpublished stories he wrote even earlier."[9] Recently, Bruce Bawer proclaims that "almost all of these stories are contrived productions of little or no literary interest."[10] Though hamstrung by such New Critical fixations as finding "who the protagonist really is," Joseph L. Blotner and Frederick L. Gwynn do offer useful thematic and topical categories— "The Lonely Girl Characterizations," for example—that might help organize an approach to these 20 stories.[11]

The uncollected stories are neither all failures nor a trove of unacknowledged masterpieces. Though linked by their author's subsequent neglect, they contain a broad range of styles, characters, and concerns. The tales include brief sentimental failures ("The Hang of It"), early drafts of later work ("I'm Crazy"), ambitious, though unformed, experiments ("The Inverted Forest"), and highly sophisticated, carefully refined pieces ("The Varioni Brothers" and "The Heart of a Broken Story").

Salinger placed most of these stories near or at the top of a competitive literary marketplace, and Ian Hamilton's claim that Salinger lost his innocence upon writing "to length and formula" (60) strains after effect. Salinger was no innocent. He was writing for money, consciously adapting his style to the demands of such diverse outlets as *Collier's* and *Esquire*. In fact, in one of his best early stories, "The Heart of a Broken Story," Salinger parodies a *Collier's* story in the pages of *Esquire*. Salinger's uncollected stories cover the spectrum from lowbrow to highbrow. They appeared in *Good Housekeeping, Mademoiselle,* and *Cosmopolitan* as well as *Story,* the *University of Kansas City Review,* and the *Saturday Evening Post*. In 1941 the first Holden Caulfield story,

5

"Slight Rebellion off Madison," was accepted by the *New Yorker* but did not appear until 1946. Salinger's celebrated affiliation with the *New Yorker* did not begin in earnest until the publication in 1948 of "A Perfect Day for Bananafish."

Salinger's uncollected stories can be classed in three distinct, though related, categories. Like "The Young Folks," the stories "Go See Eddie," "The Long Debut of Lois Taggett," "The Varioni Brothers," "Elaine," and "The Inverted Forest" examine social manners and reveal Salinger's continuing exploration of filial bonds, bleak marriages, psychological disturbance, artistic frustration, the corruption of innocence, and the cinema as vacuous diversion. World War II provides the second major focus of Salinger's early art. "The Hang of It" and "Personal Notes on an Infantryman" are one-page stories, patriotic bromides in prose that are resolved in cute-to-sickening surprise endings. "Soft-Boiled Sergeant," "Last Day of the Last Furlough," "Once a Week Won't Kill You," and "This Sandwich Has No Mayonnaise" explore the ruptures war visits upon individuals and families. Related to but extending beyond the war stories are the pieces that focus on Holden Caulfield. In the Babe Gladwaller–Vincent Caulfield serial tales, Holden is a missing-in-action soldier, Salinger's first major character who assumes the paradoxical proportions of being an "absent presence," usually an individual physically gone—missing, lost, or dead—who haunts the lives of the survivors to the point of obsession. Holden also appears in "Slight Rebellion" and "I'm Crazy," early versions of parts of *The Catcher in the Rye*. The first manifestation of Holden's *voice*, however, appears through Billy's first-person narrative in "Both Parties Concerned."

Salinger's refusal to collect these tales in hardcover derives from his conviction that they are not worth reprinting. This decision has largely preempted a developmental approach to his work, and it is generally unrecognized that the contours of Holden Caulfield's character were drawn as early as 1941. A crucial element of Salinger's career, therefore, is its lacunae: inevitably, periodical pieces are doomed to remain literary ephemera, here this month, gone the next. In the magazines a writer surely casts his bread upon the literary waters. If the pieces do not sink, they drift from sight. For every hundred or thousand readers of *Nine Stories* there may be one—or none—familiar with the metafictional playfulness of "The Heart of a Broken Story." In his collected works the young man who in 1939 sat in the back succeeded like no other of his classmates in achieving authorial visibility. It is ironic, then, that the published work of Salinger's most public period is his least known. And for a writer as elusive as Salinger it is only appropriate that one approach him through paradox: like the dead brothers and dead friends who haunt Salinger's fiction, what is left out has a telling place, even if certain artifacts remain well out of the way, in crowded stacks, or, more appropriately, on rolls of microfilm.

"The Conventional Chill"

Salinger presents a number of stories that consider characters who become involved in degrading, often phony social contexts. In "Go See Eddie" Helen becomes attracted to a world of glitter and risks losing her essentially decent self. This story introduces a central conflict in Salinger's work that has been variously defined by his readers. Warren French, for example, explores the conflict between nice and phony worlds, and Ihab Hassan discerns an informing opposition between the sensitive outsider and the assertive vulgarian.[12]

As the story opens we find that Bobby, a booking agent, is disturbed that his sister, Helen, is romantically involved with Phil Stone, a married man. Having just returned from Chicago, Bobby insists that Helen get her acting career back on track. He wants her to see Eddie Jackson, who is "going into rehearsal with a new show."[13] Once a "swell kid," Helen currently languishes in slothful, enervating elegance. In Bobby's view Helen teeters on the verge of ruining herself. In perceiving Phil as "really a grand person" and their relationship as the "real thing" ("Eddie," 123), Helen aligns herself with the forces of affectation and illusion. Bobby hates to see his sister's affiliation with a pretentious crowd. Like Holden Caulfield, Bobby has contempt for "grand" people: "You and your god damn grand persons. You know more god damn grand persons" ("Eddie," 123). "Swell kid[s]" and "grand persons" succinctly express the characteristic thematic conflict between innocence and depravity. Bobby fears that Helen will lose those qualities which are integral to her best self. At the end of the story Helen agrees to put Phil off and makes ready to pick up her career. Though slight in range, "Go See Eddie" foreshadows Salinger's more searching explorations of innocence either threatened or lost.

"The Long Debut of Lois Taggett" and "Elaine" are ambitious, sprawling stories. "The Long Debut" presents a sympathetic life study of Lois Taggett as well as a satire of upper-middle-class materialism. The third-person narrator speaks in a sarcastic voice. As a club-hopping society girl, Lois "didn't do badly. She had a good figure, dressed expensively and in good taste, and was considered Intelligent. That was the first season when Intelligent was the thing to be."[14] The story "Elaine," on the contrary, examines the tawdry lives of the lower class. The winner of two "Beautiful Child" contests, Elaine resembles Rapunzel, the golden-haired princess in the tower.[15] Unlike the intelligent Lois, Elaine is intellectually deficient. Put in the "slower class," she needs nine and a half years to graduate from elementary school. Her fate is to be both beautiful object and dumb symbol. Her role will always be to stand still and look pretty. In a school production, for example, "Elaine Cooney enacted the part of the Statue of Liberty. Hers was the only nonspeaking part in the pageant" ("Elaine," 40).

Both Lois and Elaine are victimized by social predators. Salinger makes it clear that Lois has a good soul: she has a genuine desire and capacity for love. Her wealth, however, attracts a callow fortune hunter, Bill Tedderton: he "trained himself to look deep enough into Lois' eyes to see the door to the family vault" ("Debut," 29). Similarly, Elaine's beauty makes her the prey of lascivious men. In the company of her mother, grandmother, and landlord, Mr. Freedlander, Elaine frequents the movies. The beautiful body of a woman houses the innocuous and impervious mind of a child. In the darkness of the movie theater, Mr. Freedlander "pressed his leg against Elaine's. She made no attempt to move her leg away from his. She simply was unaware of the imposed intimacy. . . . [S]he was totally unqualified to accommodate sex and Mickey Mouse simultaneously. There was room for Mickey; no more" ("Elaine," 41).

In "The Long Debut" and "Elaine" Salinger explores, respectively, the incursions of psychosis and sexual seduction. In "The Long Debut" he wrenches his focus from a parody of upper-class materialism to present the irruption of Bill Tedderton's inexplicable violence.[16] After Lois and Bill marry, the narrator reports an odd, disjunctive incident: "Bill . . . deliberately, yet almost idly, did what he had to do" ("Debut," 30). He burns Lois's left hand with a cigarette. Later, without provocation or warning, he smashes her foot with a golf club. The narrator avoids any attempt to explain these acts.

Elaine attracts the attentions of a mindless young man, Teddy Schmidt. He stands in direct contrast to the Hollywood icons who dwell in her imagination. Her innocence seems more like ignorance and foolishness. "[U]nwilling to be confused by unfamiliar, evadable issues," Elaine inhabits a media fantasyland of charming, perfect achievers. It is a "Hollywood- and radio-promoted world peopled with star newspaper reporters, crackerjack young city editors, young brain surgeons. . . . All of her men spoke in deep, trained voices that sometimes swooped pleasantly through a sixteen-year-old girl's legs" ("Elaine," 41). The movies and radio relieve the tedium of her family's everyday life. Romance is displaced into a celluloid dream. Thus Elaine is insulated from the realities of sex. She has no sense of the shallow devices of young men like Teddy, and on their date to the beach remains unaware of his character and intentions, described by the narrator in cloying moralizations: "His mediocre heart had begun to pound excitedly, because with the eternal rake's despicable but seldom faulty intuition, he knew it was going to be easy . . . so easy" ("Elaine," 45). The following month Elaine and Teddy marry, but their union does not outlast the wedding reception. In a disagreement over a movie star, the mothers-in-law get into a screaming match. After taking the uncomplaining, emotionally untouched Elaine away from "that sissy boy" ("Elaine," 47), Mrs. Cooney decides on what they need to do in order to improve the day: they go to the movies. While "The Long Debut" meanders after Bill's violent outburst, "Elaine" concludes with Salinger's comic reassertion of Elaine's safe world of movie love.

"The Varioni Brothers" and "The Heart of a Broken Story" introduce Salinger's concern with the place of art in a materialistic society, on the one hand, and the limits of conventional fictional form, on the other. Both stories offer sophisticated uses of narrative form. "The Varioni Brothers" has three separate narrators, who offer a range of public and private voices; "The Heart of a Broken Story" presents the narrator's account of his failure to concoct a sentimental *Collier's* love story. Both tales reflect Salinger's attraction to constructing multiple narrative frames and engaging in self-reflexive play.

In "The Varioni Brothers" an unnamed editor indicates that "producer, raconteur and wit" Vincent Westmoreland will be a one-shot guest columnist for Gardenia Penny's "Around Old Chi."[17] Westmoreland begins his piece by offering a wish list for a "sociable genie." After putting Hitler, Mussolini, and Hirohito "into a fair-sized cage, and promptly deposit[ing] the menagerie on the front steps of the White House," the genie would then be assigned another seemingly impossible, though eminently desirable, task: Westmoreland would like to know what became of Sonny Varioni. In "the crazy Twenties," the Varioni brothers were rich and successful songwriters (Sonny wrote the music and Joe the lyrics), but their story is "one of the most tragic and unfinished of the century." Sonny's taste for gambling brought him into arrears with a mobster, Buster Hankey, and when he refused to pay, Buster sent a hit man, Rocco. At a wild party at the brothers' mansion, a drunken blond steered the hit man toward the piano: "[Rocco] elbows his way through the crowd, fires five shots, very fast, into the wrong man's back. Joe Varioni, whom no one in the room had ever heard play the piano before, because that was Sonny's affair, dropped dead to the floor" ("Varioni," 12). Sonny soon disappeared. Seventeen years later Westmoreland sends out an appeal: "Some remote little person somewhere must have the inside dope."

Sarah Daley Smith responds with a letter. Sarah has the "inside dope" and immediately encapsulates Sonny's condition:

> He is in Waycross, Illinois. He's not very well, and he's working day and night typing up the manuscript of a lovely, wild, and possibly great novel. It was written and thrown into a trunk by Joe Varioni. It was written longhand on yellow paper, on lined paper, on crumpled paper, on torn paper. The sheets were not numbered. Whole sentences and even paragraphs were marked out and rewritten on the backs of envelopes, on the unused sides of college exam papers, in the margins of railroad timetables. The job of making head and tail, chapter and book, of this wild colossus is an immeasurably enervating one, requiring, one would think, youth and health and ego. Sonny Varioni has none of these. He has a hope for a kind of salvation. ("Varioni," 13)

Sarah's summary of Sonny's lamentable condition answers the questions of where he is, how he is, and what he is doing. But it does not provide the whole story—that is, Sarah's story, a last chapter to the tragedy. At Waycross College Sarah was a student of Joe Varioni. Though now happily married, Sarah views Joe as the love of her life. Her extreme attraction to him was matched only by his apparent unavailability. He embodies Sarah's lost idyll. In the mysterious and conflicted artist Joe Varioni Salinger creates a fit predecessor of Seymour Glass.[18] Tall, weary, thin, Joe "was brilliant. He had gorgeous brown eyes, and he had only two suits. He was completely unhappy. I don't know why." Joe combined inscrutability with artistic compulsion. While at work on his novel, he would sometimes read to the worshipful Sarah from a mess of "crazy sheets of yellow paper. . . . He could cram more writing in less space than anybody I ever knew" ("Varioni," 13).

Joe's desire to be a novelist was preempted by Sonny's desire for their joint success at popular songwriting. "Handsome, charming, insincere and bored" ("Varioni," 13), Sonny asserted his control over Joe. He used his brother's gifts for his own selfish ends and was utterly impervious to literary art: "He showed me a story once. About some kids coming out of a school. I thought it was lousy. Nothing happened" ("Varioni," 77). Their agent, Teddy Barto, blithely suggested that Joe simply keep writing his novel while living in Chicago:

> "He's a novelist," [Sarah] said. "He shouldn't be writing songs."
> "So he can write a few novels in town," Teddy said, solving everything. "I like books. Everybody likes books. It improves the mind." ("Varioni," 76)

Here Salinger indicates the conflict between the artist's need for solitude and the demands of the popular marketplace. Joe could not write novels and lyrics at the same time. By controlling Joe's activity, Sonny not only diverted his brother from his true calling, but also used him to enhance his own craft. Without Joe's words, without his company, Sonny "has an awful lot of trouble hearing the music. I need every little help I can get" ("Varioni," 77).

"The Varioni Brothers" offers an inviting psychological matrix of personal and artistic resolutions. After a period of mourning, Sarah settled for a "wonderful, ungeniuslike" husband. Her entry into the common life of domestic happiness became a necessary betrayal of her futile and idealized love for Joe. When falling in love with her husband, she danced to the music of the Varioni Brothers: "I treacherously found that I could use Varioni words and music to date and identify my new happiness for future nostalgic purposes." Her nostalgia also prompted her to recall passages of Joe's novel "best while I was bathing the children" ("Varioni," 77). In Sarah's recollection, Joe fed her emotional life. Thus Salinger links lost love, unrealized genius, and childhood innocence.

If Sarah found a way to fuse the lost idyll with present happiness, Sonny still seeks a way to reconcile himself to his self-lacerating guilt. Joe's murder manifested a grotesque, though tragic, exemplification of Sonny's selfish appropriation of Joe's artistic life. Joe's ironic death in a case of mistaken identity underscored the cost of Sonny's manipulative drive for self-gratification. For 17 years Sonny has tortured himself. He moved in with Sarah's family and forged an ironic union, a

sort of symbolic marriage: indeed Sonny and Sarah could use each
other to get close to Joe. Though broken in health, Sonny continues
his attempt to complete Joe's novel. As Ian Hamilton points out, this
attempt foreshadows "Buddy Glass's efforts on behalf of Seymour"
(75). For Sonny to piece together a novel from fragments would be
tantamount to recapturing the essence of Joe's artistic life. Sonny
might thereby achieve "a kind of salvation." Interestingly, Sonny
comes closest to his *own* art while working on Joe's manuscript: "I
hear the music for the first time in my life when I read his book"
("Varioni," 77).

In "The Varioni Brothers" Salinger constructs a tale-within-a-tale-
within-a-tale in order to explore a public mystery within the private
domains of Sarah's frustrated and Sonny's guilty love. In this story Salinger leaves open the question of whether Sonny completes Joe's book.
For Sonny to complete the manuscript would be to sentimentalize the
materials and thus vitiate the power of Salinger's tale of waste. By
attempting to reconstruct the novel, Sonny engages in a private,
though apparently futile and sadly nostalgic, effort to reconcile himself
to his brother's death. This process gives meaning to his life. Consequently, the story continues beyond the limits inscribed by its very last
words. Sarah's voice stops, but the story goes on.

"The Heart of a Broken Story" is remarkable for its surface play of
comic brilliance. Published in 1941, the story simultaneously satirizes
the kind of popular art that swallows Joe Varioni and offers multiple,
parodic versions of the very sentimentalized story that the narrator
claims to find impossible to tell. "The Heart of a Broken Story" comments on and invalidates its own premises. Well before meta-fiction
became fashionable, Salinger unmakes—that is, he deconstructs—the
form of the sentimental love story, presenting, as it were, a series of
subjunctive counterlives that emerge and dissolve in a skein of comic
improbabilities. Salinger anticipates the self-reflexivity associated with
such recent post-modern practitioners as John Barth, Kurt Vonnegut,
Thomas Pynchon, and Philip Roth. He also anticipates the self-reflexivity that characterizes the Glass stories, especially "Seymour."

Salinger begins with a straightforward description of Justin Horgenschlag on his way to work:

> Every day Justin Horgenschlag, thirty-dollar-a-week printer's assis-
> tant, saw at close quarters approximately sixty women whom he had
> never seen before. Thus in the four years he had lived in New York,

Horgenschlag had seen at close quarters about 75,120 different women. Of these 75,120 women, roughly 25,000 were under thirty years of age and over fifteen years of age. Of the 25,000 only 5,000 weighed between one hundred five and one hundred twenty-five pounds. Of these 5,000 only 1,000 were not ugly. Only 500 were reasonably attractive; only 100 were quite attractive; only 25 could have inspired a long, slow whistle. And with only 1 did Horgenschlag fall in love at first sight.[19]

Riding to work on the Third Avenue bus, Horgenschlag sees "*femme fatale*" Shirley Lester and instantly becomes "a dead duck." The narrator settles into purple prose, detailing how Horgenschlag views Shirley as "a positive cure-all for a gigantic monster of loneliness which had been stalking around his heart since he had come to New York. Oh, the agony of it! The agony of standing over Shirley Lester and not being able to bend down and kiss Shirley's parted lips. The inexpressible agony of it!" ("Heart," 32). The agony is so "inexpressible" that the narrator admits that the preceding material "was the beginning of a story I started to write for *Collier's*." A "boy-meets-girl story," he feels, is a fine thing, just what "the world needs." But the narrator encounters an arresting problem: he cannot devise a way to have the boy meet the girl, "[n]ot and have it make sense." The problem of making sense impels the narrator on an imaginative romp, during which he ridicules a variety of romantic possibilities for how this boy could meet this girl. Horgenschlag, for example, could never bend over and announce his love: "I beg your pardon. I love you very much. I'm nuts about you. I *know* it. I could love you all my life. I'm a printer's assistant and I make thirty dollars a week. Gosh, how I love you. Are you busy tonight?" The narrator considers Horgenschlag " a goof, but not *that* big a goof. . . . You can't expect *Collier's* readers to swallow that kind of bilge." Maybe not. The narrator could not give this young man "a suave serum, mixed from William Powell's old cigarette case and Fred Astaire's old top hat" ("Heart," 32). By identifying what he is "up against," the narrator confronts those points at which fictional formula cannot overcome the improbabilities of behavior.

Horgenschlag is a cross between Prufrock and Walter Mitty, a schlemiel incapable of becoming a leading man. Thus the narrator dramatizes a series of scenarios that depict what could never actually be. Horgenschlag could neither mistake Shirley for someone he knew in Seattle, nor faint in the aisle, tearing her stocking in the fall and

13

thereby giving himself an excuse to contact her later: "But what is more logical," the narrator says, "is the possibility that Horgenschlag might have got desperate. There are still a few men who love desperately. Maybe Horgenschlag was one. He might have snatched Shirley's handbag and run with it toward the rear exit door. Shirley would have screamed" ("Heart," 131). At this point the narrator surrenders his subjunctives and slips into a present-tense depiction of the projected fantasy. Horgenschlag gets chased, apprehended, tried, and imprisoned. He writes letters. Shirley answers one. He writes another. Not wanting any more to do with this crackpot, Shirley refuses to reply. Again desperate, Horgenschlag breaks out of jail with 16 other prisoners. One escapee is killed. The narrator teases,

> Guess who?
> And, thus, my plan to write a boy-meets-girl story for *Collier's*, a tender, memorable love story, is thwarted by the death of my hero.
> Now, Horgenschlag never would have been among those seventeen desperate men if only he had not been made desperate and panicky by Shirley's failure to answer his second letter. But the fact remains that she did *not* answer his second letter. She never in a hundred years would have answered it. I can't alter facts. ("Heart," 132)

The absurd play on a series of subjunctives now appears as a real event that makes further improbabilities impossible. Horgenschlag's supposed death precludes him from enacting the greatest fiction of all: writing a letter to Shirley and presenting himself as the nobody he truly is. The "unlikely" letter is no more so than Shirley's honest reply, which would ultimately reinforce the impossibility of their romance: "If only you had spoken to me instead of taking my purse! But then, I suppose I should have turned the conventional chill on you" ("Heart," 132).

In "The Heart of a Broken Story" Salinger takes the measure of wishful fantasy as the basis for popular entertainment and—at a remarkably early point in his career—registers his uneasiness with formula fiction. This story constitutes his earliest attack on phony art. Its placement in *Esquire* accentuates Salinger's capacity to discriminate among diverse markets. It is crucial to recognize that Salinger does not snub *Collier's;* rather, he simply points out the limitations of the love-story genre. By no means was Salinger above publishing such sentimental "bilge" in *Collier's*. Two months earlier, he published a syrupy piece, "The Hang of It," and more than a year later *Collier's* printed the equally sentimental "Personal Notes on an Infantryman." In minitypeface each story is crammed onto one page; each story is a glib comedy with a cloying surprise ending. These portraits offer idealized accounts of unreflecting people parading through a comic-book military. What is remarkable is that they are completely unlike Salinger's more expansive tales of men and boys at war.

"The Music of the Unrecoverable Years"

In the early 1940s a precocious and self-confident Harvard graduate enlisted in the army in hope of seeing action in the Pacific theater. In the same world war, somewhere above Italy, a curly-haired Jewish kid from Brooklyn watched as toy bridges settled into the bombardier's crosshairs. In a meat locker beneath the city of Dresden an American POW, a Hoosier, felt the percussive punches of incendiary bombs; on the surface a beautiful city was burning. Norman Mailer went to war and produced *The Naked and the Dead*, a monumental compression of at least 30 lives and two major plots. Joseph Heller needed the cold war and at least 7 years to complete Yossarian's comic nightmare in *Catch-22*, a novel depicting an army at war with itself in a distorted world of dark and maddening circularity. Kurt Vonnegut, Jr. anguished over the fire-bombing of Dresden for 25 years before fusing Billy Pilgrim's behind-the-lines bungling in *Slaughterhouse-Five*, with a satire of middle America that segues into an escape-to-the-womb, science-fiction-and-sex fantasy. Without question the great novels of Mailer, Heller, and Vonnegut derived largely from the impact of their authors' respective immersions into the psychosensual bombardment of war. The war became Mailer's rite of initiation, Heller's comedy of chaos, Vonnegut's death dance of overgrown children. In each configuration, the war took boys away from family, courtship, and budding careers and sent them off to engage the nation's enemies.

Unlike Mailer, Heller, and Vonnegut, J. D. Salinger is rarely associated with the art of the war story. Like them, Salinger left home and became a soldier. An intelligence officer, he landed at Normandy on D day and was a veteran of three major campaigns. While Salinger has yet to publish a war novel, he did explore the physical and psychological losses war inflicts on the soldier. The war provides the explicit subject in "For Esmé—with Love and Squalor," and it informs nine of his uncollected stories of the 1940s. Most significantly, the missing-in-action version of Holden Caulfield is presumably dead. It could also be argued that Seymour Glass is a psychological casualty of war; Walt Glass dies absurdly in a wartime accident. Salinger actually wrote a number of war stories while in the field; he mailed them back to be published. As John Scow writes, "With a swagger, the prospering young author in 1944 sent [Whit] Burnett a two-hundred-dollar check to help other young writers, and added: 'Am still writing whenever I can find the time and an unoccupied foxhole.' He carried a typewriter around in his Jeep, and an Army acquaintance remembers him typing away, crouching under a table, while the area was under attack."[20] However questionable this reminiscence may be, it derives its form from the perception that Staff Sergeant Salinger was an active writer whose output was not impeded by combat. As Warren French indicates, "More of his stories were published in 1945 than in any other year except 1948 (1976, 26).[21] This is not to say that Salinger was the rough-and-ready soldier, swashbuckling and sadistic like Corporal Clay in "For Esmé," a man who could blow the head off a cat and gleefully absolve himself with rationalizations of battle fatigue. In fact this fictional incident has a potential source in the mind-teasing lore associated with Salinger's reported meeting with Ernest Hemingway. According to Warren French, "A tale circulates that he met Ernest Hemingway when the author-correspondent visited Salinger's regiment, and that Salinger became disgusted when Hemingway shot the head off a chicken to demonstrate the merits of a German Luger" (1976, 25).

Except for "The Hang of It" and "Personal Notes on an Infantryman," Salinger insistently debunks the sentimentalized popularizations of war, especially the way in which movies present cosmetically serene surfaces: dying men merely settle into the big sleep without the slightest disfigurement. "Soft-Boiled Sergeant," originally entitled "Death of Dogface," offers a case in point. In a first-person vernacular narrative, Philly Barnes, a World War II veteran, wants to set the record straight about war movies. His wife is a war-movie buff. The story begins:

> Juanita, she's always dragging me to a million movies, and we see these here shows all about war and stuff. You see a lot of real handsome guys always getting shot pretty neat, right where it don't spoil their looks none, and they always got plenty of time, before they

croak, to give their love to some doll back home. . . . Then you see the dead guy's home town, and around a million people, including the mayor and the dead guy's folks and his doll, and maybe the President, all around the guy's box, making speeches and wearing medals and looking spiffier in mourning duds than most folks do all dolled up for a party.[22]

Philly tells Juanita the story of Burke so that she will "stop making me go to all them war movies all the time." The true story of the ugly, unphotogenic Burke, the "soft-boiled sergeant," provides a sobering antidote to Hollywood's fantasy portrayals. In this story, bad art— phony art—is a seductive soporific that corrupts one's sensibilities by making horror seem nice. Burke's story reflects a case of actual heroic self-sacrifice. It is also a story of injustice, waste, and tragedy.

Philly recounts his experiences as a lonely, underage (16 years old) enlisted man who is befriended by Staff Sergeant Burke. Though ugly and afflicted with a "rotten joke voice," Burke was a former hobo and is now an army lifer. Philly points out that Burke can "do things" ("Soft," 82). Most notably, he can be kind. Burke allows the innocent Philly to wear his war medals and also takes him out to see a Charlie Chaplin movie. Like Chaplin, Burke is one of the "funny-looking little guys always getting chased by the big guys. Never getting no girl, like. For keeps, like" ("Soft," 84). Philly sees Burke as a "great man" whom few people will ever know about. Apparently Burke in turn sees Philly as a youthful version of himself. Before enlisting, both Burke and Philly were drifters. When watching Philly lie on a bench, Burke sees an image of his own loneliness. He can view his own experience with nostalgia, a kind of recollected idyll. Burke composes a peaceful scene that freezes time in the midst of a passage. Burke asks, "When you was settin' on your bunk [crying] . . . was you thinking that you wanted to be laying on your back in a boxcar on a train that was stopped in a town, with the doors rolled open halfway and the sun in your face?" When Philly answers "kind of" and wants to know how Burke knew, the sergeant replies, "Mac, I ain't in this Army straight out of West Point" ("Soft," 85).

After Philly ships out he never sees Burke again, though he does learn of his fate. Burke is killed at Pearl Harbor after rescuing some buck privates who foolishly sought refuge in a large refrigerator. In giving up his life to rescue these innocents, Burke has half his jaw shot off. The materials of Burke's life and death counterpoint the stirring,

17

tear-jerking, antiseptic film scenarios. Philly presents Burke's death with a string of negatives: "He died all by himself, and he didn't have no message to give to no girl or nobody, and there wasn't nobody throwing a big classy funeral for him here in the States, and no hot-shot bugler blowed taps for him" ("Soft," 85). Salinger employs a ver-nacular tale-within-the-tale to render the account of a life for which Hollywood had no use.

The war provides Salinger's central complex in the four serial stories that feature John "Babe" Gladwaller and/or Vincent Caulfield. The form of the serial story fuses the scenic compression associated with the short story and the encompassing panorama associated with the novel. A hybrid form, the serial tale fosters the illusion that the char-acters have a real life that extends beyond a story's dramatic confines. The intrinsic concerns of the present action offer suggestive, though necessarily incomplete, relationships among the stories. "Last Day of the Last Furlough" depicts the plights of Babe and Vincent just before they go to war; "A Boy in France" presents the battle-weary Babe in search of a foxhole; "This Sandwich Has No Mayonnaise" details Vin-cent's distressed rumination over his missing-in-action brother, Hol-den; "The Stranger" chronicles Babe's trip to see the old girlfriend of his late friend Vincent.

In "Last Day" Vincent comes to Babe's house on the day before their departure. These friends both have sensitive, preadolescent sis-ters who exemplify childhood innocence. Babe's sister is Mattie; Vin-cent's is Phoebe. At the outset of the story, Babe seeks to horde the last minutes of his known, protected life by escaping into his books: "At the moment, the sergeant was at the studio of Mihailov, the painter, with Anna Karenina and Count Vronsky. A few minutes ago he had stood with Father Zossima and Alyosha Karamazov on the portico below the monastery. An hour ago he had crossed the great sad lawns belonging to Jay Gatsby, born James Gatz. Now the sergeant tried to go through Mihailov's studio quickly, to make time to stop at the corner of Fifth and 46th Street."[23] The irrepressible flow of life impinges upon the safe, static world of art. Babe must indeed "make time," for even when his mother brings him milk he is thrust from the insular aesthetic world: "*Too late, he thought. Time's up. Maybe I can take them with me. Sir, I've brought my books. I won't shoot anybody just yet. You fellas go ahead. I'll wait here with the books*" ("Last Day," 26). Babe's sardonic medita-tion reveals his recognition that the repose and civility of home are soon to be eradicated by the brutality of war. In going to meet Mattie, he achieves temporary relief from the threatening actualities. He embraces his life most fully as he recognizes its extreme tenuousness. Seeing Mattie's face "was worth fifty wars," for it means he can pull her home on a sled, an experience that briefly eclipses both his love for books and the lure of romance. By italicizing Babe's present-tense reflections, Salinger brings us directly into Babe's mind: *"This is for me. I'm happier than I've ever been in my life. This is better than my books, this is better than Frances. . . . Shoot me, all you sneaking Jap snipers that I've seen in the newsreels. Who cares?"* ("Last Day," 27).

Though disturbed by thoughts of war, Babe can still find refuge in the childhood idyll. Vincent Caulfield, however, possesses a tortured psyche; he has already been separated from the warmth of his own past. In "Last Day" Vincent appears at the Gladwaller residence to share the last hours of his furlough. When Babe and Mattie return home, Vincent greets them at the door and acts as if he does not know them. He deadpans, "If you've come to read the gas meter, you two, you've come to the wrong house. We don't use gas. We burn the children for heat. Always have" ("Last Day," 61). His dark joke implies his obsessed comprehension of how war normalizes the slaughter of children. The specific burning child in question, one might say, is Holden Caulfield. Early in the story Babe tells his mother that Vincent "has a kid brother in the Army who flunked out of a lot of schools. He talks about him a lot. Always pretending to pass him off as a nutty kid" ("Last Day," 27). To Vincent, New York is "no good" since the letter arrived informing the family that Holden is missing. Holden's absence preys on Vincent's mind. In the middle of a conversation about Babe's girlfriend, Vincent blurts a seeming non sequitur: "He wasn't even twenty, Babe. Not till next month. I want to kill so badly I can't sit still. Isn't that funny? I'm notoriously yellow. . . . Now I want to shoot it out with people" ("Last Day," 61).

"Last Day of the Last Furlough" provides a point of departure that leads Salinger to depict Babe at war in "A Boy in France" and Vincent at war with himself in "This Sandwich Has No Mayonnaise." Each story presents psychological turmoil within a fixed dramatic setting. In both tales Salinger uses present-tense interior monologues to accentuate physical discomfort and psychological misery. Exhausted by battle, Babe has trouble finding an empty "Kraut hole" in which to sleep; Vincent is waiting on an army truck in a driving rainstorm in Georgia. They are supposed to go to a USO dance, but they cannot leave until four boys drop out. Bureaucratic symmetry must be maintained: there must be a girl for every boy. In "A Boy in France" Babe's interior monologue is encased within the account of a detached third-person narrator. Salinger thereby conveys Babe's mental disarray within a framework of realistic action: "*I won't dig in tonight*, the boy thought, walking on. *I won't struggle and dig and chop with that damn little entrenching tool tonight. I won't get hit. Don't let me get hit, Somebody. Tomorrow night I'll dig a swell hole, I swear I will.*"[24] In "This Sandwich" Salinger keeps the story completely within Vincent's tortured mind. While waiting in the downpour, Vincent thinks and he thinks. His mind runs in a riot of ruminative thought:

> Who swiped my raincoat? With all my letters in the left-hand pocket. My letters from Red, from Phoebe, from Holden. From Holden. Aw, listen, I don't care about the raincoat being swiped, but how about leaving my letters alone? He's only nineteen years old, my brother is. . . . My missing-in-action brother. Why don't they leave people's raincoats alone?
>
> I've got to stop thinking about it. Think of something pleasant, Vincent old troll. Think about this truck. Make believe this is not the darkest, wettest, most miserable Army truck you have ever ridden in.[25]

He reports a brief conversation, and then his thoughts return to their obsessive track: "Missing, missing, missing. Lies! I'm being lied to. He's never been missing before. He's one of the least missing boys in the world. He's here in this truck; he's home in New York; he's at Pentey Preparatory School ('You send us the Boy, We'll mold the Man—all modern fireproof buildings . . .'); yes, he's at Pentey, he never left school. . . . Missing! Is that missing? Why lie about something as important as that?" ("Sandwich," 191).

By locating Babe and Vincent in the narrative present, Salinger gives no hint regarding the disposition of subsequent events. At the very least a first-person retrospective account guarantees the narrator's survival. Locked in an experiential present, the reader, like the characters, is awash in the moment. Will Babe survive the night? Will Holden be found? Cut off from the safety of reliable expectations, each finds the present intolerable.

Both Babe and Vincent escape into imagination. Babe fashions a compensatory fantasy future; Vincent reconstructs the memory of a past, and now lost, idyll. Their mental wanderings provide some comfort. Ironically, the association with peace, coherence, and safety reinforces the horrors of the all-too-real present. Babe, for example, finds a "Kraut hole." He digs out the blood-encrusted dirt and imagines being whisked away through "the kind of abracadabra familiar to and special for G.I.'s in combat" ("Boy," 316). His fantasy brings together his craving for female companionship and his love for literature: an American woman will come through the window and read him the poems of Emily Dickinson and William Blake. Similarly, Vincent escapes the downpour and his grief by recalling comforting scenes from the past. He relishes the memory of "that Saturday in the summer at Port Washington." In one of the more remarkable passages in Salinger's work, Vincent recalls a perfect afternoon. Vincent's siblings were all alive. At the behest of brother Red—a prototype of the late Allie in *Catcher*—Vincent took Phoebe and a friend to the world's fair. In this recollection Holden was lost, but he was easily found. At the time the Caulfield parents were performing in a play, *Death Takes a Holiday*, a title that evokes the very process in which Vincent engages. Interestingly, Vincent's language evokes Holden's voice and inflections as they appear in *Catcher*, even as Vincent's memory captures the contours of Holden's iconoclastic personality:

> Red said to me, *It won't hurt you to see the Fair either. It's very pretty.* So I grabbed Phoebe, and she had some kid with her named Minerva (which killed me), and I put them both in the car and then I looked around for Holden. I couldn't find him; so Phoebe and Minerva and I left without him. . . . At the Fair we went to the Bell Telephone Exhibit, and I told Phoebe that *This Phone* was connected with the author of the *Elsie Fairfield* books. So Phoebe, shaking like Phoebe, picked up the phone and trembles into it, *Hello, this is Phoebe Caulfield, a child at the World's Fair. I read your books and think they are very excellent in spots. My mother and father are playing in* Death Takes a Holiday *in Great Neck. We go swimming a lot, but the ocean is better in Cape Cod. Good bye!* . . . And then we came out of the building and there was Holden, with Hart and Kirky Morris. He had my terry-cloth shirt on. No coat. He came over and asked Phoebe for her autograph and she socked him in the stomach, happy to see him, happy he was her brother. Then he said to me, *Let's get out of this educational junk. Let's go on one of the rides or something. I can't stand this stuff.* . . . And now they're trying to tell me he's missing. Missing. Who's missing? Not him. He's at the World's Fair. ("Sandwich," 192–93)

"A Boy in France" and "This Sandwich Has No Mayonnaise" depict the horrors of war, while presenting literature and memory, respectively, as temporary refuges. In both stories Mattie and Phoebe embody perfect innocence. Such refuges, of course, are tenuous at best. Babe receives clippings and letters from home that provide comfort, even as they reinforce his alienation. Good memories can also be self-lacerating, especially when they recreate lost moments. At the end of the story Vincent winds up having an unspoken monologue with his missing brother: "Stop kidding around. Stop letting people think you're Missing. Stop wearing my robe to the beach. Stop taking the shots on my side of the court. Stop whistling. Sit up to the table" ("Sandwich," 197).

"This Sandwich" reflects Salinger's early preoccupation with the lost idyll, which is dramatized here in terms of a surviving brother trying to contend with the memory of his apparently dead brother. This motif achieves fullest realization in the Glass stories: Buddy, Zooey, and Franny enact similar attempts to reconstruct the past. The psychological configuration of a surviving sibling trying to regain connection to a lost brother is reinforced in "The Stranger," when Vincent Caulfield dies in combat. In the company of Mattie, Babe goes to see Vincent's old love, Helen, who lives in an "ugly, expensive little New York apartment."[26] Ostensibly, Babe makes this journey to tell how Vincent died; actually, Babe's visit has more to do with exploring his own emotions. His trip, first, pays homage to his spiritual brother—a version of himself—and, second, defines the distance between the people who stayed home and the people who went to war. According to Ian Hamilton, this story finds "the war-damaged survivor pitiably suspended between two worlds—the world of combat and the world of civilian readjustment" (91). Babe's capacity for "readjustment" depends on his ability to communicate the true nature of his war experiences. Like Philly Barnes, Babe is outraged by the difference between the Hollywood portrayals of "comfortable lies" and the brute reality of death. Babe's interior monologue, however, underscores the frustrating incommunicability of what he has seen:

> Don't let any civilian leave you, when the story's over, with any comfortable lies. Shoot down all the lies. Don't let Vincent's girl think that Vincent asked for a cigarette before he died. Don't let her think he grinned gamely, or said a few choice last words.

>   These things don't happen. These things weren't done outside
>   movies and books except by a very, very few guys who were unable
>   to fasten their last thoughts to the depleting joy of being alive.
>   ("Stranger," 77)

Babe cannot overcome the terrifying chasm between pre- and postwar
America. He is tortured by "the music of the unrecoverable years; the
little, unhistorical, pretty good years when all the dead boys in the 12th
Regiment had been living and cutting in on other dead boys on lost
dance floors" ("Stranger," 18). Salinger presents an idyllic life contained within images of the recollected dance. The dancers may be
ghosts inhabiting Babe's memory, but their "unhistorical" innocence
still lives on in children in general and Mattie in particular. After the
visit to Helen, Babe perceives a life that is still to be lived. He sees a
little boy "trying to get his small, relaxed dog . . . to get up and finish
walking across the street." The story's final image presents a distilla-
tion of the dead soldiers' lost dance. Mattie "made a little jump from
the curb to the street surface, then back again. Why was it such a
beautiful thing to see?" ("Stranger," 77).

Here an innocent expresses herself in an unconscious aesthetic act.
It anticipates Holden's partially restorative experience in *Catcher* of witnessing a little boy walking along the edge of a curb, singing and hum-
ming "If a body catch a body coming through the rye."[27] Babe's journey
is psychologically therapeutic: he confronts the past and then focuses
on the present. So much of Salinger's fiction is retrospective in focus;
characters are continually looking backward in the hope of finding ex-
planations for an ongoing chaotic reality. As a survivor, Babe came
home from war to find himself emotionally displaced in an unfamiliar
present, believing he needed what could never be restored: the lost
(br)other. Instead he is moved to see the beauty of his sister's improvisational act.

Toward *The Catcher in the Rye*

J. D. Salinger's major creation, Holden Caulfield, looms in the popular
imagination with a sort of flesh-and-blood reality. Seeming more real
than life itself, this animated voice offers a modern version of Huck
Finn. Though Huck hails from a Missouri riverside hamlet in the 1840s
and Holden inhabits an upper-class world of urbane privilege, both

relate to "sivilization" as alienated misfits. But neither is a rebel. They have no desire to overthrow any system, however oppressed they might feel. As conflicted loners, they want out; they need to get away and seek a space that combines motion and peace: they long for a noncontingent existence. Holden is an innocent adolescent caught in the body of an adult; he likes to paw girls, but he is a virgin; he loves a few people passionately, but he does not "like *any*thing that's happening" (*Catcher*, 169).

This flippant, funny, self-dramatizing oddball lived in Salinger's imagination for at least 10 years. He made his first appearance in "Slight Rebellion off Madison," a story purchased by the *New Yorker* in 1941 but not published until December 1946. According to Warren French, the delay was occasioned by the editorial decision that all able young men, even fictional ones, should be thinking about going to war (1976, 24). Salinger did indeed send Holden (who in "The Stranger" is named Curtis) to war. The attempt to make the various Holden Caulfield stories a consistent body of work would be not only futile but wrongheaded: such an attempt would belie the *process* of Salinger's discovery, disposal, and recovery of a character too significant to let go.[28]

"Slight Rebellion" focuses on Holden's afternoon date with Sally Hayes and its drunken aftermath. Salinger narrates the story in the third person: "Holden's [dancing] style was long, slow side steps back and forth, as though he were dancing over an open manhole."[29] Holden's characteristic voice emerges in dialogue: he is essentially the character who speaks in *Catcher*. While sending Holden off to war, Salinger recasts his voice in the person of Billy, the narrator of "Both Parties Concerned," a story published in February 1944, five months before the appearance of "Last Day of the Last Furlough." Essentially, Holden dies but the voice lives into another tale and under another name. Billy "sounds very much like a slightly older Holden Caulfield, even down to his favorite locutions" (French 1988, 24). Married at 20 to the 17-year-old Ruth, Billy is overwhelmed by the emotional demands of wedded life and the added shock of paternity. In this story Salinger explores the entanglements of innocence and sex, all the while refining the voice and vision that would eventually inform Holden's extended narrative. It is plausible to suspect that after this one tale Salinger let Billy lie, deciding instead to resurrect Holden for "I'm Crazy," a story published in late December 1945, three weeks after the appearance of "The Stranger."

"I'm Crazy" depicts Holden's departure from "Pentey Prep," his farewell interview with Mr. Spencer, and his journey home. Holden tells his own story in the first person vernacular. In *Catcher* Salinger combines and extends the incidents in "Slight Rebellion" and "I'm Crazy." Because *Catcher* takes place after the end of World War II, the notion of Holden-as-soldier becomes anachronistic. In the novel the dead Vincent becomes the live D.B., an ex-soldier who survived the war only to become a self-prostituting screenwriter. D.B. never makes an appearance, though sister Phoebe appears in all versions without any substantial change. Phoebe's favorite author in "This Sandwich," Elsie Fairfield, provides in *Catcher* the basis of her own pen name, Hazel Weatherfield Caulfield. Brother Red of the story turns into the deceased, red-haired brother Allie in the novel. Salinger also disposes of another Caulfield sibling: Viola, the two-year-old sister in "I'm Crazy," disappears entirely.

The apparently seamless novel was the product of a decade of literary activity that saw Salinger try out Holden's character in at least seven published stories. Jack R. Sublette summarizes events in two unpublished Caulfield stories, in which intimations of both *Catcher* and the Glass stories emerge. In "The Last and Best of the Peter Pans" Vincent makes "references to a dead brother named Kenneth." The story presents "a conversation between Vincent and his mother—Mary Moriarity, an actress. . . . The conversation . . . ends with a reference to her 'want[ing] to save a child from crawling off a cliff.'" In "The Ocean Full of Bowling Balls" brother Kenneth is dead and Holden lives. The story details Vincent's relationship with Kenneth (Sublette, 20–21). The second story also holds a surprising anticipation of "Hapworth 16, 1924." Holden writes a long letter to Kenneth from "Camp Goodcrest for slobs." It is not clear why these undated stories were not published. It is clear, however, that Salinger was experimenting with various scenarios. He found his way into *Catcher* even as the late Kenneth provides a suggestive prefiguration of Seymour Glass. As Vincent is to Kenneth, so Buddy becomes to Seymour: the brotherly amanuensis.

In "Slight Rebellion off Madison" Holden Caulfield is home on Christmas break. He has neither dropped out nor flunked out. The third-person narrator tends to reflect a less strident and dissatisfied Holden than appears in the novel. When he and Sally Hayes go to the lobby during intermission at the theater, they encounter George Harrison, who was once introduced to Sally at a party: "Now, in the lobby of the Empire, they greeted each other with the gusto of two who might frequently have taken baths together as small children" ("Slight," 76). The wry narrator dilutes and even competes with Holden's disgust with pretentiousness:

> Sally asked George if he didn't think the show was marvellous. George gave himself a little room for his reply, bearing down on the foot of the woman behind him. He said that the play itself certainly was no masterpiece, but that the Lunts, of course, were absolute angels.
> "Angels," Holden thought. "Angels. For Chrissake. *Angels.*" ("Slight," 76)

Holden's "slight rebellion" focuses not only on phony language but more sweepingly on conventional forms of behavior. In a scene revised in *Catcher* Holden vents his disgust: "Sally, did you ever get fed up? I mean did you ever get scared that everything was gonna go lousy unless you did something?" His repugnance is all-encompassing; it lacks antecedents and seems too excessive for the actual circumstances of this story. Unlike Sally, who merely finds school a "terrific bore," Holden detests school: "Well, *I* hate it. . . . Boy, do I hate it! But it isn't just that. It's everything" ("Slight," 77). Holden's subsequent rant provides a sweeping dismissal of conventional life. His solution is to fashion an escape-to-nature fantasy that, ironically, would culminate in marriage to Sally. A normal girl very much at home with convention, Sally is utterly incapable of running away. She wrestles Holden's absurd plan into a pragmatic and levelheaded deferral: running away *would* be the thing to do, certainly, but only after Holden earns his college degree. She says, "There'll be oodles of marvellous places to go to." She replaces his escape wish with a guided tour. Holden's admission that "[i]t wouldn't be the same at all" reflects his inability to imagine himself taking part in the commonplace activities of life. Holden offers a subjunctive, negative counterlife to his escape fantasy: "We'd have to go downstairs in elevators with suitcases and stuff. We'd have to call up everyone and tell 'em goodbye and send 'em postcards. And I'd have to work at my father's and ride in Madison Avenue buses and read newspapers. . . . You don't see what I mean at all."

Indeed Holden is speaking another language. He loathes the thought of being his father's good son and the prospect of being confined within the strictures of a terrible sameness. In this piece, Holden's rebellion is essentially rhetorical: his most assertive act is to call Sally a "royal pain." He then goes off on a drunken spree. He poses similar queries to the obtuse Carl Luce. What would Carl do if he were "going stark, staring mad[?] Supposing you wanted to quit school and everything and get the hell out of New York. What would you do?" Carl tells Holden to "Drink up" and he does ("Slight," 78). He gets drunk and calls Sally. She hangs up. His escape fantasy is then replayed in darker tones; he concocts a death scene from a schlock Hollywood film. He sits on a radiator, for example, and calls to the piano player: "Hiya, boy! . . . I'm on the hot seat. They pulled the switch on me. I'm getting fried" ("Slight," 79). This incident prefigures Holden's penchant in *Catcher* for playacting. He enacts a similar death scene after Maurice the pimp roughs him up (*Catcher*, 103–4).

"Slight Rebellion" depicts Holden's contempt for convention, though the story does not carry this attitude beyond a series of episodic examples. "Both Parties Concerned" extends Holden's conflict with social convention by projecting his language and behavior onto Billy. Rather than escaping to the woods, Billy finds himself enmeshed by the responsibilities of marriage. In this story Salinger drops the third-person frame, thereby unifying narrating voice and acting self. The authority normally invested in the detached third-person voice dissolves into Billy's improvisational and provisional account of his attempt to understand his confusion. Like Holden in *Catcher*, Billy tends to repeat rhetorical tropes. Speaking of Ruthie, Billy claims, "I know her like a book. I mean I know her like a book."[30] This instinctual redundancy expresses Billy's nervousness, urgency, and insecurity. Repeatedly the past tense narrative passes into the present tense, a shift that accentuates his continuing attempt to assert what "I mean." He reports on a band playing in a bar: "They started playing 'Moonlight Becomes You.' It's old now, but it's a swell song. I mean it isn't a bad song" ("Both," 47). His use of the present tense allows the thoughts of one instant to be revised, if not contradicted, in the next. Speaking of Ruthie, he says, "She was being very cynical like. I don't like that. It don't bother me, but I don't like it" ("Both," 14).

The story's major conflict derives from Billy's insistence on going out every night with Ruthie. This practice allows them to evade the demands of parenthood, while nestling into a false paradise of music, drinks, and dancing. Billy's obsession with nightlife lets him extend his adolescence and continue his truncated period of dating. Like Holden in "Slight Rebellion" Billy longs for the noncontingent life. Ruthie is tired of going out but is unable to make Billy settle down. Consequently, the marriage nearly founders. Fed up, Ruthie moves out. Her good-bye letter jars Billy and initiates a series of disjunctive, neurotic actions. With his hand shaking from the shock of having just read the letter, Billy answers the door to find Moriarity, who wants to play basketball: "Then I did something nuts. I slammed Moriarity on the back like he was my long-lost brother—and I can't even stand the guy!" ("Both," 48). Like Holden playing a man in the electric chair, Billy starts to play Bogart in *Casablanca:* "I began to make believe Sam was in the room with me. Boy was I nuts!"

Essentially, Billy needs to grow up, give up his adolescent desires, and contend with the demands of marriage. Ruthie returns, but their relationship begins to become consolidated only after he wakes up during a thunderstorm, finds the bed empty, runs downstairs and discovers the frightened Ruthie sitting alone in the kitchen, and tells her she can "wake me when it thunders"—an indication that he is prepared to support another person. His concern for her "made her cry harder." Billy does not seem to understand the symbolic implications of this moment: "Funny kid. But she wakes me now, that's what I mean. It's okay with me. I mean it's okay with me. I mean I don't care if it thunders every night." Their unification derives from the acknowledged need for mutual dependence. "Both Parties Concerned" ends with the beginning of Billy's prospective passage into adulthood.

"I'm Crazy" presents an outline of the novel's major action. Holden flunks out of Pentey Prep and journeys home. Significantly, Holden tells his own story. "I'm Crazy" offers a version of Holden's interview with Mr. Spencer and his climactic conversation with Phoebe in her bedroom. A number of minor differences appear between the two works. For example, at the outset of "I'm Crazy" Holden stands alone on a Pentey hilltop, not outside a football game, as in *Catcher,* but outside a basketball game. It is not afternoon but evening. Holden is about to leave school. Salinger emphasizes Holden's alienation through his chosen dissociation from his peers as well as his morbid sensibility that has been formed from exposure to too many movies: "It was almost eight o'clock at night, and dark, and raining, and freezing, and the wind was noisy that way it is in the spooky movies on the night the old slob with the will gets murdered."[31] Trying to work up a good-bye feeling, Holden manifests his chronic self-effacement. First he views himself as an old man; then he imagines attending a funeral: "Boy, I was cold. Only a crazy guy would have stood there. That's me. Crazy. No kidding. I have a screw loose. But I had to stand there to feel the goodby to the youngness of the place, as though I were an old man. . . . I knew I'd never throw a football around ever again with the same guys at the same time. It was as though Buhler and Jackson and I had done something that had died and been buried, and only I knew about it, and no one was at the funeral but me" ("Crazy," 36).

Holden's interview with Mr. Spencer in *Catcher* virtually replicates the scene in "I'm Crazy." The aged Spencer attracts and repulses Holden. The teacher delivers an exasperated harangue about "life being a game . . . you should play . . . by the rules and all" ("Crazy," 48). Holden has as little interest in history as he does in the rules. His history exam is a jumble of freely associated pseudofacts on the science of embalming. As Spencer reads the exam aloud, Holden drifts into reverie. His meditation is a symbolic counterpoint to Spencer's dead Egypt. Holden wonders about the ducks: "I was sort of wondering if the lagoon in Central Park would be frozen over when I got home, and if it was frozen over would everybody be ice-skating when you looked out the window in the morning, and where did the ducks go, what happened to the ducks when the lagoon was frozen over." The ducks represent a vestige of natural life amid the encompassing concrete and steel of New York City. Holden's concern for the ducks suggests his preoccupation with threatened innocence. Holden never sees or finds out anything about the ducks in either work. The missing ducks haunt him.

On the train to the city, Holden has an opportunity to exercise his facility for narrative invention. While in *Catcher* Holden admits he is a liar, Salinger presents him in both works more as a fiction maker, an artist in life, a performer in a series of role-playing identity games. In "I'm Crazy" Holden meets the mother of Andrew Warbuck (Ernest Morrow in *Catcher*). "Strictly a louse," Warbuck is "the kind of guy, when you were a little kid, that twisted your wrist to get the marbles out of your hand." Holden speaks glowingly of Warbuck. His lies are designed, first, for self-entertainment and, second, to encourage a nice woman to have grand notions about her son. This penchant for story-telling reflects Holden's abiding desire to recast the true materials of experience into forms he can control.

Holden's nagging dissatisfaction with life assumes incipient form and partial resolution in "I'm Crazy." Here he has no horrific nighttime experiences. The scene on the train is followed by the final scene at his family's apartment. He returns home and goes to see his two sisters, the 10-year-old Phoebe and the 3-year-old Viola. Regarding Phoebe, Holden says, "She sounds like a goody-good, but it was only when it came to me. That's because she likes me. She's no goody-good, though. Phoebe's strictly one of us, for a kid." Similarly, Viola is "one of us." She is also at odds with the adult world. Hypersensitive, she tells Holden that "Jeanette [the maid] *breathes* on me all the time" and she took away Donald Duck. As in *Catcher,* Phoebe confronts Holden about his chronic dissatisfaction. He tells her, "They kept shoving stuff at me, exams and all, and study periods, and everything was compulsory all the time. I was going crazy. I just didn't like it." Phoebe proclaims, "But, Holden . . . you don't like *anything*" ("Crazy," 48, 51).

As a story, "I'm Crazy" trails off into underdeveloped suggestiveness. Holden faces his parents, though what transpires is not reported. He again visits his sisters' room, where he puts Donald Duck in Viola's crib and at her request lines up some olives for her to eat. "I'm Crazy" presents Holden's conflicted feelings about childhood, adolescence, and adulthood; his affiliation with childhood preempts his embrace of responsibility. Hung up between worlds, Holden climbs into his own bed. While waiting to fall asleep he realizes that "everybody was right and I was wrong" ("Crazy," 51). He fears the prospect of office work and wonders again about the whereabouts of the Central Park ducks. He falls asleep.

In *Catcher,* following his discussion with Phoebe, Holden avoids his parents and heads into the night. He is a prematurely gray-haired wanderer in an after-hours world that taunts, exhausts, and teaches him. But that is another story, a longer and much richer one.

Nine Stories

These Cryptic Fictions of Openness

With the 31 January 1948 publication of "A Perfect Day for Banana-fish" Salinger initiated a practice that would continue for 15 years: the publication of his short fiction in periodicals would be followed by hardback (and then paperback) collections. Had Salinger drawn his line a month earlier, *Ten Stories* would have included "The Inverted For-est."[32] We have nine stories rather than eleven or twelve because Sal-inger did not collect "A Girl I Knew" and "Blue Melody," both of which appeared after "A Perfect Day." Clearly, Salinger chose the stories he wished to stand on.

Once collected, these nine stories lost their vagrant, and separate, existences as periodical pieces and became part of a sequence. Each story assumes a relationship with its companion pieces. But how does one approach a collection? Does one see the stories as constituting a version of the novel? Are they merely stories that the author admired enough to collect? What is the cumulative effect of disparate tales on related themes?

Such questions have invited vexed critical inquiry into matters of theme and genre. Warren French, for example, argues for what he calls a short story cycle with a "progression based upon the slow and painful achievement of spiritual enlightenment" (1988, 63–64). French sees the stories as parts of an ordered thematic continuum with a beginning, middle, and end. James E. Miller, Jr., finds alienation to be Salinger's dominant theme, giving "the volume a singleness of impact which be-lies its multiplicity" (20).[33] Without question, *Nine Stories* resonates with those thematic complexes which animate the uncollected stories. For example, Salinger explores the conflict between the innocent, if problematic, world of children and the decadent, sterile world of adult-hood ("A Perfect Day," "Uncle Wiggily in Connecticut," "The Laugh-ing Man," "Down at the Dinghy," "For Esmé—with Love and Squalor");[34] the alienation of a postadolescent youth not yet initiated into manhood ("Just before the War with the Eskimos," "The Laughing Man," "De Daumier-Smith's Blue Period"); the ravages of war as a source of psychological breakdown ("A Perfect Day," "For Esmé"); and the use of cryptic fables and self-reflexive fiction-making ("A Perfect Day," "The Laughing Man"). Revealing his preoccupation with human beings living in the aftermath of some fall from a once-saving grace, Salinger presents in *every* story some version of a lost idyll, lost innocence, lost past, or lost opportunity. Indeed Salinger's characters frequently seem like posthumous survivors of a better world. It is also possible to view *Nine Stories* as being unified by Salinger's devotion to characters who belong to a recognizable socioeconomic world. They are white upper-middle-class residents of New York City or the surrounding suburbs. If Salinger's characters are on vacation, as they are in "A Perfect Day," "Down at the Dinghy," and "Teddy," or at war, as Sergeant X is in "For Esmé," then they are only temporarily displaced.

The presence of related themes, characters, and settings does not settle the issue of genre, the matter of what happens when one puts distinctive short stories together in the same book. On what aesthetic ground does one stand? Regardless of the reaches of critical ingenuity, *Nine Stories* can be classed neither as a novel nor as a serial story, nor, I submit, as reflecting an intelligible thematic organization with a beginning, middle, and end. The primary danger of pursuing self-contained artistic unity as a desirable critical goal derives from privileging the problematic New Critical axiom that successful works of literary art possess demonstrably coherent and cohesive structures. Second, applying such an axiom to a collection of stories presupposes that there is such a thing as The Novel (there are only multiple versions of novelized form) and that The Novel is the standard form to which modern prose fiction aspires. Once one points out that *Nine Stories* begins with the account of Seymour Glass's suicide and ends with Teddy's probable, though unconfirmed, death, one has little to go on regarding plot.

Nine Stories, as a whole, has its generic analogue not in well-wrought novels but in those fictional domains which create the *context* for establishing interconnections yet steadfastly refuse to impose the fiction of completed wholeness. As a collection, *Nine Stories* should be classed with such modernist works as James Joyce's *Dubliners*; Sherwood Anderson's *Winesburg, Ohio*; Ernest Hemingway's *In Our Time*; William Faulkner's *Go Down, Moses*; and Eudora Welty's *The Golden Apples*. Contemporary collections that suggest relationships but deny narrative completion can be found in John Barth's *Lost in the Funhouse*, Susan Minot's *Monkeys*, Lee K. Abbott's *Strangers in Paradise*, and Richard

Ford's *Rock Springs*. Barth presents a series of self-reflexive, ingenious narrative frames; Minot's Vincent family, living north of Boston, provides the focus for nine teasingly short stories; Abbott depicts the doings of hell-raisers, desperadoes, obsessives, and loners in the country-club desertlands of Deming, New Mexico; Ford explores the monotones of assorted Montana lowlifes who grope toward the wisdom that is sadness. Like *Nine Stories*, these works evoke the presence of an encompassing fictional world where characters in one tale would be (and sometimes are) at home in another. What is crucial is that the authors refuse to impose the fiction of closure. Instead they celebrate the entanglement of many loose ends. Rather than supporting the notion of unity and resolution, these collections, and *Nine Stories* in particular, raise possibilities but frustrate hopes for full disclosure. The tales tend to conclude with open-ended suggestion and sometimes even epiphany.[35] What always looms is the blank space between stories.

One has intimations of a larger, more complex world operating beyond the confines of the present narrative. For example, in *Nine Stories* four members of the Glass family appear or are mentioned: Seymour in "A Perfect Day," Walt in "Uncle Wiggily," and Boo Boo and Webb (presumably Buddy) in "Down at the Dinghy." Questions arise that are never addressed. What, for instance, is the significance of Lionel's attachment to the late Seymour's diving goggles in "Down at the Dinghy?" Is it a mere detail? Does it make Boo Boo afraid that Lionel might eventually share his uncle's fate? The appearance of family members in separate stories suggests a complex ongoing life that remains unreported. These connected stories—as in Joyce, Salinger, Ford—attempt to render life as a series of loose-fitting fragments. The encompassing form—suggested by titles that are matter-of-fact (*Nine Stories*), geographical (*Dubliners, Rock Springs*), or symbolic (*Strangers in Paradise*)—identify the perimeters within which the juxtaposition of related themes or characters will deny aesthetic closure.

The famous epigraph to *Nine Stories*—"We know the sound of two hands clapping. / But what is the sound of one hand clapping?"—provides access to Salinger's mysterious and open-ended narratives. The epigraph is a Zen koan, an epigrammatic form designed to eclipse the pursuit of solutions through logic and rationality. Its prominent placement has invited speculation regarding the relationship between Eastern thought and these stories about urbane Americans, especially insofar as Eastern philosophy offers a religious and experiential alternative to materialistic America. As James Lundquist remarks, "The word *Zen* means thinking, meditation, to see, to contemplate."[36] A koan offers an intense focus for this meditative process. Salinger's epigraph seems to be a riddle that has no solution per se: Is silence the sound of one hand clapping? Is it the sound a tree makes when it falls in the forest with no one there to hear? In focusing meditation, any koan releases the tranquil play of mind. Ostensibly, the koan presents a riddle; actually, it constitutes an approach to experience: intuitive rather than rational, poetic rather than empirical, connotative rather than denotative. A koan opens one's being to the impress of intuition, which achieves its most conscious expression through the experience of epiphany. Many of the nine stories turn on a character's apparently stunning realization. Often the character achieves such insight in response to some physical object: the intoxicated Eloise in "Uncle Wiggily" weeps over her daughter's eyeglasses; Sergeant X begins to regain his faculties after unwrapping the gift from Esmé. Such moments of awakening have their counterpoint in more cryptic endings usually characterized by odd, disjunctive events. At the end of "Just before the War," Ginnie decides to keep Franklin's chicken sandwich, an act that presumably has something to do with the fact that it once took her three days to dispose of a dead Easter chick. Booper's scream at the end of "Teddy" suggests (but does not confirm) that she, as Teddy had predicted, shoved him into an empty swimming pool.

At issue is Salinger's insistence on interpretive openness, an antidote, as it were, to Holden Caulfield's rigid and prescribed reading of the world. Holden views himself, for example, as a self-proclaimed Messiah, a catcher of children who might otherwise tumble off "some crazy cliff" (*Catcher,* 173). His realization that he has to let the children fall constitutes an acceptance of random cause and effect. However frightening, the world must remain open. It is from this perspective, then, that Salinger offers a sequence of tales that excite, even as they frustrate, the activity of reading.

"A Perfect Day for Bananafish"

"A Perfect Day for Bananafish" presents the circumstances immediately preceding the suicide of Seymour Glass. On their second honeymoon, Seymour and his wife, Muriel, are staying in a hotel in Miami Beach. The vacation is to be not only recreational but restorative: Seymour is not himself. While serving in the military he had to be hospitalized for mental problems. He was not, it appears, cured. But to approach the story with the expectation of forming a clinical diagnosis is, as James E. Miller, Jr., observes, a reductive venture: "To assume that Seymour is simply a psychotic is to render the story meaningless. To interpret his suicide as his simple and direct device to sever his marriage to a vacuous, spiritually shallow girl is to reduce the story to the dimensions of the daily tabloid" (27–28).

"A Perfect Day" contains two primary scenes. In the first, Muriel speaks to her mother on the telephone. They discuss Seymour's condition, especially his odd actions. Their dialogue provides details from the past that heighten the uncertainty about the present. Is Seymour really crazy? If he is, what will he do? Mrs. Fedder thinks Seymour is a psychotic. On the phone she is nervous and upset; she feels that Muriel wasted herself on an unfit husband; now the crazy man threatens her daughter's safety. In the second scene Seymour is lying on the beach, where he is joined by the four-year-old Sybil Carpenter. Seymour is calm, engaging, wry, playful. He seems anything but a "raving *maniac*."[37] Seymour talks to Sybil, takes her into the ocean, and tells her a fable about bananafish.

The conversations in these two scenes juxtapose two competing frames of reference: a normative adult world of materialistic concerns and a child's world of imaginative play. Muriel is very much at home in a hotel that houses "ninety-seven New York advertising men" (3).[38] Having tied up the phone lines, these working men make "the girl in 507 . . . wait from noon till almost two-thirty to get her call through. She used the time, though." Muriel reads an article, "Sex Is Fun—or Hell." She also performs a number of minor practical chores: she cleans her comb and brush, removes a spot from a skirt, rearranges a button, paints her nails. Though having waited for hours, Muriel does not leap when the phone rings. In fact "she was a girl who for a ringing phone dropped exactly nothing." Her conversation with her mother offers an incomplete account of Seymour's apparently psychotic episodes. He does and says strange, even violent, things: he drove a car into a tree; he called his wife "awful things"; now, Muriel reports, he "has something new. . . . He calls me Miss Spiritual Tramp of 1948" (5). He also insisted that Muriel read Rilke's poems in the original, even though Muriel cannot read German.[39] Recently, we find, Mr. Fedder consulted a psychiatrist: "He told [Dr. Sivetski] everything. . . . The trees. That business with the window. Those horrible things he said to Granny about her plans for passing away. What he did with all those lovely pictures from Bermuda—everything" (6). In the face of her mother's distress, Muriel remains calm.

Though generally seen as a crass and shallow woman, Muriel does not seem anything other than resolutely normal: in fact she seems supportive and tolerant. She appears genuinely mindful of Seymour's well-being. If anything, she underestimates the seriousness of Seymour's condition, seeming instead to feel that a nice vacation will start them on the road to happiness. She has none of her mother's rancor.

Salinger always portrays psychiatrists in a negative way. He associates them with a destructive tendency toward obtuse generalization—a denial of the unique complexity of each individual. Mrs. Fedder reports Dr. Sivetski's fear that Seymour will lose control of himself. Muriel also spoke briefly to a psychiatrist who claimed he "had to have more facts. . . . They have to know about your childhood—all that stuff" (8). Salinger debunks the notion that sufficient "facts" will allow a trained professional to identify the disease and prescribe a cure. A belief in such "stuff" belies the possibility that Seymour's recent wartime experiences could have upset his balance. In light of the subsequent Glass stories, it is possible that Seymour might be crazy only from the conventional point of view. Perhaps Seymour opted out of the Fedder world. In any event the pursuit of "facts" runs in complete opposition to the imagistic contexts supplied by Seymour's language. For example, he explained why he lies on the beach all covered up: "He won't take his bathrobe off. . . . He says he doesn't want a lot of fools looking at his tattoo" (9–10). On the surface, the statement is preposterous: Seymour has no tattoo. Imagistically, however, Seymour does feel marked, disfigured, at odds, perhaps, with anything resembling machismo.

Seymour seeks emotional sustenance in the company of a child. Sybil Carpenter's name and personality, however, collide with the expectations of childhood innocence. The name Sybil evokes the prophetic seer and harbinger of death who is given eternal life without eternal youth. In T. S. Eliot's *The Waste Land*, the epigraph, attributed to the Sibil of Cumae, reads, "What do you want? I want to die."[40] Seymour quotes a phrase from the poem, accentuating his sense of entrapment. When reminded of a nice little girl, Sharon Lipschutz, he remarks, "How that name comes up. Mixing memory and desire" (13). What may be remembered and desired is the childhood idyll, an experiential counterforce to spiritual tramps. Sybil's surname suggests the material realm, which aligns her with the world of things. Eberhard Alsen in fact views Sybil as "a miniature Muriel" (13). By any estimation she is not a darling child; she is mean-spirited, irritable, and demanding. She was ready to push Sharon Lipschutz off a piano stool.

Seymour compliments Sybil on her blue bathing suit—the color of his suit. In fact her bathing suit is yellow, a point that associates her with the fabled bananafish. After they go into the water, Seymour tells her a story about the bananafish: "They lead a very tragic life. . . . [T]hey swim into a hole where there's a lot of bananas. They're very ordinary-looking fish when they swim *in*. But once they get in, they behave like pigs. Why, I've known some bananafish to swim into a banana hole and eat as many as seventy-eight bananas. . . . Naturally, after that they're so fat they can't get out of the hole again. . . . They die" (15–16). Dallas E. Wiebe convincingly argues that when Sybil goes underwater and comes up claiming to have seen six bananafish, she is actually seeing Seymour's toes sticking out of the sand.[41] By seeing his six toes Sybil in effect tells him that he is abnormal. In Wiebe's view she can be seen as unwittingly sentencing him to death: a child has identified him with a bananafish. Seymour is very sensitive about his feet. On the way back to his room he angrily denounces a woman for staring at them. He insists his feet are quite normal. At the least Seymour's vision of a normal fish becoming glutted reveals a disgust with sensuality. To view the fish as phallic and the banana hole as vaginal may well provide a context for Muriel's concern for whether "Sex Is Fun—or Hell." Certainly, Seymour's gun is phallic: "He cocked the piece. Then he went over and sat down on the unoccupied bed, looked at the [sleeping] girl, aimed the pistol, and fired a bullet through his right temple" (18).

The narrator of "A Perfect Day" is detached, retentive, cryptic, relaying surface action but rarely explaining or judging events. The reason for Seymour's suicide offers, consequently, an open field for speculation. Alsen locates the causes in Seymour's spiritual deterioration (202–9). French argues that Seymour pulls the trigger because he sees himself as a "failed guru" (1988, 68). Bryan considers this death a response to sexual guilt.[42] Salinger fashions an interpretive enigma: Seymour's suicide is the mystery at the center of his fiction.

Salinger insists that the reader, like the psychiatrist, *not* be given adequate facts. One can only formulate a series of questions: What was the nature of Seymour's breakdown during the war? Which Rilke poems did he send? What did Seymour do to those "lovely pictures"? What is the nature of his relationship with Muriel? Why does he kiss

Sybil's foot? Why does he shoot himself in the head? From Mrs. Fedder's perspective, Seymour is a psychotic. Or, as Buddy later indicates, he might be a man who has seen through the masks of materiality, the empty forms of maya. Having repudiated the phenomenal realm, Seymour must then eradicate the vessel that contains, restricts, and possibly defiles his spirit. Regardless of one's speculations, the basic critical problem in "A Perfect Day" and in *Nine Stories* is to contend with one's limited and provisional interpretive authority. Salinger's teasing use of numerology offers not so much a series of coded keys as a set of questions. Why, for example, does the number six figure so prominently? Six tigers run around the tree in "Little Black Sambo." Sybil sees six bananafish. Seymour's gun is an "Ortega calibre 7.65," while his hotel room number is 507.[43]

The first of *Nine Stories* introduces the Glass family saga. The lives of the surviving family members lead up and point back to (but never get away from) this awful event in 1948. By taking his own life Seymour achieves the status of an absent presence, a haunting specter. He is either lost man or holy man, a zero or a circle, a fractured man or a sainted man. His absence focuses the mystery that haunts their lives.

"Uncle Wiggily in Connecticut"

Eloise and Mary Jane, former college roommates, have plans to get together for lunch. Neither graduated; both left school after their sophomore year. Having had one daughter named Ramona, Eloise is now a housewife married to Lew, for whom she feels contempt. After a disastrous marriage, Mary Jane became a career woman. She is coming out to Eloise's swank, Connecticut suburb, where the two will be able to catch up on each other's lives. Mary Jane gets lost on the way. She is late for lunch, but it does not matter: there is plenty of time; they can have a few drinks.

In "Uncle Wiggily in Connecticut" the afternoon confab gradually reveals the frustrations that make Eloise's life miserable. Out there in the suburbs she suffers in exile from a better self that was lost a long time ago when her boyfriend, Walt, was absurdly killed in a freak wartime accident. In retaliation Eloise lashes out at the people around her: with racist hauteur she lords it over the black maid; she mocks old friends; her contempt for her husband is leavened only by a self-effacing humor. Speaking of her daughter, Eloise says, "She looks like Lew. When his mother comes over the three of them look like triplets. . . .

What I need is a cocker spaniel or something. . . . Somebody that looks like me" (24). Eloise has consigned herself to an emotional penal colony: she imprisons herself and tortures others. Her chief victim is her daughter—emotional neglect and incessant nagging characterize Eloise's relationship with Ramona.[44]

Ramona, afflicted with myopia, peers at the world through thick lenses. An introverted, withdrawn child of approximately four years of age, she picks her nose, scratches herself, and uses faulty grammar, all of which elicit irritated correctives from her mother. Ramona is both truculent and honest. When Mary Jane asks for a "little kiss," she replies, "I don't like to kiss people" (25). Because she has no playmates, Ramona resorts to invention. Her imaginary boyfriend, Jimmy Jimmereeno, focuses and feeds her inner life. Jimmy has "green eyes and black hair. . . . No mommy and no daddy. . . . No freckles." He also has a sword. Mary Jane wonders whether he took off his galoshes:

> "He has boots," Ramona said.
> "Marvellous," Mary Jane said to Eloise.
> "You just think so. I get it all day long. Jimmy eats with her. Takes a bath with her. Sleeps with her. She sleeps way over to one side of the bed, so's not to roll over and hurt him." (26–27)

Ramona's boyfriend provides a compensatory world. Jimmy is hers; he is not afflicted by parents; his sword provides an image of power and romance.

Ramona is actually living out the stunted, frustrated inner life of her mother. Eloise, too, has an invisible boyfriend. The dead soldier, Walt, had the capacity to "make me laugh. I mean really laugh" (28). Walt represents Eloise's lost idyll. She recalls how "nice" he was: "[H]e showed up late once just as the bus was pulling out. We started to run for it, and I fell and twisted my ankle. He said, 'Poor Uncle Wiggily.' He meant my ankle. Poor old Uncle Wiggily, he called it" (29). Walt was an unusual person. He often made strange, humorous remarks. Once they were on a train, and "he sort of had his hand on my stomach. You know. Anyway, all of a sudden he said my stomach was so beautiful he wished some officer would come up and order him to stick his other hand through the window. He said he wanted to do what was fair" (30). Walt's odd remarks seem to be a way of speaking about love, the words suggesting rather than denoting the nature of the feeling. His words are as enigmatic as his brother Seymour's clasp of Sybil's ankles. Conventional words cannot express certain notes on the emotional register. Eloise's recollections of Walt exacerbate her loneliness. She seems close to desperation, and her language, at times, betrays a fixation with death. For example, when Mary Jane refuses another drink because she is supposed to be working, Eloise blurts, "Call up and say you were killed. Let go of that damn glass. . . . Go phone. Say you're dead. . . . Gimme that." Her emotional life, as it were, is buried with Walt.

Like Ramona, Eloise is "lousy with secrets." She will not tell Lew that Walt was a private. Nor would she let him know that Walt is dead. Lew would be "worse [than jealous]. He'd be a *ghoul*. . . . The last thing I'd do would be to tell him he was killed. But the last thing. And if I did—which I wouldn't—but if I *did*, I'd tell him he was killed in action" (32). At this point Mary Jane presses Eloise for details of Walt's death. She tells her: "Walt and some other boy were putting this little Japanese stove in a package. Some colonel wanted to send it home. . . . Anyway, it was all full of gasoline and junk and it exploded in their faces. The other boy just lost an eye" (33).

Ramona functions as an unconscious secret sharer in her mother's emotional life. Ramona announces that Jimmy is dead. Her loss of Jimmy emphasizes as it replicates her mother's loss of Walt. With Ramona, however, there is a startling difference. Later, when drunk, Eloise goes upstairs and finds her daughter all the way over in the bed. Remembering that Jimmy is dead, Eloise wakes Ramona and demands an explanation. Ramona does not want to hurt her new beau, Mickey Mickeranno. Eloise becomes extremely disturbed and orders her daughter to the center of the bed. When she does not budge, Eloise drags her. Essentially, Ramona is able to see what is not there—a Jimmy or a Mickey—and thereby has an emotionally sustaining bond with this imagined presence. Moreover, unlike Walt, Jimmy is replaceable. The power of imagination—the safe world of Ramona's solipsistic retreat—can overcome death. The problem with Eloise is that Walt *is* dead: her memories, however wonderful, emphasize distance. Walt's death began a process that mutated Eloise's decent, kind, and loving personality.

Following this outburst, Eloise "stood for a long time in the doorway. Then, suddenly, she rushed, in the dark, over to the night table, banging her knee against the foot of the bed, but too full of purpose to feel pain. She picked up Ramona's glasses and, holding them in both hands, pressed them against her cheek. Tears rolled down her face, wetting the lenses. 'Poor Uncle Wiggily,' she said over and over again" (37). She then kisses her daughter and goes down to awaken the drunken Mary Jane. Eloise now recalls herself as the young Idaho innocent who arrived in Manhattan and was mocked for having a "brown-and-yellow dress" from Boise. The fact that Eloise then "cried all night" suggests, she hopes, that she "was a nice girl" (38).

Salinger's retentive narrator withholds psychological access; he does not explain these events. They appear in sequence. Separately and collectively, however, they do imply the nature of Eloise's epiphany: she now views herself in all her meanness, once a nice girl, now a muddled failure. Ramona's glasses connect her to her own innocent and lost world of Walt Glass, a connection reinforced by the association with the children's story of Uncle Wiggily. Because her insight is contained within her drunken spree, she might merely be wallowing in boozy self-pity. Salinger offers no inkling as to what might come next. In effect, he concludes "Uncle Wiggily" by dramatizing a potentially restorative insight that is never tested by subsequent action. Like the ending of "A Perfect Day," the ending of "Uncle Wiggily" evokes meditation on the story's unresolved emotional matrix.

"Just before the War with the Eskimos"

"Just before the War with the Eskimos" reflects Salinger's preoccupation with centering the drama of his short stories in partially self-revelatory conversations. Ginnie Maddox goes to Selena Graff's apartment in order to be reimbursed for cab fare. Following their weekly tennis match Ginnie is tired of "getting stuck—every single time—for the whole cab fare" (39). Selena supplies the balls but does not pay for them. Salinger presents an atmosphere of petty nagging and "hostile silence" (41). Ginnie insists on getting her money and refuses to be deterred by Selena's passive aggression, especially her apparent strategy of making Ginnie wait. While sitting in the living room, Ginnie meets Selena's brother, Franklin, who barges in, excited over his cut finger. He asks whether Ginnie ever cut her finger " 'right down to the bone and all?'. . . There was a real appeal in his noisy voice, as if Ginnie, by her answer, could save him from some particularly isolating form of pioneering" (42–43).

Franklin's cut finger offers access to his conflicted inner life. Through his conversational posturing—his tough-guy bravado, his swearing, his slang, his smoking, his caustic, though playful, assertions—Franklin is obliquely soliciting Ginnie's friendship. The story depicts a subtle interaction between surface details and psychological implication. In Ginnie's case the question of Franklin's "appeal" focuses her growing interest in him. She seeks an appropriate posture. She, too, is playing a role. She wants to talk with him but is wary of showing too much. At one point she feels "her answer was too civil under the circumstances" (45). At issue is the nature of Ginnie's response. At the least their conversation wins her away from her dour mood.

Just as Seymour opens himself to the companionship of children, and Ramona fabricates playmates, so too does Franklin fashion a persona that might compensate for his deficiencies. Like Holden Caulfield, Franklin hangs suspended between adolescence and adulthood. At age 24 he is too old to be a boy, but that is what he seems most to be. He has quit his job and will not return to college. His heart condition keeps him in a state of emotional and social paralysis. Because of his bad "ticker" he could not be drafted, and thus he performed alternative service in an airplane factory. There he became friends with Eric, a young man who manifests cartoonish, effeminate affectations. Using the hated word *grand*, he speaks in an ornate manner: "You may quote me wildly on that" (51). Eric apparently was released from service because he is a homosexual. The story's implied drama suggests that Franklin's inability to participate in conventionally masculine domains are leading him toward homosexuality. Franklin's sense of manhood is further threatened by his lack of success with women, particularly Ginnie's older sister. A failed suitor, Franklin wrote Joan eight unanswered letters. When Franklin calls her "Joan the Snob," Ginnie tacitly defends her sister but secretly enjoys his gibe.

The dialogue suggests, but does not detail, the story's informing psychodrama. Franklin's need for female companionship emerges through his insistence that Ginnie take his leftover chicken sandwich. Like Walt Glass, Franklin Graff seems to be talking in some strange language that connotes, but does not spell out, his specific emotional desires. The chicken sandwich is an odd gift: it has no context. The enigmatic offering, which Ginnie accepts, establishes the perimeters of the story's unexplained content. There is a connection between Ginnie's relationship with Franklin and her own emotional uplift. When Selena finally returns with the money, for example, Ginnie tells her she does not want it. She gives up her plans for the movies and asks Selena whether she can come back that night, presumably in hope of encountering Franklin.

The detached narrator denies access to Ginnie's motives. By investing the day-old sandwich with unresolved interpretive significance, Salinger focuses attention on these odd reciprocal gestures. The story's final sentence creates uncomfortable ambiguities regarding Ginnie's motives: "A few years before, it had taken her three days to dispose of the Easter chick she had found dead on the sawdust in the bottom of her wastebasket" (55). This cryptic statement invites rumination. Does Ginnie have a tendency to retain dead things? Is her retentiveness a sign that she is open to Franklin, or is it a reflection of futile, misplaced sentimentality? Since Franklin is neither dead nor a chicken, perhaps he is capable of being restored by Ginnie. However one reads the ending, the primary critical fact is that the narrator, though having made numerous judgments earlier, now refuses to resolve lingering questions. It seems that Ginnie herself is not sure why she is interested. She has been touched emotionally and alerted to the possibility of a new friendship. She will supposedly come back to try to find what she feels, but Salinger does not take us back with her.

"The Laughing Man"

In "The Laughing Man," one of Salinger's best stories, the unnamed adult narrator recounts his childhood escapades as a member of the Comanche Club. Under the protective tutelage of the Chief—a young NYU law student named John Gesudski—the boys experience in the heart of New York City the high life of sport and the imaginative life of a serial story narrated to them by Gesudski. Gesudski's job is to pick the boys up after school and take them out to play. The Chief stands not only as surrogate big brother but also vatic mentor. They play baseball. When it rains they go to the museum. The daily activities always include an installment of the Chief's running narrative of the Laughing Man: "It was a story that tended to sprawl all over the place, and yet it remained essentially portable. You could always take it home with you and reflect on it while sitting, say, in the outgoing water in the bathtub" (58). In looking back, the narrator reflects on the childhood idyll with good humor and warm spirits. He evidences none of the alienation of Seymour or the rancor of Eloise.

Comic play and zany invention characterize the Chief's story. He makes a new world: Paris borders France and Tibet is by the sea. The tale obliterates boundaries between human beings and animals. A lonely, deformed bandit, the Laughing Man wears a poppy-petal mask to hide his ugliness. In the forest "he befriended any number and species of animals. . . . Moreover, he removed his mask and spoke to them, softly, melodiously, in their own tongues. They did not think him ugly" (59). He lived with a small band of "blindly loyal Confederates," among whom are Black Wing, "a glib timber wolf" and Omba, "a lovable dwarf" (61). The serial tale zooms along in a wild foray of complication and resolution. Suffused with gruesome violence, the story chronicles the Laughing Man's continuing battle with his archenemies, Marcel Dufarge and "his daughter (an exquisite girl, though something of a transvestite). . . . Time and again, they tried leading the Laughing Man up the garden path. For sheer sport, the Laughing Man usually went halfway with them, then vanished, often leaving no even faintly credible indication of his escape method" (60).[45] The Laughing Man repeatedly displays his resilience. His antagonists cannot contain him. An outlaw, the Laughing Man is a Robin Hood. He gives his loot "anonymously to the monks of a local monastery—humble ascetics who had dedicated their lives to raising German police dogs" (61). For the narrator, the storytelling Chief testifies to the power of imagination, especially its capacity to vitalize experience: "I regarded myself not only as the Laughing Man's direct descendant but as his only legitimate living one. I was not even my parents' son in 1928 but some devilishly smooth impostor" (61). His most real life exists within the expanding reaches of the tale. The Chief's story gives the Comanches a secret life, an internal kingdom of magical transformation. The children are "circulating ominously, and incognito, throughout the city, sizing up elevator operators as potential archenemies, whispering side-of-the-mouth but fluent orders into the ears of cocker spaniels, drawing beads with index fingers, on the foreheads of arithmetic teachers. And always waiting, waiting for a decent chance to strike terror and admiration in the nearest mediocre heart" (62).

The exuberant narrator presents, on the one hand, the action as a child would perceive it and suggests, on the other, the meaning of the story from an adult perspective (though he does not specify this meaning). To balance the innocent and knowing points of view, the narrator employs a parenthetical style. He frequently ruptures his syntax with interpolated commentary. For example, in speaking of the Laughing Man's "flesh-sealed nostrils," the narrator describes the way in which "the hideous, mirthless gap below his nose dilated and contracted like (as *I* see it) some sort of monstrous vacuole. (The Chief demonstrated, rather than explained, the Laughing Man's respiration method)" (59). The first parentheses draw attention to the narrator's subjective viewpoint; the second gives the reader a descriptive overview of the Chief's antics. Not only does the pervasive use of parentheses reinforce the narrator's retrospective focus, but it also celebrates the (apparently) offhanded spontaneity of the narrative itself. The parentheses amend, as they comment on, the narrator's tale.

The Laughing Man's story exists not only as a wild escapade but also as veiled autobiography. The Chief's tale provides an oblique parallel to his life. As Richard Allan Davison argues, the Laughing Man is a caricatured self-portrait of the Chief.[46] Gesudski feels he is ugly: he is short and stocky; he has a "large and fleshy" nose. Just as the animals love the Laughing Man, so too do the children love the Chief. To them he is an amalgam of "Buck Jones, Ken Maynard, and Tom Mix" (58). Like the Laughing Man, the Chief is lonely. One day, however, the Chief violates the "general men-only decor of the bus" by putting up his girlfriend's photo. Soon Mary Hudson becomes part of the retinue. As James E. Miller, Jr., notes, "when the young man's relationship with Mary Hudson blossoms . . . the plot of his tale proliferates with great energy and gusto" (21).

Eventually signs of tension show. The Chief's tale reflects the strain in the couple's relationship. Not only is Mary late for a rendezvous, but the Laughing Man becomes trapped by the Dufarges. While barbed-wired to a tree, the infuriated Laughing Man pushes off his mask, causing Mlle. Dufarge to pass out. Possibly, Gesudski has been revealing unsavory aspects of himself and Mary is repulsed. Certainly John and Mary hail from different social classes: he has to scrape his way through law school; she comes from money. As Warren French suggests, "it seems possible that the Chief is using his fantastic narrative to objectify his own problems with his girl's disapproving father" (1988, 74).

While the actual causes of the rupture remain hidden, the narrator employs his parenthetical style to suggest without defining the fact of the romantic breakup: "I had no idea what was going on between the Chief and Mary Hudson (and still haven't, in any but a fairly low, intuitive sense), but nonetheless, I couldn't have been more certain that Mary Hudson had permanently dropped out of the Comanche lineup" (70). The playful tone indicates that the story is not tragic. People

Part 1

break up. The Chief's disappointment apparently leads him to conclude the running saga of the Laughing Man. In the final installment,
which follows Mary Hudson's tearful departure, the Laughing Man
dies after finding out that the Dufarges killed his beloved Black Wing.
The hero refuses nourishment and orders Omba the dwarf to pull off
his mask: "The story ended there, of course. (Never to be revived)"
(73).

The Chief's imposition of closure might derive from his own psychological inadequacies. For example, Richard Allan Davison argues,
"[The Chief] engages in what is a symbolic suicide and murder, a
murder not only of the Laughing Man but also of the dreams of twenty-
five children" (13). Such a reading, however, overstates the story's
ominous implications. Rather than being a sadistic killjoy, the Chief
simply continues what he has been doing all along: rendering his inner
life in fable. Far from being tragic, the story's ending marks a rupture
that in effect is a point of passage. In seeing "a piece of red tissue paper
flapping in the wind," the narrator recalls that it "looked like someone's poppy-petal mask" (73). The opiate of story is gone, as is a bit
of childhood. The child winds up in bed with a cold—a necessary sub-
mission to the facts of life. Irving Deer and John H. Randall III remark
on the ending: "By the use of myth, the Chief has conveyed to the
boys the essential inner meaning of adult experience."[47] The narrator's
abiding good humor reflects his balanced attitude: he can review the
childhood idyll in all its escapist splendor; he can perceive its dissolu-
tion as necessary for (rather than inimical to) one's sane adaptation to
a postadolescent world. The geography of experience has returned to
its customary coordinates. Paris and China no longer share a border;
landlocked Tibet remains far away from any "stormy coast" (61).

"Down at the Dinghy"

"Down at the Dinghy" juxtaposes two conversations. In the first, Sandra, the maid, and Mrs. Snell, a pretentious, label-conscious cleaning
woman, discuss Lionel, the four-year-old son of Sandra's employers,
Mr. and Mrs. Tannenbaum. The family is in the waning days of their
summer vacation at a lake within commuting distance of New York
City. In the second conversation Mrs. Beatrice (Boo Boo) Tannenbaum
(née Glass) goes down to the dinghy to try to convince Lionel not to
run away.

Sandra is worried that Lionel heard her make an undivulged disparaging remark. She projects her guilt onto Lionel, blaming the secretive boy for his silent arrivals. He might be anywhere: "[I]t drives ya loony, the way that kid goes pussyfootin' all around the house. Ya can't *hear* him, ya know. I mean nobody can *hear* him, ya know. . . . I mean ya gotta weigh every word ya say around him" (75). Sandra feels no remorse over what she said; she only fears that Lionel heard and might tell his mother. Sandra's characteristic response is to snort as she "malcontentedly" and "rancorously" (76) registers her disdain for her employers and her hatred for "this crazy place." Her anti-Semitism allows her to forge a facile sense of superiority. After Mrs. Snell remarks that Lionel is "kind of a good-lookin' kid," Sandra replies, "He's gonna have a nose just like the father" (76). Salinger does not limit his attack on phonies to the elite classes. His portrait of Sandra savages her smug self-righteousness and vile prejudices.

The "Lady of the house," Boo Boo, enters the kitchen. In comparison with her employee, Boo Boo appears childlike, pure, and bright: "She was a small, almost hipless girl of twenty-five, with styleless, colorless, brittle hair pushed back behind her ears, which were very large. . . . Her joke of a name aside, her general unprettiness aside, she was—in terms of permanently memorable, immoderately perceptive, small-area faces—a stunning and final girl" (77). In distinction to the hateful and pretentious domestics, Boo Boo retains the spirit of innocence. She comes into the kitchen looking for pickles. Apparently she has already gone once to entice Lionel to return. This time she will try to bribe him. With Boo Boo's arrival Sandra and Mrs. Snell adjust their attitudes. They feign concern. Mrs. Snell says, " 'I hear Lionel's supposeta be runnin' away.' She gave a short laugh." Boo Boo answers, "He's been hitting the road regularly since he was two. But never very hard" (77–78). When confronted by anything disagreeable, Lionel flees. According to Boo Boo, he once heard a child tell him, "You stink, kid." Another time a girl told him that "she had a worm in her thermos bottle." He then "sought refuge under a sink in the basement of our apartment house" (79). In the present case, Lionel's flight carries him to the family's rented boat.

A sensitive, brooding, withdrawn child, Lionel tends to take words literally. Unlike the Comanches, he does not inhabit a safe, fictive world where horrors can be accommodated. This story continues Salinger's exploration of the relationship between fiction making and self-expression begun in the first five stories. In "A Perfect Day" Seymour's fable provides an indictment of adult experience; in "Uncle Wiggily" Ramona creates a compensatory world; in "Down at the Dinghy" Boo Boo attempts to use role-playing to cure Lionel of his strident literalness. She tries to talk her way into his separate world. When Boo Boo claims to be an admiral, Lionel replies, "You aren't an admiral" (81). He refuses to allow his mother her fiction. Instead he defines her as an adult: "You're a lady all the time." He is not, certainly, *playing* sailor. He is truly running away. As Seymour Glass's sister, Boo Boo must fear the onset of a similar psychological alienation. Salinger forces the association between Seymour and Lionel by placing Seymour's underwater goggles in the boat. The petulant child flips them overboard. "'That's constructive,' said Boo Boo. . . . 'They once belonged to your Uncle Seymour'" (84). Salinger captures the inscrutable obstinacy of a precocious child bent on living out what seems to be a perverse whim. Boo Boo responds to this act by holding up a key chain that is "[j]ust like Daddy's. But with a lot more keys on it" (85). Lionel wants the keys. "It's mine," he tells her. Boo Boo replies, "I don't care." This verbal jousting makes an impression on Lionel: "His eyes reflected pure perception, as his mother had known they would." What this perception might include is not made known.

Here one must listen for the sound of one hand clapping. Salinger is suggesting that an ineffable transaction is taking place. Boo Boo tosses Lionel the keys. He drops them overboard, giving up what he wanted. This action seems to make Lionel cry. He tells his mother why he is running away:

> "Sandra—told Mrs. Smell—that Daddy's a big—sloppy—kike."
> Just perceptibly, Boo Boo flinched. . . . "Well, that isn't *too* terrible. . . . Do you know what a kike is, baby?" (86)

Lionel thinks he does: "It's one of those things that go up in the *air.* . . . With *string* you hold." Lionel does not need to know the meaning of words. While he does not understand ethnic prejudice, he does understand the universal language of hate. He translates the tone of Sandra's ethnic slur into the closest literal equivalent. He is horrified, therefore, to think of a "big, sloppy" father floating in the sky. Lionel's unwitting declaration of innocence reunites him with his mother. His safe return from the dinghy significantly culminates with his act of play: "They didn't walk back to the house; they raced. Lionel won." He is indeed safe within a game in which his mother, unbeknownst to him, controls the outcome.

"For Esmé—with Love and Squalor"

"For Esmé—with Love and Squalor" is Salinger's most successful war story. Like "Soft-Boiled Sergeant," "For Esmé" offers a first-person, present-tense narrator who frames the retrospective tale.[48] Just as Philly looks back on his relationship with Burke, so too does the narrator review his relationship with Esmé. While serving as a preinvasion intelligence trainee in Devonshire, England, he meets and converses with the orphaned, 13-year-old Esmé and her young brother, Charles. In the second half of the story he presents himself as a psychologically shattered veteran of five military campaigns. The "soft-boiled" narrator cannot tolerate the horrors of war. Consequently, he does not emerge from the action "with all his faculties intact" (104). Both Philly and the unnamed I-narrator of "For Esmé" tell their stories in response to their respective wives. Juanita, the war-movie buff, accepts Hollywood's antiseptic fantasies as depictions of real life; the narrator of "For Esmé" pens his story because his wife, "a breathtakingly level-headed girl," will not allow him to attend Esmé's wedding—"a wedding I'd give a lot to be able to get to" (87).

In fact he *does* give "a lot" and the gift is the story, these "few revealing notes" designed to keep the "wedding from flatting." The succeeding story actually fulfills Esmé's strange, ingenuous request from six years before. Upon hearing that her newfound companion considers himself a not-so-prolific writer, Esmé says, "I'd be extremely flattered if you'd write a story exclusively for me sometime. . . . It doesn't have to be terribly prolific! Just so that it isn't childish and silly. . . . I prefer stories about squalor" (100).

This story about love and squalor reflects Salinger's intense commitment to debunking all clichés and roles that depict war as glory and death as apotheosis. In "For Esmé" the narrator's training-camp comrades-in-arms are not swashbuckling rogues, smiling automatons incapable of dread. Rather, they are no company at all. There is no esprit de corps, just sheer loneliness and blandness and boredom. These men are all "letter-writing types" (88) who live in self-imposed limbo.[49] They pen their letters to avoid direct human contact. The narrator feels hostile toward both his fellow troops and his own correspondents (88–89). One afternoon he comes in out of the rain to listen to a children's choir in rehearsal, an antidote to the dour atmosphere of camp: "Their voices were melodious and unsentimental, almost to the point where a somewhat more denominational man than myself might, without straining, have experienced levitation" (90). The narrator's laconic, perhaps mildly sarcastic, tone does not deter him from being enthralled. He wants the singing to go on and on. From out of the harmony of voices, he fixes on Esmé's: "Her voice was distinctly separate from the other children's voices, and not just because she was seated nearest me. It had the best upper register, the sweetest-sounding, the surest, and it automatically led the way."

Esmé inhabits the nexus between childhood and adulthood. With the innocence of a child, she has the poise of an adult. Self-possessed beyond her years, Esmé has primary responsibility for Charles.[50] When the narrator has tea with Esmé, he finds that the children's parents were both killed in the war. True to her position as Charles's protector, Esmé spells out that her father was s-l-a-i-n. Her self-possession becomes manifest in a humorless, high-toned seriousness. Her occasional malapropisms indicate the fragility of her order, the tenuousness of her pose. She also tends to project her own feelings onto the exuberant Charles. For her to say that "Charles misses [their father] exceedingly" is to articulate (as she displaces) her own sense of loss. Indeed she worships her late father: "He was an extremely gifted genius. . . . He was an exceedingly lovable man. He was extremely handsome, too. Not that one's appearance matters greatly, but he was. He had terribly penetrating eyes, for a man who was intransically [*sic*] kind" (97–98). Propelling her performance is her need to impress the narrator with her intelligence and, as the story intimates, to find in him a surrogate father. Esmé's instinctual craving for relation informs her request that the narrator write her a story both "squalid and moving" (103)—a story, in other words, that thematically encompasses the horror and beauty of her own experience. The story *for* Esmé will constitute an aesthetic analogue to her own heroic attempts to order her life.

Their conversation implies, but does not explicitly record, the extent of each character's emotional reaction. Beneath these polite, congenial conversational surfaces resides an intimation that each possesses what the other most deeply needs. The narrator, disgusted by the petty actualities of his wife's middle-class concerns and alienated from the letter-writing types in camp, senses in Esmé a saving balance between the "silly-billy" (89) innocence of children and the squalor of adulthood. Neither character is fully aware of the implications of this meeting. When the narrator prepares to leave he experiences "mixed feelings of regret and confusion. . . . It was a strangely emotional moment for me" (101–2). As time passes, each retrospectively achieves insight into the nature of their love, and the capacity to respond finds issue in heartfelt forms of expression. Only later, with Esmé's letter and the loan of her father's watch, do we find that she recognized the import of their meeting. For the narrator, the telling of the tale—the artistic process itself—fulfills his pledge to write a story especially for her.

Following the meeting in the tearoom the narrator changes the scene. He moves ahead and presents "the squalid, or moving, part of the story. . . . I've disguised myself so cunningly that even the cleverest reader will fail to recognize me" (103). He now speaks of himself in the third person. Having been released too soon from a hospital, Sergeant X is still breaking down: he is hypersensitive and nervous; his hands shake; his gums bleed; he chain-smokes; his mind teeters "like insecure luggage on an overhead rack" (104). His experiences have dissociated him from his prewar life. He is not himself. He is not "I." He is X, a crossed-off, anonymous integer.[51] He sits in his room among "at least two dozen unopened letters and at least five or six unopened packages, all addressed to him" (105). The only message that gets through is an inscription on the flyleaf of Goebbels's "Die Zeit Ohne Beispiel"—"The Unexampled Time." The inscription reads, " 'Dear God, life is hell'. . . . [T]he words appeared to have the stature of an uncontestable, even classic indictment. . . . Then, with far more zeal than he had done anything in weeks, he picked up a pencil stub and wrote down under the inscription, in English, 'Fathers and teachers, I ponder "What is hell?" I maintain that it is the suffering of being unable to love.' " X looks at his words and recoils in horror: his words are illegible. He becomes even more unstrung over his brother's request for war souvenirs. He tears up the letter and throws it into the trash.

Corporal Z, X's companion, has a mindless insensitivity to horror that allows him to pass through the war psychologically unscathed. He uses the excuse of battle fatigue as an outlet for sadism. To X's disgust, Z once shot a cat. To Z, the war is an engaging spectacle, a bit of fun, something to write home about. Z's girlfriend, Loretta, takes special delight in using X as a case-study exhibit for her college psychology class. As Z points out, it is her inane contention that X could not have got a "nervous breakdown just from the war and all. She says you probably were unstable like, your whole goddam life" (109).

Neither insensitive correspondence, nor talking to Z about Loretta, nor listening to Bob Hope on the radio can help X recover his faculties. Instead he needs contact with someone who has a sensitive understanding of the way war can destroy one's being. Like X, Esmé has been ravaged by the war. By chance, X opens Esmé's letter and receives help from the only available source. Her envelope contains her father's watch and a postscript from Charles. The letter is a communication of one war victim to another. In Esmé's case she is holding up. As befits a "statistics-lover" (92), she has an obsession with detail:

> Dear Sergeant X,
>
> I hope you will forgive me for having taken 38 days to begin our correspondence but, I have been extremely busy . . . and I have been justifiably saddled with one responsibility after another. However I have thought of you frequently and of the extremely pleasant afternoon we spent in each other's company on April 30, 1944 between 3:45 and 4:15 P.M. in case it slipped your mind.
>
> We are all tremendously excited and overawed about D Day and only hope that it will bring about the swift termination of the war and a method of existence that is ridiculous to say the least.
> (112–13)

Her affection for the sergeant informs this letter. As a token of her love, she includes her father's watch, offering it as a "lucky talisman": it is "extremely water-proof and shock-proof as well as having many other virtues among which one can tell at what velocity one is walking if one wishes" (113). Like the sergeant, the watch did not survive the trip intact. The crystal is cracked. The letter and contents, however, do carry the narrator back to his "strangely emotional moment." He holds the watch for a long time: "Then suddenly, almost ecstatically, he felt sleepy" (114).

Sergeant X's sleepiness initiates the therapeutic process of self-recovery that finds completion in his wedding gift. To the extent that the present story is a gift, it is, in Ihab Hassan's words, a "modern epithalamium" (147), a tale about love expressed in the celebration of marriage, specifically the narrator's love. As a marriage hymn, the story celebrates the fusion of lives in the hopes of defeating alienation. As the classic comic ending, marriage symbolizes the future of society made manifest as the unification of separate lives. Love thus relieves, because it displaces, misery. "For Esmé" celebrates the open future by rendering the "squalid and moving" experiences of the past. As epithalamium, the tale is not merely a celebration of unity but a reconstruction of fragments, specifically the narrator's fractured psyche. The marriage between groom and bride parallels the symbolic unification of X and Esmé, not as husband and wife but as father and daughter.

"For Esmé" offers a summation of Salinger's major subjects and themes: war, childhood, married life, the breakdown of communication, the phoniness of convention, the difficulty of friendship. Esmé's symbolic gift constitutes something of a riddle. It is a sign that suggests an emotional reality deeper than language. Warren French sees Esmé as embodying "the highest potential of the human being who chooses to remain firmly earthbound within a squalid society. . . . Her story is one of the rare ones of the victory of the 'nice' world over the 'phony'" (1988, 78). Unlike most Salinger stories, "For Esmé" concludes with a closed ending. In the process of telling the tale, the narrator reconciles himself to the problem that was his past. Through wry good humor, he reflects those attributes which allow him to function in postwar America "with all his fac—with all his f-a-c-u-l-t-i-e-s intact" (114). For the moment he puts his life to rest.

"Pretty Mouth and Green My Eyes"

The highly refined diction of Salinger's detached narrator in "Pretty Mouth and Green My Eyes" provides an ironic counterpoint to the story's brutal double betrayal: "When the phone rang, the gray-haired man asked the girl, with quite some little deference, if she would rather for any reason he didn't answer it" (115). The language of civility deftly serves the cause of cynicism. The gray-haired man, Lee, is in bed with the girl, Joanie. At the other end of the line is Arthur, Lee's junior law colleague and supposed friend. Joanie is Arthur's wife. This ironic circumstance inspires Lee's self-conscious performance. With Joanie as his rapt audience, Lee combines the roles of *fidus Achates* and wise mentor. Arthur bares his soul, becoming both cuckold and dupe. His self-lacerating honesty and insistent self-exposure, however, endow him with the dubious, though sympathetic, stature of the long-suffering romantic fool who recognizes his folly a few years too late.

Part 1

"Pretty Mouth" chronicles Lee's shameless performance—What else could he do? The poor guy's wife was in bed next to him—as an urbane play of words, a display of feigned compassion and tough talk. From Arthur's benighted perspective, Lee's advice and analysis seem generous, caring, and reasonable. It is a late night's early morning after a long party. Joanie is not home; Arthur is certain she is in bed with another man; he wonders if Lee saw her leave with anyone. Lee saw nothing, though he feels the sensible thing to do is "to put the thing out of your mind. . . . For all you know, you're making—I honestly think you're making a mountain—" (119). Arthur interrupts to make another point. Their dialogue is riddled with such fragmented sentences. These syntactic ruptures accentuate both Arthur's rattled, drunken condition and Lee's reasonable, but phony, attempts at calming him: "'You actually go out of your way to torture yourself. As a matter of fact, you actually in*spire* Joanie—' He broke off. 'You're bloody lucky she's a wonderful kid'" (120). Lee finds himself close to speaking something like the truth: that Arthur's nagging anxiety drives Joanie into another man's arms. He catches himself in time to compliment his attentive lover.

Arthur's sympathetic stature does not derive from his victimization; as a person, he appears weak, whining, and ineffectual. Yet despite his flaws, he emerges as a voice speaking in defense of the human, especially in his refusal to acquiesce in Lee's glib, comfortable view that human beings are predators. To Lee's remark that Joanie is a "wonderful kid," Arthur replies, "She's an animal!" When Lee rejoins, "We're all animals. . . . Basically, we're all animals," Arthur disagrees: "Like hell we are. I'm no goddam animal. I may be a stupid, fouled-up twentieth-century son of a bitch, but I'm no animal. Don't gimme that. I'm no animal." Lee's world-weary summation is a self-justifying rationalization. Once he reduces the ontological status of the human, he surrenders moral imperatives. Anything goes. All acts are equal because choice devolves into instinct. Arthur, at least, has standards. He is capable of being appalled. With sardonic gusto he indicts Joanie for being a pretender: "She thinks she's a goddam intellectual. That's the funny part, that's the hilarious part. She reads the theatrical page, and she watches television till she's practically blind—so she's an intellectual. . . . You want to know who I'm married to? I'm married to the *greatest living undeveloped, undiscovered act*ress, *nov*elist, psychoanalyst, and all-around goddam unappreciated celebrity-genius in New York. . . . Madame Bovary at Columbia Extension School." Arthur's

54

tirade reflects his anguished amazement that he could ever have felt what he used to feel. Nevertheless, he retains ambiguous feelings for Joanie. Though recognizing that she has contempt for him, he finds himself lapsing into self-deluding, romantic hope. Either they have a good evening or he indulges in nostalgia. His lost idyll mocks him: "I start thinking about—Christ, it's embarrassing—I start thinking about this goddam poem I sent her when we first started goin' around together. 'Rose my color is and white, Pretty mouth and green my eyes.' Christ, it's em*bar*rassing—it used to *remind* me of her. She doesn't have green eyes—she has eyes like goddam *sea* shells" (125). He perceives her shabbiness but is paralyzed by his past. Arthur is in love with an idea of himself that he associates with another time. The memory of past splendor—sending a poem to a new girl—becomes his most stable reality.

When Arthur and Lee hang up, Joanie finally speaks. She seems to justify Lee's sweeping assessment that "[w]e're all animals." She congratulates him on his telephone performance. "You were wonderful. . . . I'm *limp*. I'm absolutely *limp*. . . . God, I feel like an absolute *dog*" (127–28). Joanie's self-admission is prelude to the story's most arresting irony. The phone rings again: Arthur has called back to tell Lee that Joanie just came in the door. He reports that they might move out of the city, this breeding ground for neurotics. His past idyll is now transposed into the fantasy of suburban escape. With this phone call Arthur attempts to regain lost dignity. He apparently feels that he might have been pathetic. Once again, Arthur becomes the unwitting victim of a wrenching irony. His fabricated happy ending is nothing more than a face-saving lie. In playing this part Arthur becomes more ridiculous than ever.

In this story Salinger does not take us inside any character's mind. In the end we are left with Lee telling Arthur that he has a splitting headache. He hangs up and orders Joanie to "*sit still*" (129). Salinger concludes without interpreting Lee's condition. To the sentimentally inclined, the ending could be construed as Lee's epiphany. But what does he see? Does he feel remorse? Or does Lee simply have a splitting headache? Perhaps the performance has strained him.

"Pretty Mouth," a powerful story of dual infidelity, constitutes Salinger's most withering portrait of phony, self-absorbed people. In a world of disposable friendships and easy betrayals, these animals are animals with a purpose. They are self-conscious players. All three characters are enmeshed by the roles that point away from, but ultimately confirm, the squalid self: Joanie plays at being an intellectual, but she is really giggling and mindless; Lee plays the role of faithful friend, but he is actually humiliating Arthur; Arthur tries to recoup his losses with the scenario of a false alarm and a happy ending. At the least, by the end Lee's headache has disconcerted him enough to wrench him from his duplicitous role.

"De Daumier-Smith's Blue Period"

"De Daumier-Smith's Blue Period" presents the first-person account of a 19-year-old painter who, after his mother's death, returns to New York City from Paris in the company of his stepfather. At loose ends, the narrator wanders the city's galleries and spends a good deal of time reading. He is obsessive about his art: "In one month alone . . . I completed eighteen oil paintings. Interestingly enough, seventeen of them were self-portraits" (132–33). His appearance must indeed be strange: "Three late afternoons a week I spent in a dentist's chair, where, within a period of a few months, I had eight teeth extracted, three of them front ones" (132). In his self-absorption he translates his disfigurement into surreal cartoons. In one of them he "shows a cavernous view of the mouth of a man being attended by his dentist. The man's tongue is a simple, U.S. Treasury hundred dollar bill, and the dentist is saying, sadly, in French, 'I think we can save the molar, but I'm afraid that tongue will have to come out'" (133). The narrator's art reflects both his sardonic sensibility and his disdain for economic pursuits. He is isolated. He is an out-of-place oddball whose return to New York "threw me, and threw me terribly" (131).

"Blue Period" recounts the various disturbances in the narrator's life. A Francophile, he is given to self-dramatization. The young painter's penchant for surrealism also finds expression in his weird reconstruction of the most commonplace situations. His descriptions express his loneliness. For example, a simple event like coming out of the Ritz Hotel unleashes a surreal comic tirade that reflects his extreme frustration:

> [I]t seemed to me that all the seats from all the buses in New York had been unscrewed and taken out and set up in the street, where a monstrous game of Musical Chairs was in full swing. I think I might have been willing to join the game if I had been granted a special dispensation from the Church of Manhattan guaranteeing that all the other players would remain respectfully standing till I

was seated. When it became clear that nothing of the kind was forthcoming, I took more direct action. I prayed for the city to be cleared
of people, for the gift of being alone—a-l-o-n-e: which is the one
New York prayer that rarely gets lost or delayed in channels, and in
no time at all everything I touched turned to solid loneliness. (132)

This remarkable passage manifests the narrator's strained state of
mind. He cannot cope with the frenetic city flux.

To get away from the United States, the narrator answers a help-
wanted ad for instructors in a Montreal correspondence art school. To
compensate for his addled condition, he fabricates an identity. He
claims to be on intimate terms with Picasso; he says his paintings are
well placed in private collections; he invents an agent and a dead wife;
he adopts the name Jean de Daumier-Smith, which might mean that
his name is John Smith. He puts together a portfolio and gets a job
from M Yoshoto. The school turns out to be a run-down, one-room
dump, where de Daumier-Smith works alone all day on the paintings
of untalented students. At night the noisy sexual frolics of M and Mme
Yoshoto keep him awake.

The problematic center of "Blue Period" concerns the narrator's response to one of his students. Sister Irma's envelope contains not a
personal photo but a snapshot of her convent. At best she seems unprepared to draw anything; at worst she seems a simpleton: "She said
she had '34 kittys in my cooking class and 18 kittys in my drawing
class.' Her hobbies were loving her Lord and the Word of her Lord and
'collecting leaves but only when they are laying right on the ground.'
. . . She said her kittys always like to 'draw people when they are running and that is the one thing I am terrible at.' She said she would work
very hard to learn to draw better, and hoped we would not be very
impatient with her" (148). Her sample includes "a highly detailed depiction of Christ being carried to the sepulchre" (149). She painted
this watercolor on brown wrapping paper. Some critics have gyrated
over Sister Irma's putative greatness. John Russell refers to the "unmistakable genius in the drawings" of this nun.[52] Howard M. Harper,
Jr., somehow concludes that Sister Irma has "real talent" (77). What is
irrefutable is that de Daumier-Smith develops an obsessive love for his
correspondent. He perceives her as a great artist; he writes her long
letters that provide detailed commentary on every piece; he queries
her about her life, even proposing a visit to her convent. Like his surreal renderings of New York, the narrator's version of Sister Irma is the

product of a diseased imagination. His response to her is so excessive and the material that inspires it so meager that one must question his judgment.

"Blue Period" in fact depicts the runaway imagination of the narrator. On one level, Salinger presents a mixed-up young man who so craves a relationship that he fabricates one; on another level, the story offers a Salinger riddle: how do we read, and take seriously, the perceptions of a narrator who mistakes the origin of the "moaning sound" coming through the wall? The narrator translates the human noise of sexual intercourse into a fiction that elevates, in a nearly demented manner, his own self-importance:

> Just before I fell asleep, the moaning sound again came through the wall from the Yoshotos' bedroom. I pictured both Yoshotos coming to me in the morning and asking me, begging me, to hear their secret problem out, to the last terrible detail. I saw exactly how it would be. I would sit down between them at the kitchen table and listen to each of them. I would listen, listen, listen, with my head in my hands—till finally, unable to stand it any longer, I would reach down into Mme. Yoshoto's throat, take up her heart in my hand and warm it as I would a bird. Then, when all was put right, I would show Sister Irma's work to the Yoshotos, and they would share my joy. (155)

This story is a trap: it invites the reader to invest confidence in a narrator whose personal account demonstrates his preposterous powers of misinterpretation. At the least, one must entertain some doubts about the authenticity of the story's peak moments of rhetorical intensity. One day, looking into the "lighted display window of the orthopedic appliances shop," the narrator has an "altogether hideous" experience: "The thought was forced on me that no matter how coolly or sensibly or gracefully I might one day learn to live my life, I would always at best be a visitor in a garden of enamel urinals and bedpans, with a sightless, wooden dummy-deity standing by in a marked-down rupture truss" (157). One must consider the possibility that Salinger's narrator is involved in self-parody. As he has been all along, the narrator is prone to wild imaginings. After this view of himself as visitor in a medical-supply "garden," he escapes into his mind, where he visualizes himself visiting Sister Irma. He now translates her into a sentimental heroine out of stock romance (158). Sister Irma, however, never responds to any of the narrator's letters. Insistently the story depicts his tendency to inflate his own craving into ludicrous scenarios.

The climax of the story takes place later, when the "hideous" vision gives way to a putative experience of the sublime. The narrator watches a girl changing the truss of a wooden dummy: "I stood watching her, fascinated, till suddenly she sensed, then saw, that she was being watched. . . . She blushed, she dropped the removed truss, she stepped back on a stack of irrigation basins—and her feet went out from under her" (163). De Daumier-Smith then has what he calls "my Experience. Suddenly . . . the sun came up and sped toward the bridge of my nose at the rate of ninety-three million miles a second. Blinded and very frightened—I had to put my hand on the glass to keep my balance. The thing lasted for no more than a few seconds. When I got my sight back, the girl had gone from the window, leaving behind her a shimmering field of exquisite, twice-blessed, enamel flowers" (164).

This vision leads him to give "Sister Irma her freedom to follow her own destiny. Everybody is a nun." Warren French, among others, finds this moment "inexplicable except as a mystical experience" (1988, 81).[53] There is another explanation: the event may be a parody of transcendence. The narrator's mixture of bombast and self-inflation seems to burlesque the literary epiphany.[54] A pronounced incongruity exists between the girl's pratfall and the rhetoric reporting the "Experience." Thus the narrator presents the activities of a neurotic mind bent on wresting grandiose meanings from the most pedestrian of materials. One must be suspicious of a tale that so blatantly delivers its own explanation. To invest this moment with sublimity is to miss the joke perpetrated by the narrator, who is looking back on his younger self. Edward Stone suggests, "The once-mad but now sane . . . can give an account of his earlier condition either by analysis or, if he is an artist, by the implicit judgment of echo and allusion put to the uses of comedy. What folly, back then!" (139). At one point the narrator diagnoses his own condition. In a letter to Sister Irma he muses whether the woman in blue is Mary Magdalene: "If she is not, I have been sadly deluding myself. However, this is no novelty" (153). No novelty indeed.

Among the pieces in *Nine Stories* "De Daumier-Smith's Blue Period" is most odd and disjunctive. It offers, in my view, a satire of closed thematizing, of the tendency to interpret life in terms of broad and seemingly significant generalizations. It would be as valid and illuminating to say, "Not everybody is a nun." Where does either formulation lead? The narrator recounts, as it were, a tale of his own lies, an account of his obsessive desire to make things come out nicely even when the world is eloquent only with enamel urinals. Significantly, he leaves Montreal and joins his stepfather in Rhode Island. Finally he does something sane. He investigates "that most interesting of all summer-active animals, the American Girl in Shorts" (164–65).

"Teddy"

"Teddy," the last of *Nine Stories,* presents the vacationing McArdle family; they are returning on a cruise ship from England to the United States. Teddy McArdle is a child. He is also a seer and a mystic, a devotee of Eastern religion, most notably Advaita Vedanta.[55] As a precocious genius, Teddy is unemotional and unflappable. An object of study to professors of psychic phenomena, he subscribes to the Vedantic theory of reincarnation. Through deep meditative trances, he purports to know his nine earlier lives. In his preceding incarnation, he tells fellow passenger Bob Nicholson, he was "making very nice spiritual advancement" until he "met a lady, and I sort of stopped meditating" (188). The fallout—his bad karma—leads Teddy's soul to a sort of penal stop in America: "I wouldn't have had to get incarnated in an American body if I hadn't met that lady. I mean it's very hard to meditate and live a spiritual life in America. People think you're a freak if you try to. My father thinks I'm a freak, in a way." Salinger accentuates the differences between Teddy and the rest of his family. Teddy's father, for example, speaks in the tough-guy tones of American slang. Teddy's sister, Booper, is a truculent brat, a young soul, in his view, only recently born into the cycle of reincarnation. Unlike de Daumier-Smith, Teddy is never ironically rendered. The third-person narrator presents Teddy in distinctly sympathetic terms. Teddy inhabits his own plane: he "gave his father a look of inquiry, whole and pure" (167). His rarefied sensibility, reflected in his face, "carried the impact, however oblique and slow-travelling, of real beauty" (168). The narrator betrays a weakness for precious diction and forced analogy: "His voice was oddly and beautifully rough cut, as some small boys' voices are. Each of his phrasings was rather like a little ancient island, inundated by a miniature sea of whiskey" (169).

Throughout *Nine Stories* Salinger tends to associate childhood with purity and innocence. Ramona, Lionel, and Charles, for example, have prelapsarian qualities. Teddy's purity, however, does not reflect preexperience; rather, his purity derives from the fact that his soul has evolved away from material, sexual, and social impediments. His dissociation from the American milieu is philosophical and religious. In Teddy's view, the separation between material and ideal realms is an illusion fostered by the conceit that human beings are trapped within "finite dimensions" (190). Teddy replaces metaphysical duality with an all-pervading monism. At the age of six, for instance, he had a mystical vision when Booper was pouring milk. At that instant he "saw that everything was God. . . . I saw that *she* was God and the *milk* was God. I mean, all she was doing was pouring God into God" (189). In discussing the Edenic myth of the Fall, Teddy argues that logic is the forbidden fruit of the Tree of Knowledge: "You know what was in that apple? Logic. Logic and intellectual stuff. That was all that was in it. So—this is my point—what you have to do is vomit it up if you want to see things as they really are. . . . You won't see everything stopping *off* all the time" (191). Teddy's vision conflates the ancient concept of atavism—the world suffused with spirit—and pantheism—God is everywhere in everything—to propose the notion that materialistic distinctions are illusions. For Teddy, matter has *no* intrinsic reality or essence outside the mind that perceives it. When looking at floating orange peels, for example, Teddy posits that they actually "started floating" inside his mind (172). His monism offers an alternative to the phony world of role-playing, materialism, and spiritual corruption. "Teddy" most clearly initiates Salinger's serious preoccupation with displacing American culture in favor of an approach to experience that honors simplicity, spirituality, intuition, and egolessness. Specifically, in "Teddy" Salinger has transposed the myth of childhood innocence into a philosophy of antimaterialistic transcendence—with the means of eventual spiritual salvation, or nirvana, generating from a succession of soul-cleansing reincarnations.

Crucially, Teddy's philosophy has no social context. He is alone with his consciousness and his diary. He placidly endures, even embraces, his estrangement. Nothing in the story suggests that his vision might be passed on. Teddy is a Seymour without disciples. Marginalized as a "freak," he becomes an object of study. He can disturb his inquisitors by offhandedly predicting their deaths, but he does not belong within any social framework. He feels an "affinity" for his parents. At the core of his philosophy is the notion that society and history—and even family—are not simply impediments to The Way but are essentially irrelevant. He also repudiates the reality of sequential time. His trances provide access to future events. When Teddy writes in his diary, "It will happen today or February 14, 1958, when I am sixteen," he identifies his death day. To break the chains of maya is to perceive events as synchronous. Thus the future has already occurred; *when* he dies is of no moment. Such a perspective inevitably separates him from social concerns. His only nod toward the possibilities of affiliation is his desire to teach children the spiritual benefits of disaffiliation.

When Nicholson inquires how he would change the educational system, Teddy replies, "I think I'd first just assemble all the children together and show them how to meditate. I'd try to show them how to find out who they *are*. . . . I'd get them to empty out everything their parents and everybody ever told them. . . . I'd just make them vomit up every bit of the apple their parents and everybody made them take a bite out of" (195–96). Teddy elevates perception to the status where it makes one's world. As one sees, so one is: "The reason things *seem* to stop off somewhere is because that's the only way most people know how to look at things" (189–90). The spiritual concerns of "Teddy" anticipate the Glass family stories, in which Salinger examines precocious children, society, and the possibility of developing alternative spiritual values.

At the conclusion of "Teddy" Salinger offers the possibility that Teddy did in fact predict his death. He told Nicholson that his sister may shove him into an empty pool. Calmly, Teddy goes off to meet her. Rather than following Teddy, the narrator remains with Nicholson, who decides to follow Teddy to the pool. As Nicholson approaches he "heard an all-piercing sustained scream—clearly coming from a small female child" (198). The story and the collection ends with this scream "reverberating within four tiled walls." The silence evoked by the volume's epigraph stands in contrast to what presumably are Booper's screams. Salinger suspends exact knowledge of what transpired. Characteristically, he refuses to close off meanings. He encourages open-ended engagements with multiple possibilities rather than resting with the kind of fixed interpretations that he parodies in de Daumier-Smith's "Experience."

The Glass Family

The Babe Gladwaller–Vincent Caulfield serial tales provide artistic and thematic antecedents to the Glass family stories. At least three complexes from the early tales inform Salinger's treatment of the family that has absorbed his attention in his last five published pieces of fiction: first, Salinger explores the conflict between the alienated artistic temperament and the crass, despiritualized environment; second, childhood—and a vision of a nostalgic past—offers a tenuous refuge from the vapid and corrupt adult world; and third, the death of a beloved brother removes him from the seedy entanglements of life, while the memory of this brother provides his survivors with a recollected sanctuary and/or psychological incubus. Indeed, dead brothers inhabit a conspicuously prominent place in Salinger's fiction: Vincent loses Holden; Phoebe loses Holden and Vincent; in *Catcher* Holden and Phoebe lose Allie; the Glass children lose Walt and Seymour.

By inventing seven siblings Salinger creates an extensive fictional domain. His primary complication resides in the tribe's obsessive insularity. Encounters with outsiders—non–family members—are at best problematic. If the interactions are not outright failures, then they are so odd as to constitute blatant attacks on the most conventional forms of social affiliation. For example, the story of Seymour's prospective wedding in "Raise High the Roof Beam, Carpenters" becomes an account of his nonwedding. The children feel as though they inhabit a separate class. They are *of* one another. Salinger's dedication to them has, it seems, become total, an immoderate interest that, in John Updike's view, creates its own form of entrapment: "Salinger loves the Glasses more than God loves them. He loves them too exclusively. Their invention has become a hermitage for him. He loves them to the detriment of artistic moderation."[56]

Their tribal insularity, however, has a paradoxical counterpoint in their theatrical heritage. The children of Les and Bessie Glass, two former vaudevillians, are gifted. They sing; they dance; they are intellectual prodigies. Each child came and went as contestants on "It's a Wise Child," a radio quiz show. Mrs. Glass has the children perform under pseudonyms because she once read an article "on the little crosses professional children are obliged to bear—their estrangement from normal, presumably desirable society—and she took an iron stand on the issue and never, never wavered" (*RH*, 7). Her fears were justified. Four of the children are especially gifted in artistic matters, and they are the most estranged. Seymour, the eldest, is his mother's "favorite, her most intricately calibrated, her kindest son."[57] When he turned 15, Seymour entered Columbia University and went on to a college professorship. He is also a poet who has a deep attachment to Haiku. The second eldest, Buddy, is a writer and recluse, the chief chronicler of the family saga. He is narrator and chief actor in "Raise High," the author/compiler of "Zooey," and the narrator of "Seymour: An Introduction." The youngest zon, Zooey (Zachary), is a handsome, successful television actor. As a child, Zooey shared Teddy's predicament of being an object of intense professional scrutiny. Specialists wondered how he could be so brilliant. Of all the children, Zooey was the "most voraciously examined, interviewed, and poked at." Unlike Teddy, Zooey seems to have suffered "costly" emotional damage from the attempts "to isolate, and study if possible, the source of Zooey's precocious wit and fancy" (54–55). Zooey's relationship with Seymour and Buddy is extremely strained: he feels that their indoctrination into Christian mysticism and Buddhist philosophy turned him (and Franny) into "freaks" (103). The baby of the family, Franny is also a gifted actress. In summer stock she played a brilliant Pegeen in Synge's *The Playboy of the Western World*. According to Zooey, "[Franny] held that goddam mess up" (197). The remaining siblings include the elder sister, Boo Boo, who appears in "Down at the Dinghy." She seems to lead the most conventional life. The latest we hear of her is that she has three children and is happily married. Bessie's "only truly lighthearted son" (90), Walt, was killed in a noncombatant accident during World War II. (Walt Glass is Eloise's dead boyfriend in "Uncle Wiggily in Connecticut.") Waker is Walt's surviving twin. An adult, he is a Jesuit priest and seems to possess a delicate sensibility. Of the Glass children, Waker is least known.

In presenting the Glass family story, Salinger makes the self-inflicted death of Seymour on 18 March 1948 the central point of reference. Following "A Perfect Day" the five Glass stories published in the *New Yorker* concern themselves with Seymour's life and legacy. In order of publication they are "Franny" (29 January 1955); "Raise High the Roof Beam, Carpenters" (19 November 1955); "Zooey" (4 May 1957);

"Seymour: An Introduction" (6 June 1959); and "Hapworth 16, 1924" (19 June 1965). *Franny and Zooey* appeared as a collection in 1961; *Raise High the Roof Beam, Carpenters and Seymour: An Introduction* was published in 1963. "Hapworth" remains uncollected. The order of publication in no way coincides with the order of incident. In fact "Hapworth" records the earliest extended treatment of Seymour, a 30,000-word letter that he wrote in 1924 on his sixteenth day at Camp Hapworth in Maine. Throughout the series, Seymour's legacy as poet, seer, and gentle individual vies with the less flattering (though not mutually exclusive) portrait of Seymour as narcissist, psychotic, and manipulator. Supposedly a poet of great talent, he is capable of perpetrating physical and emotional violence on himself and others. "A Perfect Day" introduces Seymour's mystery: Is his artist's soul too pure for this world, or is he an addled psychotic, a shattered, suicidal victim of the war?

It is impossible to say whether Salinger had projected the Glass family saga in 1948 when he told the story of Seymour's suicide. Seymour does have antecedents in the haunted artist Joe Varioni of "The Varioni Brothers," in the inexplicably deranged Bill Tedderton of "The Long Debut of Lois Taggett," and in the enigmatic poet-drunk Raymond Ford of "The Inverted Forest." It seems plausible that in 1948 Salinger had at least an inkling of the possibilities of expanding his materials. In "A Perfect Day," however, there is not a single hint regarding the existence of other Glass family members. The Walt of "Uncle Wiggily" is not identified as a Glass until his death is mentioned in "Raise High." In "Down at the Dinghy" Boo Boo's maiden name is Glass. Over the years, Seymour certainly grows in Salinger's imagination, even to the point where Salinger attempts to reconcile discrepancies between the amiable young man on the beach in "A Perfect Day" and the guru of later stories. Sally Bostwick remarks on Salinger's tendency "to expand, delete, and experiment with his material before he knows quite what he wants to focus on" (35). After claiming authorship of "A Perfect Day," for example, Buddy points out—as members of the family have made clear to him—that the Seymour of the story bears little resemblance to the Seymour of real life. In fact, Seymour on the beach is essentially a self-portrait of Buddy. As Salinger's alter ego, Buddy also claims authorship of "Teddy" (*RH*, 176), even quoting some lines.[58] In having Buddy mention that he has one extremely successful novel about a young person, Salinger insinuates that Buddy may have written *Catcher*. In light of such recastings, it seems that Salinger views the making of literary art as an ongoing process in which the present tale can alter the contexts of earlier tales. New material provides emendations of existing materials, a situation that leads John Updike (55), Eberhard Alsen (90–91), and Warren French (1988, 89–93) to consider the disjunctions that exist between "Franny" and "Zooey." The fiction that a real-life Buddy Glass is the actual author of some of J. D. Salinger's works has the primary effect of displacing Salinger; his published work thereby furthers his disappearing act. Buddy's claim for authorship also reinforces the notion that the Glasses are flesh-and-blood creatures. Indeed, in his preface to "Zooey" Buddy reveals that Zooey, Franny, and Mrs. Glass have each advised him on reconstructing their story. Each also finds something wrong with Buddy's finished product.

In these stories Salinger offers a fictional world that contains the kind of open endings he so frequently uses in *Nine Stories*. The open ending flaunts the artistic convention favoring thematic resolution and replaces it with the provocative, if not teasing and cryptic, cessation of artistic process. Salinger's open endings are appropriate to the serialization of a family's life: indeed, putative endings are actually contained within the ongoing life. All endings, then, are beginnings. A particular action might achieve apparent resolution, but its ramifications inform subsequent events. Significantly, the end of Seymour's life is the procreant, if tragic, beginning that feeds the lives of his siblings. Seymour's death is as unavoidable as it is inexplicable. It focuses past and present. On the dust jacket of the first edition of *Franny and Zooey* Salinger himself refers to the Glass stories as "a long-term project, patently an ambitious one." He points out that he has "a good deal of thoroughly unscheduled material on paper, too, but I expect to be fussing with it, to use a popular trade term, for some time to come."[59]

All the Glass stories, except perhaps "Franny," tend to be digressive. Salinger consciously eschews the formal constraints of genre, whether short story or novel. For example, Buddy identifies "Zooey" not as a long short story or novella but as a "prose home movie" (47), an artistic creation, semiprofessional, designed for in-house viewing, a form of discourse wherein events are captured by Buddy's camera eye and translated into images that the subjects themselves might watch and critique. In attempting to depict the unfolding life, Salinger often has Buddy speak of himself in the narrative present. Indeed the plot of "Seymour" is no more than Buddy's account of the conditions that impinge on his attempt to write an introduction to Seymour's life. Given such insularity of focus, the notion of having a public readership becomes more and more remote. "Seymour" and "Hapworth" seem self-consciously haphazard. The materials are admittedly arbitrary. "Hapworth" in particular reflects no attempt to tell a story in *any* conventional sense. Possibly the least structured and most tedious piece of fiction ever produced by an important writer, "Hapworth" seems *designed* to bore, to tax patience, as if Salinger might be trying to torment his readers away from ever wanting the next new thing from him. These kinds of compositions—"prose home movie" and letter to mother and father—depict Salinger's attempt to shrink his readership to a closed community. This preoccupation pervades the Glass stories. The family members' best audience is always one another, just as their primary activity is the self contemplating the meaning of the self. For the Glass children, the obsession with self-consciousness in the cause of overcoming the entanglements of "ego" constitutes the series' abiding dilemma. The Glass children's burden calls forth the abrasive fabric of their brilliance.[60]

"Franny": "A Special Semblance of Absorption"

With its sense of heightened expectation in relation to a facile reality, the opening scene of "Franny" evokes the spirit of F. Scott Fitzgerald. Ivy League undergraduate men wait at a train station for the arrival of their dates. Once the train pulls in, the football weekend—the opponent is Yale—can begin with its rounds of expensive lunches, cocktail parties, postgame receptions, and fancy dinners. It will be a carefully choreographed public exhibition. The college boys cannot wait to perform their parts in the pas de deux, a strained display of confected elegance. Behind his urbane narrator, Salinger directs all his contempt for Ivy League phonies into his mocking depiction of their pseudointellectuality. They speak in "voices that, almost without exception, sounded collegiately dogmatic, as though each young man, in his strident, conversational turn, was clearing up, once and for all, some highly controversial issue, one that the outside, non-matriculating world had been bungling, provocatively or not, for centuries" (3). Salinger's general target is phoniness. More precisely, it is the pretentiousness associated with smug intellectuality, the presumption of analytical superiority.

Among the collegians waiting on the platform is Lane Coutell, Franny Glass's boyfriend. He whiles away the time rereading what might appear to be a conventional love letter. Actually it reflects the tensions that exist between the smooth surfaces of their romantic discourse, on the one hand, and those disquieting forces which undermine the idyll, on the other. As a correspondent, Franny is both affectionate and resentful, laudatory and critical, adoring and irritable, effusive and retentive. Lane reads words that express ardor: "I just got your beautiful letter and I love you to pieces, distraction, etc." (4). On the one hand, she longs to see him; she cannot wait to go dancing. She tries to allay his apprehensions over whether her parents heard them come in and, apparently, make love: "[Y]ou can *relax* about that Friday night. I don't even think they heard us come in" (5). Her complimentary close reads "All my love," followed by sixteen X's.

On the other hand, this breathless letter contains material that ruptures the sense of romantic rapture. While she "absolutely adore[s] [Lane's] letter, especially the part about Eliot," she goes on to write, "I think I'm beginning to look down on all poets except Sappho. I've been reading her like mad, and no vulgar remarks, please" (4–5). Assuming that Lane praised Eliot—a reasonable surmise given Eliot's preeminence among conservative intellectuals in the mid-1950's— Franny's quotation of decidedly nonmodernist lines reflects a radical divergence in the couple's artistic tastes. Furthermore, Franny is both compliant and complaining. She accepts Lane's advice about using a dictionary but chides him for his machismo: "I hate you when your [*sic*] being hopelessly super-male and retiscent (sp.?). Not really *hate* you but am constitutionally against strong, silent men" (5). In the P.P.S. her self-effacement betrays lurking insecurity: "I sound so unintelligent and dimwitted when I write to you." Behind this feeling is her dislike for Lane's tendency to analyze "everything to death" (6).

Like any piece of prose, Franny's letter is a text awaiting interpretation. It directly reflects her divided mind, yet Lane construes the text as a placid sign of stable love. Later, at lunch, for example, when Franny admits to having felt "*destructive*" all week, Lane reveals himself to be a selective reader: "Your letter didn't sound so goddam destructive." Franny replies, "I had to strain to write it" (15), a remark that undercuts the authority of Lane's one-dimensional reading. The letter indeed reveals "strain" and self-division. It offers signs of Franny's inchoate breakdown. She even writes, "I've been going i.e. crazy lately" (4). This sentence could mean "crazy in love"; it could mean "emotionally disturbed." It might mean both. Throughout the Glass stories, Salinger continues this practice of incorporating texts-within-the-text—letters, quotations, diary entries, poems, book titles—in order to highlight the thematic context. Franny's letter marks the beginning of her attempt to recast the meaning of her words, not in relation to Lane or T. S. Eliot but in relation to what she considers *real* poetry, a literature of spiritual fulfillment.

Salinger presents Lane as a shallow, fatuous performer. When the train arrives, for example, he "empties" his face of expression. By affecting nonchalance, he prepares a face to meet the face he is about to meet. He takes great pleasure in kissing Franny's coat, a pathetic, if comic, gesture that reduces Franny to a sensation he has sequestered in his mind. Similarly, when he takes her into Sickler's, the "highly favored place among, chiefly, the intellectual fringe of students at the college" (10), he appreciates Franny's appeal as an admirable object. The narrator mocks Lane's self-satisfied hauteur: he "briefly looked around the room with an almost palpable sense of well-being at finding himself . . . in the right place with an unimpeachably right-looking girl—a girl who was not only extraordinarily pretty but, so much the better, not too categorically cashmere sweater and flannel skirt" (11). When Franny perceives his "momentary little exposure . . . she elect[s] to feel guilty for having seen it, caught it, and sentence[s] herself to listen to Lane's ensuing conversation with a special semblance of absorption." She is a victim of her own consciousness. For her to perceive that *she* is perceived as special is for her to be doubly punished: first, by the tacit admission of vain superiority, the conviction that she is worth being seen in such a way, and, second, by the masochistic decision to torture herself by faking interest in the bore's heady lucubrations.

At the outset of the story Franny upholds surface expectations only through her capacity for repression. On the platform, upon making her entrance she does not reveal her "impatience over the male of the species' general ineptness and Lane's in particular" (9) but instead squeezes his arm with "simulated affection" (10). After claiming to have missed him, Franny takes mental note of the falsity of her words. She then feels guilty for not feeling as she thinks she should. The scene at the train station introduces the story's pervading thematic conflict between public form and private consciousness, between public action and private conscience.

The primary action of "Franny" takes place at Sickler's restaurant. It provides a forum for a dialogue on competing intentions and alternative principles. In this debate Lane Coutell is a cardboard player—Zooey describes him as a "big nothing" (98)—a self-absorbed bore, impressed by his snobbish "A"-paper analysis of Flaubert. In Lane's company Franny questions the ground of being. Torn and disturbed, she is coming emotionally undone: she is disgusted by her culture's artistic, educational, and religious forms of self-making. Salinger presents the conflict between Lane's attempts to maintain (and advance) bourgeois conventions through his self-congratulatory social performance, on the one hand, and Franny's insistent challenge to these postures, on the other, first, through her withering critiques of them and, second, through the introduction of spiritual correctives. Lane wants not only to maintain conventional surfaces but to orchestrate her movements across these surfaces. He wants her to be an extension of himself, an appendage who is also a worshipful audience. The restaurant—"Sickler's was snails"—epitomizes Lane's world. He can drink martinis with a right-looking girl and mime the manners of adult, upper-class sophisticates. With hearty appetite, Lane orders Sickler's haute cuisine of snails, frogs' legs, and salad, while Franny orders a chicken sandwich, which she does not eat. With Franny across the table, Lane pontificates on Flaubert's lack of "testicularity" (11). Such a perspective on the master novelist no doubt informs his essay, which he wants to read to Franny. In summarizing his views Lane talks nonsense—a mixture of psychobabble, cant, slang, aspersion, and name-dropping: "I think the emphasis I put on *why* he was so neurotically attracted to the *mot juste* wasn't too bad. . . . I'm no Freudian man or anything like that, but certain things you can't just pass over as capital-F Freudian and let them go at that. I mean to a certain extent I think I was perfectly justified to point out that none of the really good boys—Tolstoy, Dostoevski, *Shakes*peare, for Chrissake—were such goddam word-squeezers. They just *wrote*. Know what I mean?" (12–13). Franny does not know what he means; she has not been paying attention, though she acts like she has. When she asks for his martini olive she deflates the impact of his grand conclusion: his professor thinks Lane "ought to publish the goddam paper somewhere" (13–14).

Franny's abstraction precedes her explicit refusal to play the role of supportive, adoring female. She accuses Lane of sounding like "a section man"—an instructor or graduate assistant who runs "around ruining things for people" (14–15). Franny hates the process of reducing the experience of literature to dry, analytical terms. She is torn between "self-disapproval and malice" (14). While loathing herself for speaking up at all, she nevertheless levies blast after blast at the "pedants and conceited little tearer-downers" (17). Franny's attack on pedantry is but one aspect of her dissatisfaction with the university intelligentsia, a class that includes poetasters and egotists. Franny reviles the pedagogical structures that support a glorification of Self as an autonomous intellectual agent. As G. E. Slethaug points out, Franny "strenuously objects to the various kinds of hollow formalism evidenced by students, academics, and poets."[61] Franny dismisses, for example, the well-published Manlius and Esposito: "[T]hey're not *real* poets. . . . If you're a poet, you do something beautiful. I mean you're supposed to *leave* something beautiful after you get off the page and everything" (18–19). This affirmation of the poet implies her love for her brother, Seymour; she sees him as the apotheosis of the pure poet.

Her repudiation of Manlius and Esposito reflects her rage against whatever might be understood as conventional life. When Lane mentions having seen Wally Campbell, Franny launches a diatribe against affectation and money; she registers her disgust with safe and predictable social manners (25–26). Wally Campbell represents mere conformity. As Franny argues, once the individual has become co-opted by the mores of a self-consciously recognizable class, then that individual renounces the possibility of direct experience. Even Bohemians, in Franny's view, are conformists: their act is only apparently iconoclastic; they simply conform to a beard and black clothing stereotype. The Wally Campbells, essentially, are "tiny and meaningless and—sad-making" (26).

In fact, as far as Franny is concerned, any action that projects a self in the costume of *any* social form becomes tainted. The actor necessarily involves what Franny denounces as "ego," a narcissistic preoccupation with the self as social (as opposed to spiritual) entity. Ego is to be condemned because it informs any self-conscious action that issues in social performance. Stage acting, then, constitutes an extension and intensification of the egotistical role-playing that Franny associates with conventional behavior in everyday life. Franny quits the theater in order to evade such vain self-dramatizations: "It seemed like such poor taste, sort of, to want to act in the first place. I mean all the *ego*. And I used to hate myself so, when I was in a play, to be backstage after the play was over. All those egos running around feeling terribly *char*itable and *warm*" (28).

Critics of the Glass children fault them for a presumption of vain superiority, the notion that they inhabit an Archimedean position of judgment.[62] To give him a bit of credit, Lane accuses Franny early in their discussion of making "one *hell*uva sweeping generalization" (17). It is her way. While Franny's diatribe attacks sterile convention, its "sweeping" virulence is in itself a reflection of pathology: she complains too much; indeed any form of behavior, under her strictures, can be abstracted, or generalized, into phoniness. There is no room for the possibility that someone circulating backstage might be sincere in tendering congratulations. Franny is afflicted with the Holden Caulfield disease so deftly identified by Phoebe: "You don't like *any*thing that's happening" (*Catcher*, 169). Crucially, Salinger presents Franny's eruption as a symptom of her breakdown. She would be the first to admit that her mind is not right: "All I know is I'm losing my mind. . . . I'm just sick of ego, ego, ego. My own and everybody else's" (29). Franny's diagnosis identifies a vexing problem that inhabits the center of Salinger's work: at one extreme, social roles can be phony evasions of genuine identity; at the other extreme, the abolition of all social roles coincides with one's annihilation. Over here, Lane Coutell preens his feathers; over there, Seymour Glass blows his head off. Franny's sickness leads her to the dichotomous conclusion that one is either an ego or a nobody: "I'm sick of not having the courage to be an absolute nobody" (30).

The pervading irony of the story is that Franny tenders both her diagnosis and her conflicted soul to a most unworthy audience. In listening to her, Lane feels "worried and vaguely, unfairly conspired against." He compensates by adjusting his demeanor so that he looks "attractively bored" (21). On a number of occasions Lane perceives Franny's outburst as a "goddam bug" (15) that threatens to "bitch up the whole weekend." Franny's jeremiad does not—and will not—wrest Lane from his impregnable self-absorption. In fact the long dialogue dramatizes the limitations of language. By meeting words with words Franny fails to make herself understood. Her discomposure, especially her fainting spells, is to Lane merely a symptom of her "bug." Franny's critique does not provide catharsis. In speaking her mind she becomes more self-divided.

Like Holden in *Catcher*, she thinks she might simply disappear: "Maybe there's a trapdoor under my chair and I'll just disappear" (18).

Such a wish points to the dark underside of Salinger's fiction: the desire to disappear coincides with a rejection of one's place in the social world. Disgusted with everything, one opts for invisibility, self-erasure. Holden and Franny want to disappear; Seymour commits suicide; the reclusive Buddy absents himself. The author himself drops way out of sight. The possibility of securing a balance between the extremes of solipsism and phoniness, the possibility, as it were, of securing peace so that Franny might find a way to live *in* the world, does not engage Salinger's attention in "Franny," though it does become the central focus of "Zooey."[63] "Franny" dramatizes Franny's dis-ease with social performance as it issues in her longing for self-renunciation. The specific causes (and effects) of her breakdown are not made clear. Instead Salinger presents an accumulation of overlapping contexts—romance, guilt, pedagogy, art, and at the end, biology—any one of which provides access to a consideration, but not an explanation, of her tortured condition.

The dialogue between Franny and Lane has its climax in the examination of the efficacy of an alternative way of life. Franny's obsession with *The Way of a Pilgrim* and the Jesus Prayer presents in a literary and religious paradigm a potential corrective to the horrors of ego.[64] *The Way of a Pilgrim* is an anonymous personal narrative that Franny claims she found out about in religion class. (Later Zooey reports that she got the book and its sequel, *The Pilgrim Continues His Way*, from Seymour's desk.) *The Way* depicts the quest of a 33-year-old Russian peasant who in the nineteenth century wanders the countryside in order to discover what it means "in the Bible when it says you should pray incessantly" (33). Franny's enthusiastic report on his progress culminates with her account of the Jesus Prayer. One can pray incessantly, she reports, by repeating, "Lord Jesus Christ, have mercy on me" (36). Franny's celebration of the pilgrim contrasts with Lane's analysis of Flaubert. Through prayer the pilgrim achieves oneness with the mystical rhythms of life; through pedantry Lane abstracts literature into an egotistical display. The Jesus Prayer offers an antidote to the entanglements of ego. The repetition of the prayer subsumes the self in the reflexes of spiritual process. The prayer, Franny explains, "becomes self-active. Something *happens*. . . . and the words get synchronized with the person's heartbeats, and then you're actually praying without ceasing. Which has a really tremendous, mystical effect on your whole outlook" (37). Franny insists that the quantity of rote repetitions "becomes quality by itself." This process is not limited to one's sectarian affiliation. Rather, the effacement of ego as a means of transcendence can be achieved in either Western or Eastern religious traditions. She links the experience of saying the Jesus Prayer with a similar practice in "the Nimbutsu sects of Buddhism" (38).

Franny's account of the pilgrim does not relieve her psychological distress. The story offers, perhaps, the form within which her self-therapy might be achieved. It is inviting, certainly, to see Franny's celebration of the pilgrim as authorially endorsed. Salinger would, then, be affirming the pilgrim's narrative as a self-help book. However plausible this view might be, it must be qualified by the underlying psychological reality of the story: Franny is having, as Bessie and Zooey so clearly recognize, a nervous breakdown. The Jesus Prayer reflects both her genuine desire for spiritual fulfillment and a dangerous symptom of mental instability. To merge one's very being with a self-active prayer would eliminate identity. This condition should not be understood as the goal of the surviving Glass children, most notably Franny, Zooey, and Buddy. Rather, what one *does* with personal identity is the tortuous dilemma with which they wrestle.

Certainly Franny's quest for the spiritual life seems preferable to Lane's fatuous lit. crit. sensibility. Ironically, and comically, Lane can view the self-active Jesus Prayer only as inducing "heart trouble." His most obtuse and reductive contribution is the notion that "all those religious experiences have a very obvious psychological background" (40). Salinger hates psychoanalysis, especially for its tendency to de-mythologize religious sensibility into self-inflated wish-fulfillment fantasies and to transform creative idiosyncrasy into white-bread normality.

Shortly after Lane's reductive summation, Franny faints on the way to the lavatory. After this incident Salinger proposes another explanation for her discomfiture: she may be pregnant. Throughout the story Franny suffers from poor appetite, and she feels waves of nausea. After she revives, Lane is solicitous: he insists that she rest all afternoon in her room. He hopes, he tells her, that he "can get upstairs somehow" (43). Franny does not reply. Lane laments their dearth of sexual activity: "You know how long it's been? . . .When was that Friday night? Way the hell early last month, wasn't it? . . . Too goddam long between drinks. To put it crassly." In no subsequent published piece has Salinger addressed the issue of Franny's possible pregnancy. It does not come up in "Zooey." The events of "Raise High" and "Hapworth" precede 1955. In "Seymour" Buddy makes no mention of Franny having ever been pregnant. The intimation of pregnancy, while it does not mitigate her attacks on the conventional life, certainly does remind us that Franny is a creature of flesh as well as spirit. Salinger's teasing implication seems to be a playful gambit designed to stir debate, a way of unsettling the issues the story addresses. The story ends, therefore, on a note of irresolution. Salinger depicts Franny in terms of motion and silence: "Her lips began to move, forming soundless words, and they continued to move" (44). The narrator stays outside Franny's mind, letting the story trail away into the repetitions of the Jesus Prayer.

"Zooey": "A Sort of Semantic Geometry"

In the preface to *Typee* Herman Melville claims to offer the "unvarnished truth" about the Polynesian cannibals he visited after jumping ship. Nathaniel Hawthorne's "The Custom-House" asserts the essential "authenticity" of *The Scarlet Letter*; Hawthorne's narrator establishes his "true position as editor, or very little more" of the newly-found, aged manuscript that sketches the life of Hester Prynne. To vouch for the credibility of a preposterous incident in *Bleak House*, Charles Dickens, in a prefatory note, asserts the scientific credibility of spontaneous combustion: human beings can (because some reportedly did) self-immolate without the help of an external combustive agent.[65] Frequently an author's preface locates such professions of truth in the context of personal experience. Such practices identify the perimeters of authorial credibility, especially when a writer defines, as Hawthorne does, the *limits* of his authority. He might be guilty of "dressing up" the tale, but he does not deviate from "the authenticity of the outline" (Hawthorne, 63). In each case the author purports to serve (in truth) some essential, indisputable entity called real life—things as they are or were. In each case these confidential claims to truth rest upon a scaffold of lies. Their truth, in short, is a fiction.

The narrator of Salinger's "Zooey" joins the rank of authors seeking to identify the nature or degree of truth one might expect to find in the succeeding pages. By adopting the moldy old technique of "the author's formal introduction," the narrator self-consciously and wryly tests his readers' patience: "This everfresh and exciting odium," he avers, "not only is wordy and earnest beyond my wildest dreams but is, to boot, excruciatingly personal" (47). The author introducing himself is not J. D. Salinger but Buddy Glass. The fiction that Buddy Glass is author and alter ego allows Salinger to retreat behind a projected mask. The implication is that there is a real Buddy who discusses his work with a living Zooey. The preface, indeed, asserts the truth of the fiction. The personality of Buddy Glass provides a buffer, a self-protecting screen from behind which Salinger can playfully comment on his own image. Zooey feels, for example, that Buddy ought to "call off the production. *He* feels that the plot hinges on mysticism, or religious mystification" (48). Zooey fears that the tale will lead to Buddy's "professional undoing," no doubt reflecting Salinger's awareness of some readers' chagrin over his exploration of religious issues. As Buddy remarks, "People are already shaking their heads over me, and any immediate further professional use on my part of the word 'God,' except as a familiar, healthy American expletive, will be taken—or, rather, confirmed—as the very worst kind of name-dropping and a sure sign that I'm going straight to the dogs." These critics, Salinger admits through Buddy, give him (that is, both of them) pause. "But only pause."

In asserting the truth of the fiction, Buddy considers the nature of his genre. In fact this very process becomes the means through which he affirms the real-life existence of the fictional characters. As compiler of a "prose home movie" (47), Buddy rejects conventional expectations of the short story genre, especially the prescription for "brevity of detail and compression of incident" (49). He unashamedly celebrates verbosity. He also parodies conventional acts of literary naming. Crucial to any approach to the Glass stories is a recognition of Salinger's refusal to recast standard literary forms, a tendency that becomes most manifest in the diffuse and digressive "Seymour" and the shapeless and interminable "Hapworth." In making "the prose home movie," Buddy engages in "a rather unholy collaborative effort" (49). He reconstructs "Zooey" after extensive interviews with the three principals—Franny, Bessie, and Zooey. Each finds something wrong with Buddy's final version. Bessie and Franny do not like their unflattering appearance; Zooey fears that the tale dissolves into a mystical fog. This collaboration reinforces the insularity of the Glass tribe: "We are, all four of us, blood relatives, and we speak a kind of esoteric, family language, a sort of semantic geometry in which the shortest distance between any two points is a fullish circle" (49).

The language of paradox appropriately links Buddy's individual performance as writer with the tribal forces (and resources) that inform his tale. Any plot line that Buddy might fashion—the narrative distance, as it were, between two points—can be drawn only by incorporating a broad, often digressive range of associated contexts. The tribe's disagreements with Buddy's choices are part of the story. His response to these disagreements adds to the story. For example, Buddy refutes Zooey's charge of mysticism by formulating his own explanation: "I say that my current offering isn't a mystical story, or a religiously mystifying story, at all. *I* say it's a compound, or multiple, love story, pure and complicated."

What this statement might mean is anybody's guess. What it does indicate is Salinger's insistence on grounding his aesthetic experiments in a careful rendering of enigmas. It is Salinger's admission of this process—that is, Buddy's admission of his "unholy collaboration"—that winds up imbuing Buddy's authorial acts with provisional authority: none of the principals agree *entirely* with Buddy's reconstruction. Though each would propose specific emendations, each in turn affirms the basic authenticity of the account. Salinger thereby fosters the illusion that these events did happen at some time in some way. By prefacing his tale with a critique of the tale, he identifies divergences in opinion that are never resolved. No reconstruction can capture the reality, especially insofar as the reality in question has to do with transactions among brilliant and mercurial persons, each of whom is open and closed to others, aware and unaware of the oscillating motions of their minds. Nevertheless, the story is now fixed in form. As a compositional event, the preface takes place after the penning of the narrative proper. The reading of the tale by the principal parties stirs objections that become part of the self-critical, self-regarding process Buddy is, in his narrative present, now living. The implication is that literary art is most mimetic when it reveals its own inconclusiveness, especially when a present-tense, first-person narrator points out that the uncertainty of his account has already stirred divergent opinions.

Salinger's sensitivity to the interaction between fact and fiction goes back at least 15 years to "The Heart of a Broken Story" and its playful spinning out of unlived scenarios. In his later stories Salinger rejects the smooth surfaces of well-crafted fiction in favor of an art that seems spontaneous and improvisational, even conversational.[66] Having written the "author's formal introduction" in the present tense, Salinger (through Buddy's agency) merges events being narrated with the act of narration itself, a technique that later governs "Seymour." Consequently, Buddy expresses the process of thinking in the activity of writing. The first-person actor in the preface is also the present-tense teller. What is Buddy doing? He is writing to his readers. By the time Buddy slips into the third person, past tense, to run through his "prose home movie," he has already undermined the prospect of seeing his narrative from the omniscient point of view. Buddy's prefatory account reflects Salinger's experimentation with the prospects and limitations of a fiction maker's authority.

The action of "Zooey" picks up two days after Franny fainted at Sickler's restaurant. It is Monday morning at the Glass family's Manhattan apartment. Franny's breakdown continues, and Mrs. Glass does not know what to do—her husband is ineffectual; Buddy is unreachable. Zooey, her youngest son, made an attempt to speak with Franny the night before. He seems, in Bessie's view, to be the only one available who might be capable of helping Franny get beyond her exasperating and frightening behavior. Zooey himself lounges in the bathtub, rereading a letter Buddy wrote to him four years earlier. To speak of the story's action, however, belies its static design. There are few events. Zooey rereads Buddy's letter; his mother comes into the bathroom; Zooey pulls the shower curtain; they discuss Franny. Zooey gets dressed, goes to the living room, and converses with Franny. Their conversation makes her more distraught. Zooey then goes into the old bedroom of Seymour and Buddy, where their phone is still connected. Mimicking the voice of Buddy, Zooey dials Franny, a ruse that works briefly. After Franny exposes Zooey, they continue their phone conversation, which concludes with Franny's experience of peace and sleep.

"Zooey," then, resembles a one-act play of three scenes in which the players transact their business almost solely through dialogue. Even Buddy's letter possesses a conversational quality. One wonders why Zooey decides to reread Buddy's letter at this particular time. At the least Zooey can feel he is listening to his older brother. Like Franny's letter to Lane, Buddy's letter to Zooey offers direct access to its author's mind. As author, Buddy engages in the familiar Glass activity of self-examination, evaluating his own letter as "virtually endless in length, overwritten, teaching, repetitious, opinionated, remonstrative, condescending, embarrassing—and filled, to a surfeit, with affection" (56).

Buddy composed the letter on the third anniversary of Seymour's death. He addressed a 21-year-old Zooey, who was trying to decide whether to become an actor. The letter functions as both a eulogy for Seymour and a self-reflexive rumination. Buddy considers the problematic issue of "*why* S. and I took over your and Franny's education as early and as highhandedly as we did" (64). Buddy tries to fight through "the usual stench of words" in order to argue that all education should expose the pupil to a direct apprehension of God. By adopting paradigms of Eastern religion, the two brothers try to counteract the Western pedagogical premise that knowledge is a matter of acquisition, a brick-by-brick approach to building the domain of consciousness. In this view, education should not

> begin with a quest for knowledge at all but with a quest, as Zen would put it, for no-knowledge. Dr. Suzuki says somewhere that to be in a state of pure consciousness—*satori*—is to be with God before he said, Let there be light. Seymour and I thought it might be a good thing to hold back this light from you and Franny (at least as far as we were able), and all the many lower, more fashionable lighting effects—the arts, sciences, classics, languages—till you were both able at least to conceive of a state of being where the mind knows the source of all light. (65)

As in "Teddy," the child does not merely reflect natural innocence. In Salinger's later stories the child stands close to a sense of primal unity, a spiritual oneness that pervades creation. Buddy reports an epiphany he had—"a perfectly communicable little vision of truth" (67). In the supermarket Buddy happened to ask a little girl how many boyfriends she had. The little girl replies that "her boy friends' names were Bobby and Dorothy." This encounter leads Buddy to share some words from the master: "Seymour once said to me . . . that all legitimate religious study *must* lead to unlearning the differences, the illusory differences, between boys and girls, animals and stones, day and night, hot and cold" (67–68).[67] Thus the innocence of children is not merely a matter of preexperience or cute, ingenuous behavior; rather, it is a matter of *being*, of essence. Children are both embodiments of and metaphors for a religious state of perfection. Consequently, in the education of Zooey and Franny, Seymour and Buddy sought to suspend the epistemological process and thereby defer acquisition. At the same time they not only imbued their charges with a corpus of supportive rituals and chants, but they assigned a reading list that included Dr. Suzuki, the Upanishads, and the Diamond Sutra. Somehow this ponderous indoctrination into self-erasing metaphysics is not to be confused "with the cumbersome baggage of a too formal education" (60).

At the very least, Seymour and Buddy must share responsibility for possibly having made Zooey and Franny into neurotic, obsessive "freaks" (103). Was their education an induction into heightened spiritual identity? Or was it irresponsible brainwashing, a golden path away from social and communal existence and toward the isolating confines of neurosis? Buddy's letter to Zooey, like Franny's letter to Lane, introduces major issues of the story: education as learning to unlearn; the presence of the past; the conflict between the religious life and the actor's vocation; Seymour as guru or manipulator; Buddy's alienation; the complex relationship between religion and neurosis; Zooey's bitter resentment of what Buddy calls the "home seminars, and the metaphysical sittings in particular" (66). Indeed Salinger's tendency to embed one text within another emphasizes his central preoccupation: self-consciousness *is* his subject.

"Zooey" presents a series of interactions among self-examining voices. Zooey and Franny struggle incessantly with the issue of what it means to be so aware of being so aware. These voices—in both epistolary and conversational forms—seek to overcome the void left by the absent significant other. In "Zooey" the attempt to make contact with two absent figures—Seymour and Buddy—impels Bessie, Zooey, and Franny. While Bessie is beside herself because Buddy is unreachable, Zooey strikes her as his appropriate substitute; Franny offers the wistful, whining lament "I want to talk to Seymour" (151). The entire story, then, might be viewed as a series of negotiations in which the maimed survivors of Seymour's suicide and Buddy's decampment attempt to cope with the eldest brothers' emotional and ideational legacy.

Zooey is not his mother's compliant, obliging son. Instead he is truculent, haughty, judgmental, obnoxious, rude. After Mrs. Glass enters the bathroom to discuss Franny's condition—she won't eat, she cries, she mumbles—the high-strung Zooey bombards her with insults. He mocks her without mercy. Bessie, however, is undaunted: she merely chides him for his superiority complex. Like Holden Caulfield and Franny, Zooey does not like many people. Zooey's hypersensitive intellect separates him from other people. His mother tells him, "You can't live in the world with such strong likes and dislikes" (99). His particular problem is that he cannot live in the inner world fashioned by his older brothers. His abrasive behavior may well provide the least destructive alternative. While it keeps others away, it also allows him to distance himself from the psychological enclosures of their indoctrination. Bessie seems to realize that Zooey's outbursts are diversionary, his "method of dealing with problems" (95). His "style of bullying" (81) constitutes a histrionic evasion of the tortuous introspection that is Seymour's legacy. Zooey's outbursts are ways to purge his conflicted inner life. He seems most aware that Buddy and Seymour's emphasis on egolessness has led him to become self-absorbed, haughty, and isolated. In fact the separation of the Glass family from the communal life offers the central complex in Salinger's serial story.

Salinger does not merely present the Glasses as adorable paradigms; rather, he explores the positive and negative ramifications of their privileged condition. Zooey consciously tries to escape the legacy. He is as tempestuous as Seymour (usually) was placid. If Seymour and Buddy took liberties with their siblings' lives, then Zooey reveals his wariness of involvement: "What would you like us to do, Bessie? Go in there and live Franny's life for her?" (84). He believes Franny should be left alone: "If she's determined to have a nervous breakdown, the least we can do is see that she doesn't have it in peace" (85). For Bessie, Zooey nevertheless provides hope for giving some insight into Franny's predicament. Bessie's belief that Franny is a "rundown, overwrought little college girl that's been reading too many religious books" (87) may well be accurate. Nonetheless, Zooey has the background needed to consider how these religious books have affected this "*ter*ribly impressionable" young woman.

As the conversation continues, Zooey becomes less strident. He reaches a point where he speaks to his mother without insult. He sees the issue, in fact, as "strictly non-sectarian" (95). He explains that Franny got the two *Pilgrim* books from Seymour and Buddy's room. The real issue is not Franny's putative impressionability but the current effects of their early education. Zooey surrenders his pose of obnoxious banter to register his disgust and fury at being held hostage. Franny and Zooey are held in thrall by these absent presences who, in Buddy's words, stalk "in and out of the plot with considerable frequency, like so many Banquo's ghosts" (52). The Glass stories *are* ghost stories. Zooey, for one, is fed up with being haunted, especially by Buddy: "I'm so sick of their names I could cut my throat. . . . This whole goddam house stinks of ghosts. I don't mind so much being haunted by a dead ghost, but I resent like *hell* being haunted by a half-dead one. I wish to *God* Buddy'd make up his mind. He does everything else Seymour ever did—or tries to. Why the hell doesn't he kill himself and be done with it" (103).

The story focuses as much on Zooey's fragile, conflicted psyche as it does on Franny's more overt breakdown. As Zooey tells Bessie, "We're *freaks*, the two of us, Franny and I. . . . I'm a twenty-five-year-old freak and she's a twenty-year-old freak, and both those bastards are responsible. . . . I swear to you, I could murder them both without even batting an eyelash. The great teachers. The great emancipators. My God. I can't even sit down to lunch with a man any more and hold up my end of a decent conversation" (103–4). Related to Zooey's rage is his desire to rectify the damage done by their odd education.

Zooey no longer wishes to be a freak. His estrangement has become self-consuming. It is also crucial that this critique of the Glass distinctiveness comes from *within* the family itself, a position not recognized by those who charge the Glass children with complacent elitism. However one may view this family, one cannot read *Franny and Zooey* with an open mind and find much complacency. The collection depicts the family in crisis. The two youngest children are coming apart. Bessie does not understand what happened to the children who used to be "so—smart and happy and—just *lovely*" (118).

What animates "Zooey" is the question of whether Franny (and Zooey) might achieve therapy from within the family without having recourse to a psychotherapist. As Zooey tells Bessie, "Just think of what analysis did for Seymour" (106–7). Zooey has contempt for psychoanalysis and its attempt to impose prefabricated solutions. In Franny's case professional consultation would only exacerbate the malady; she would become a religious zealot, a Joan of Arc turned loose on a mad, self-destructive crusade: "You just call in some analyst who's experienced in adjusting people to the joys of television, and *Life* magazine . . . you just *do* that, and I swear to you, in not more than a year Franny'll either be in a *nut* ward or she'll be wandering off into some goddam desert with a burning cross in her hand" (108).[68]

In other words, Franny does not need to be adjusted to the conventional world of Wally Campbell. Rather, both Zooey and Franny need to be reconciled to the ghosts. They must achieve therapy in *relation to* rather than in *flight from* the conditions that shaped their unusual lives. They must thereby find a way to live out the dictates of their vocational identities as actor and actress without entirely severing connection to Seymour and Buddy. Zooey seeks to rehabilitate his relationship with the ghosts. This process cannot be separated from Zooey's attempt to determine what Buddy or Seymour would do, which is to wonder what they might say.

Zooey's encounter with Franny issues in a series of mutual diagnoses delivered through recriminatory speeches and conversational repartee. Throughout their exchange it becomes clear that Zooey and Franny are versions of each other. Both are serious actors; both were students of the "great emancipators"; both are enmeshed by their pasts. Each has a tendency to define people and experiences by using reductive rubrics. Franny's hypersensitivity to pretentiousness emerges in her attack on Professor Tupper: "I can never bring myself to smile back at him when he's being charming and Oxfordish. . . . He has no enthusiasm whatever for his subject. Ego, yes. Enthusiasm, no. . . . [H]e keeps dropping idiotic hints that he's a *Realized Man*" (127–28). Similarly, Zooey savages formula television, especially the promulgation of stereotypes in the service of commercialism. Regarding a script that his producer is promoting, Zooey says, "It's down-to-earth, it's simple, it's untrue, and it's familiar enough and trivial enough to be understood by our greedy, nervous, illiterate sponsors" (135). Their repudiations of the Phony, however justified any particular attack may be, winds up paralyzing them. They have difficulty moving beyond their own categories of judgment. In fact they may simply be substituting one constricting set of categories for another—the pieties of Eastern religion for the slogans of Madison Avenue, the Jesus Prayer for a soap-opera script.

The narrative's greatest tension, however, derives not from their conflicts with the crass Western world; rather, it comes from their own reflexivity, their self-lacerating doubts regarding the efficacy of their own judgments. As Franny remarks, "Don't you think I have sense enough to *worry* about my motives for saying the prayer? That's exactly what's *both*ering me so. Just because I'm choosy about what I want—in this case, en*light*enment, or *peace*, instead of money or pres*tige* or *fame* or any of those things—doesn't mean I'm not as egotistical and self-seeking as everybody else" (149). While Franny suffers from guilt, Zooey suffers from the strangling effects of his superior pose. Both are sick and tired of themselves; they are disgusted by their obsessive self-scrutiny. Zooey in particular laments his tendency to continue living in a condition he finds so oppressive: "I'm tired as hell of getting up furious in the morning and going to bed furious at night. . . . I sit in judgment on every poor, ulcerous bastard I know" (137). What bothers him most is the way he demoralizes others into compromising their standards. He feels responsible for making people surrender "good work" in favor of work "that will be thought good" (138). *Why* he feels responsible is a mystery, though this very tendency to assume responsibility for a decadent popular art in itself evidences megalomania.

Caught up in the very processes he hates, Zooey fully appreciates his paradoxical position: though a man of beautiful surfaces, a media star, he despises the forces that make him popular, even as he continues to seek the very popularity that comes from performing his roles. Attacking others is a roundabout way for Zooey to attack himself; similarly, going crazy is Franny's way of punishing herself. Like Zooey, Franny feels she demoralized Lane by "picking and picking and picking at all his opinions and values. . . . It's a wonder he didn't shoot me. . . . I'd have absolutely *congrat*ulated him if he had" (138–39). Likewise Zooey remarks, "I could happily lie down and die sometimes" (144). Given Seymour's suicide, such ominous statements are not mere figures of speech. Instead they reflect the dangers inherent in self-absorption. Franny drifts toward lunacy; Zooey angles toward misanthropy.

Franny and Zooey must reconcile the conflicting, if not inimical, demands of artistic self-expression and religious self-effacement. What at first seem to be correctives are actually evasions. When Franny repeats the Jesus Prayer, she hopes to displace identity into mechanical process. When Zooey engages in his truculent and insulting pontification, he enacts a form of self-destructive and self-isolating role-playing. Such behavior seems to be consuming him. He is tired of always playing the "heavy" (169). Zooey needs to find a way to accept other people, not in general but in particular. Especially he needs to reconcile himself to the ghosts. Franny needs to find a language that is genuinely expressive of the soul's needs without leading her to reject the elements of her vocational, intellectual, and emotional life.

Zooey begins to ameliorate his anger when he looks out the window and watches a street scene five flights below: "[H]e let his attention be drawn to a little scene that was being acted out sublimely, unhampered by writers and directors and producers" (151). A child is hiding from her dog; the dog, sniffing to find her, suffers the "anguish of separation" (152). Soon there is a joyful reunion. In witnessing this real-life scene, Zooey translates it into artifice. He composes the scene and imbues it with order. The girl's red tam evokes the red blanket "on the bed in Van Gogh's room at Arles. Her tam did, in fact, from Zooey's vantage point, appear not unlike a dab of paint" (151). The scene has a beginning, middle, and end; it also culminates in a genuine display of emotion. Zooey is moved. He says, "God damn it . . . there are nice things in the world—and I mean *nice* things. We're all such morons to get so sidetracked. Always, always, always referring every goddam thing that happens right back to our lousy little egos" (152).

This aesthetic moment dramatizes the reality of emotional loss and gain, yet it is depersonalized. The young girl could be anybody. Zooey momentarily transcends his state of tortured self-consciousness. Significantly, he recalls an artistically cognate image that comes from one of Buddy's "reasonably sensible" notions: "He said that a man should be able to lie at the bottom of a hill with his throat cut, slowly bleeding to death, and if a pretty girl or an old woman should pass by with a beautiful jug balanced perfectly on the top of her head, he should be able to raise himself up on one arm and see the jug safely over the top of the hill" (153–54). This scenario offers a parable of how one might maintain composure in the face of death: one fixes one's attention on a beautiful image. Zooey's view from the window and Buddy's parable do not so much efface the self as allow it to mediate between inner and outer frames of reference. The perceiver is a passive observer who is also a conscious arranger and interpreter of the scene he is witnessing. His aesthetic consciousness organizes without directly manipulating the objects under scrutiny. Both scenes celebrate a noninvasive relationship among a perceiver, another person, and selected objects. They provide contrasts to Franny's putative cures. While offering spiritually exciting alternatives to the sterile environment Franny associates with college life, the *Pilgrim* narratives and the Jesus Prayer do not draw her out of the solipsistic retreat but instead make her more self-absorbed.

Rather than working from his experience of composure, Zooey conducts a "siege" (156). Franny's narcissistic *manner* most disturbs him. He is repelled by her way of "going at this business" of breaking down. In the climax of their dialogue, he lets loose a barrage. He does not like "this Camille routine"—that is, Franny's way of upsetting their parents and giving "off a little stink of piousness" (159–60). Her "blanket attack" on the Professor Tuppers and the "system of higher education" leaves no room for individual exceptions (161). Franny does not, he tells her, "just despise what they represent—you despise them.

It's too damn personal" (162). Zooey implicates himself in this particular charge; he too lets his "feelings about television and everything else get personal" (163). According to Zooey, Franny's absolutism, manifest as unstinting personal antagonism, becomes most problematically reflected in her notions about Jesus. She wants St. Francis of Assisi to be Jesus of the Gospels. Informing Zooey's indictment is his conviction that Franny wants to dissolve all distinctions. She wants to love a gnat and a human being equally, thereby replacing a hierarchy in the value of created things with an emotional democracy.

In such a world one would not have to make choices; one could inhabit an all-embracing, egoless domain of narcotic bliss. Ego is nothing less than the collective force of those psychological and behavioral attributes which identify one as a unique person. Zooey's point is that the historical Jesus made distinctions. He had a self and an ego. Indeed he got angry and threw "tables around." Zooey tells Franny, "And you're constitutionally unable to love or understand any son of God who says a human being, *any* human being—even a Professor Tupper—is more valuable to God than any soft, helpless Easter chick" (165). Thus Franny loves not Jesus but a self-serving, sanitized Jesus that will allow her to opt out of the human condition, the realm of limitation, differences, and choice. The Jesus Prayer, then, disengages her from, rather than connects her to, the actualities of earthly life with all their ego-ridden complexities.

Zooey's attack is unrelenting: he adopts a kind of polemical scorched-earth policy. He even disparages her motives in coming home to have her breakdown: "The service is good, and there's plenty of hot and cold running ghosts. What could be more convenient? You can say your prayer here and roll Jesus and St. Francis and Seymour and Heidi's grandfather all in one" (166). He dismisses her attacks on "ego, ego, ego" as "tenth-rate thinking" and her fixation on the Jesus Prayer as a mere soporific. Franny especially perverts the Jesus Prayer: "[It] has one aim, and one aim *only*," Zooey says. "To endow the person who says it with Christ-Consciousness." Whatever this state might be, it is not a "little cozy, holier-than-thou trysting place" (172). Franny must follow the path of "Christ-Consciousness" *into* rather than *away from* the imperfect world.

There is only one problem with Zooey's diagnosis and treatment: he almost loses the patient. Franny is facedown and sobbing. Zooey concludes his rant with a ruptured sentence. He recognizes that he failed to help her, though he brilliantly describes the symptoms of their related maladies. Zooey's diatribe especially underscores the psychological dangers that attend their strained, intense, involuted, and fragile minds. He does succeed, however, in dismantling any simple approach to the story that sees the Jesus Prayer as Salinger's (or Buddy's) cure-all.

After his barrage, Zooey leaves the prostrate Franny. He goes into his room, gets a cigar and handkerchief, and then crosses into the bedroom once shared by Seymour and Buddy. The room remains as they left it; the phone is still connected and listed in Seymour's name. At this point Buddy offers no access to Zooey's mind; he merely presents surfaces. Zooey stares at a sheet densely packed with eclectic quotations from a "variety of the world's literatures" (176). The citations appear in no particular order and lack thematic cohesion. Zooey stops reading and then sits at Seymour's desk, where he covers his face with his hands. He remains "inert" for 20 minutes. After reading a seemingly inconsequential entry from Seymour's diary, he sits motionless for another half-hour. Upon moving to Buddy's desk, Zooey places the handkerchief over the phone to muffle his voice. Zooey imitates Buddy. Why Zooey waits all this time is never considered: perhaps he needs to absorb the atmosphere of his brothers' room.

In any event Zooey seeks to become at one with the ghosts. By taking on the role of Buddy, by calling Franny on Seymour's phone, Zooey attempts to effect their mutual therapy. Initially he fools Franny. She tells "Buddy" what she thinks of Zooey. The exchange constitutes an unwitting counterpoint to Zooey's diatribe against her. She sees Zooey as "com*plete*ly destructive. . . . He's just so er*rat*ic. I mean he goes around and around in such horrible *cir*cles" (190). Zooey is caught in an intellectual whirlwind: "He has about *forty* definitions for everything" (191). The prospect of Zooey trying to cure her, she feels, resembles the crazy helping the insane: "It's like being in a *lun*atic asylum and having another patient all dressed up as a *doc*tor come over to you and start taking your pulse or something" (192).

Buddy presents a Zooey presenting a Buddy who is laconic, funny, and relaxed. Significantly, this Buddy gives no advice. He listens; he asks questions. Ironically, Zooey's wittiest rejoinder leads Franny to see through the ruse. After Franny complains of Zooey's cigar smoke, he replies, "The cigars are ballast, sweetheart. Sheer ballast. If he didn't have a cigar to hold on to, his feet would leave the ground. We'd never see our Zooey again" (193). This exchange alters their rancorous mood. Zooey's Buddy has a receptive, nonjudgmental voice. In this performance Zooey embraces his vocation, a movement away from his pontifical diatribe. Now he realizes he has "no goddam authority to be speaking up like a *seer*. . . . We've had enough goddam seers in this family" (195).

Zooey also makes a crucial distinction between the life of a religionist and the life of an actor. The respective problems of Zooey and Franny derive from their attempts to remake themselves in a way that is inimical to the essential demands of their beings. If, as Zooey says, "de*tach*ment" and "[d]esirelessness" ground the religious life, then the very opposite informs the actor's craft: "It's this business of de*sir*ing . . . that makes an actor in the first place" (198). In Zooey's view, Franny is a first-rate actress and she is "stuck" with this condition. In both their cases the "only re*lig*ious thing you can do, is *act*." The artist must aspire to "some kind of perfection, and *on his own terms*, not anyone else's" (199). They should not be concerned with the failures of audiences, but they should play to an ideal audience. Zooey recalls Seymour's insistence long ago that Zooey shine his shoes when he went on the radio: he should "shine them for the Fat Lady. . . . He never did tell me who the Fat Lady was, but I shined my shoes for the Fat Lady every time I ever went on the air" (200).[69] Zooey has an image of the Fat Lady as a heat-afflicted wretch, swatting flies and listening to the radio.

Similarly, Seymour told Franny to "be funny for the Fat Lady." Franny imagines a woman with "very thick legs, very veiny. I had her in an *aw*ful wicker chair. She had cancer, *too*, though, and she had the radio going full-blast all day" (201). The Fat Lady, then, is that person out there who needs the performance to get through the day. She is the grotesque and lonely integer—humanity stripped down, the lowly outcast. Just as Zooey rehabilitates Buddy by playing him, so too does he rehabilitate Seymour by recalling the Fat Lady. Seymour's image links the performer to an indigent other. One performs in the service of art and thereby enacts the dictates of religion. The Fat Lady is not a single being, finally, but a synoptic metaphor for everyone. Zooey tells Franny "a terrible secret. . . . *There isn't anyone out there who isn't Seymour's Fat Lady.*" All are needy; all are fused in a single image. The Fat Lady, as Zooey proclaims, is "Christ Himself. Christ Himself, Buddy" (202). The actor pursues the possibility of "Christ-Consciousness" not through detachment but through engagement—the self-redemptive act of playing to a crowd of Fat Ladies.

The conclusion of "Zooey" resolves the crisis presented in "Franny." The unity of artistic and religious purposes establishes a basis for a healthy communal interaction. Salinger presents this resolution as an untried perception, valid in the moment certainly but untested in experience. Nevertheless, the (at least momentary) achievement of peace suggests the possibility of a full-hearted embrace of spiritual identity that is compatible with ego. It is with such a vision of joy that Franny hangs up the phone and falls asleep.

The Seymour Narratives

On the dust jacket of the first edition of *Raise High the Roof Beam, Carpenters and Seymour: An Introduction,* J. D. Salinger addresses the reader in an engaging, lively, teasing voice. He identifies his reasons for reprinting these distinct, though related, *New Yorker* pieces:

> Whatever their differences in mood or effect, they are both very much concerned with Seymour Glass, who is the main character in my still-uncompleted series about the Glass family. It struck me that they had better be collected together, if not deliberately paired off, in something of a hurry, if I mean them to avoid unduly or undesirably close contact with new material in the series. There is only my word for it, granted, but I have several new Glass stories coming along—waxing, dilating—each in its own way, but I suspect the less said about them, in mixed company, the better.
>
> Oddly, the joys and satisfactions of working on the Glass family peculiarly increase and deepen for me with the years. I can't say why, though. Not, at least, outside the casino proper of my fiction.[70]

With the appearance of this volume Salinger ends the practice begun in 1948 of collecting companion pieces in book form. His claim that this particular pairing has been done "in something of a hurry" looms as an oddity. The stories were published in 1955 and 1957, respectively. If Salinger desired to separate the 1963 collection from the advent of "new material in the series," then the "hurry" was unwarranted. It was not until 1965 that Salinger published "Hapworth 16, 1924." Since then, "Hapworth" has remained uncollected and without companion. Either Salinger changed his mind about continuing publication or he was teasing his readers about the existence of forthcoming materials.

While the Glass stories remain a "still-uncompleted series," Salinger's remarks reflect his desire to keep these tales from having "undesirably close contact" with any successive work. It seems, then, that Salinger was not working toward a multivolume novelistic matrix, a

Proustian search for lost time, all parts related to an informing design. Rather, he seems conscious of offering a focused series that goes backward and forward in time or that locates itself in an experiential present wherein the narrative self and the acting self are one. Salinger suggests, and the individual tales confirm, that each piece has a distinct artistic integrity, a notion reflected in Salinger's diverse array of narrative techniques. The relation of tale to tale is not an easy fit. The progression from "Franny" to "Zooey" is interrupted by Buddy's self-reflexive prologue; "Raise High" contains Buddy's first-person account of his experiences on Seymour's wedding day; "Seymour" offers Buddy's present-tense, self-consciously improvisational narrative of his *failed attempt* to introduce his brother's personal and artistic attributes; the form of "Hapworth" is epistolary, a 30,000-word letter in which the seven-year-old Seymour renders the contents of his mind in the act of writing.

What the Seymour narratives have in common, of course, is Salinger's "main character." More precisely, each tale explores the mystery of Seymour's nature. The contours of this mystery assume shape as Buddy provides conflicting views of Seymour's enigmatic actions and words. For example, from the socially normative perspective of Mrs. Fedder and the matron of honor, Edie Burwick, Seymour is deranged; in Buddy's view, Seymour is guru and poet, a spiritual and artistic master. Complicating the portrait are the words and ideas Buddy extracts from Seymour's conversations and texts, most notably his diary and his poems. The Seymour narratives all concern the conflict between Seymour's thoughts and action, on the one hand, and his relationship to conventional expectations, on the other. In the sum of their sometimes-ragged parts, the three pieces formulate the unanswered question, What does Seymour mean, in his thoughts, his words, and his actions and especially in his absence?

"Raise High the Roof Beam, Carpenters": "A Day . . . of Rampant Signs and Symbols"

In Buddy's present-tense prologue to "Raise High the Roof Beam, Carpenters," he recalls Seymour's administration of a "good prose pacifier" to the 10-month-old Franny, who was moved into her brothers' "ostensibly germ-free" room during an outbreak of mumps. To soothe the crying infant Seymour reads her the Taoist tale of Duke Mu's attempt to acquire a great horse. The duke seeks the advice of

Po Lo, who understands the distinction between a good and a super-lative animal: "A good horse can be picked out by its general build and appearance. But the superlative horse—one that raises no dust and leaves no tracks—is something evanescent and fleeting, elusive as thin air" (4).[71] Po Lo recommends Chiu-fang Kao, who embarks on a three-month quest. After returning with a horse, Kao describes it to the duke, mistaking its sex and color. The duke is irritated until Po Lo explains how Kao is indeed the true master: in ascertaining the essen-tial, he "forgets the homely details; intent on the inward qualities, he loses sight of the external" (5).

The parable celebrates the realm of spirit and introduces Seymour's own preoccupation with "inward qualities." The Taoist tale also asso-ciates Seymour with Eastern religion, a point on which Buddy elabo-rates in "Seymour": "Would it be out of order for me to say that both Seymour's and my roots in Eastern philosophy—if I may hesitantly call them 'roots'—were, are, planted in the New and Old Testaments, Ad-vaita Vedanta, and Classical Taoism?" (208). The implication that Sey-mour, like Kao, does not attend to "homely details" must be viewed in relation to Buddy's punning insistence that his own narrative "has a beginning and an end, and a mortality, all its own" (5). "[H]omely details" and human "mortality" suggest the comic and tragic contexts of the tale.

The central issue of "Raise High" involves Seymour's failure to show up for his wedding. As Dennis L. O'Connor remarks, "The bridegroom . . . never appears but his absence dominates the entire day" (328). This failure to take care of his "homely" responsibilities initiates a series of digressive and delaying actions. The wedding does not take place as planned; Buddy winds up in a car with strangers; they are stymied by a parade; the passengers abandon the car and head to Schraft's; here they cannot make a phone call; by default they proceed to Seymour and Buddy's nearby apartment, where the matron of honor has trouble getting her call through to the Fedder home. Finally she completes the call and reports that Seymour was waiting at the Fed-ders' all along. He and Muriel have eloped. The comic resolution, with its imposition of a putative domestic order and its implication of a pos-sible happy future, cannot be dissociated from the morality and "mor-tality" that attends both Seymour's dereliction and his truncated life with Muriel.

As the matron of honor repeatedly makes clear, Seymour inflicts damage on a number of people, most notably Muriel. The tale is especially darkened by its second ending, its "mortality." In the prologue Buddy observes, "I feel I must mention that the bridegroom is now, in 1955, no longer living. He committed suicide in 1948, while on vacation in Florida with his wife." As described in "A Perfect Day for Bananafish," the vacation offers—and then withholds—the prospect of a new start, a second honeymoon. It might be said that the last scene of the action initiated in "Raise High" is played out in "A Perfect Day." As Theodore L. Gross argues, "however much [Buddy] has conceived of Seymour as joyful and saintly, precocious and prophetic, we know that this man will finally take his own life—his suicide is a response to the outside world, and though we do not know the full terms of that response, it nevertheless conditions Seymour's former affirmation and makes that affirmation macabre and less conclusive, less authoritative."[72]

What centers "Raise High" is the unfolding of competing perspectives that speak explicitly to Seymour's fitness for marriage and implicitly to his relationship to those who survive his death. He is absent on his wedding day; he is absent after "A Perfect Day." Thirteen years after the nuptials, Buddy's allegiance is to Seymour as seer, a man who "forgets the homely details" in order to recognize the superlative horse. Indeed Buddy cannot "think of anybody whom I'd care to send out to look for horses in his stead" (5). Buddy affirms those spiritual qualities which are very difficult, if not impossible, for the Fedders of the world to perceive. "Raise High" considers the conflict between the "homely" imperatives of the common life and the spiritual imperatives that baffle conventional wisdom with the specter of seeming madness.

"Raise High" considers the basic propriety of Seymour's behavior from multiple (and conflicting) perspectives. In a letter Boo Boo Glass informs Buddy of Seymour's impending marriage to Muriel Fedder. Buddy is the only member of the family who has any chance of attending the ceremony. Along with her appeal that Buddy do everything possible to attend, Boo Boo registers her impressions of Muriel. She is "a zero. I mean she hardly said two words the night I met her. Just sat and smiled and smoked, so it isn't fair to say" (8–9). Muriel's mother, we find, dabbles in the arts and undergoes Jungian analysis. Her fix-it approach to matters of psychological abnormality makes her a mouthpiece for society's norms and mores. While Mrs. Fedder claims she "just loves" Seymour, she also wishes that he "would *relate* to more people" (9). Boo Boo also identifies her own misgivings: "He weighs about as much as a cat and he has that ecstatic look on his face that you can't talk to."

Boo Boo's fear of Seymour's ecstatic estrangement is justified when he fails to appear. His absence creates confusion: no one knows what to do. After 90 minutes the "unmarried bride" is led away (13). The service is replaced by screaming headlines: "It was an excessively graphic moment—a tabloid moment—and, as tabloid moments go, it had its full complement of eyewitnesses." The action takes on a disjointed quality. Buddy helps people into cars. On impulse he "lunge[s] into one of the freshly loaded cars" (15). Buddy rides away with the matron of honor, her husband, Mrs. Silsburn, and an old man who turns out to be a deaf-mute, Muriel's father's uncle. In the car Buddy listens to a series of attacks on Seymour.

His assailant, the matron of honor, functions as a surrogate for Mrs. Fedder and, by extension, the normative social order. Edie Burwick is an irrepressible, brash, angry young woman, one whose stridency deters Buddy from declaring his allegiance to Seymour: "You'd better not say you're a friend of the *groom*. . . . I'd like to get my hands on him for about *two minutes*. Just *two minutes*, that's all" (19). It may be tempting to see her as an object of Salinger's satire. James E. Miller, Jr., for example, argues that her views "are shown to be vacuous, inane, and almost brutally gross" (37). She might *seem* a caustic loudmouth blunted to Seymour's heightened spirituality. Such a position, however, can only be entertained through one's unwavering, and unreflecting, prejudice in Seymour's favor. Without question the matron of honor has a point and it has nothing to do with her inability to appreciate the spiritual dimension. She feels that Seymour violated a most basic sense of decency: "You can't just *barge* through life hurting people's feelings whenever you feel like it" (21). The matron of honor could understand a prospective groom coming down with cold feet: "If he'd changed his *mind*, why didn't he write to her and at least break it off like a gentleman, for goodness' sake? Before all the damage was done" (24). It never occurs to her that Seymour might not have "changed his *mind*." Nor can she comprehend that he might fail to recognize the impropriety of his actions.

As in "Zooey," Salinger does not simply present a glorious celebration of Glass behavior; rather he offers a critical examination of the effects of Seymour's estrangement. Even Buddy does not completely dismiss Edie's charges. While finding this "one-woman mob" intimidating, he still "had a feeling that, for all her stagy indignation and showy grit, there *was* something bayonetlike about her, something not altogether unadmirable" (29). While listening to her attack, Buddy admits to feeling "a small wave of prejudice against the missing groom . . . a just perceptible little whitecap of censure for his unexplained absenteeism."

Her attack is a prelude to her analysis of Seymour. Since Buddy is initially known merely as Seymour's boyhood friend, her diagnosis proceeds without deference. According to Mrs. Fedder, Seymour is a "latent homosexual" with a "schizoid personality" (36–37). Mrs. Fedder "didn't say it nasty or anything. She just said it—you know—intelligently" (36). To the matron of honor, Seymour's own explanation is further proof of his derangement: "But what man in his right mind, the night before he's supposed to get married, keeps his fiancée up all night blabbing to her all about how he's too *happy* to get married and that she'll have to post*pone* the wedding till he feels *steadier.* . . . [H]e's terribly sorry but he can't get married till he feels less *happy* or some crazy thing! . . . Does that sound like somebody *normal?* . . . Or does that sound like somebody that should be stuck in some booby hatch?" (39). To clinch her case, she insists that Seymour is violent. She recounts something like a "tabloid version" of a disturbing incident that took place when Seymour was 12. In discussing the partial facial paralysis of Charlotte Mayhew, a famous actress, she remarks, "This *normal* Seymour person apparently hit her and she had nine stitches taken in her face" (41). In ignoring time and place, Edie recounts a stark portrayal of surface details, an analogue to the reductive techniques of psychoanalysis.

Eventually, after their arrival at the brothers' apartment, Buddy defends Seymour, dismissing all charges against him, affirming his identity as a poet: "I said I didn't give a good God damn what Mrs. Fedder had to say on the subject of Seymour. Or, for that matter, what any professional dilettante or amateur bitch had to say. I said that from the time Seymour was ten years old, every *summa-cum-laude* Thinker and intellectual men's-room attendant in the country had been having a go at him. . . . I said that not one Goddamn person, of all the patronizing, fourth-rate critics and column writers, had ever seen him for what he really was. A poet, for God's sake. And I mean a *poet*" (59–60). Buddy's unanswered declamation counterpoints the matron of honor's sensible conclusion that Seymour is crazy. In order to appreciate Seymour's attributes, one must appropriate a distinctive frame of reference.

"Raise High" contains a number of characters who function as doubles or surrogates for absent people. The matron of honor stands in for Mrs. Fedder; the absent Muriel resembles the doubly absented Charlotte Mayhew; the old man with the top hat and cigar provides a suggestive figuration of Seymour. Amid the confusion of the nonwedding the old man remains self-contained and unflappable. Buddy admires his calm, even-tempered, and eventually cheerful demeanor. He inhabits his own plane: "He remained sublimely out of touch" (33). Buddy later "glanced . . . to see if his insularity was still intact. It was. No one's indifference has ever been such a comfort to me" (42). As a deaf-mute, the old man lives in a world of silence. His communication consists of gestures and one-word written replies. While Buddy jots a note to outline their plans to get out of the broiling car, the "tiny old man . . . read it, grinning, and then looked at me and wagged his head up and down several times vehemently" (48). He extends his "perfectly eloquent" reply via the pad of paper. He writes, "Delighted" (49).

To Buddy the message is a revelation. From a man of silence comes a compact poem: "I quickly looked over at the great writer and tried to show by my expression that all of us in the car knew a poem when we saw one, and were grateful." The old man's insularity and silence—his poetry—remove him from the mainstream. Buddy considers him a living parable of the artist. From his own world the old man emanates a sense of joy and beauty. When Buddy takes the matron of honor to the telephone in the bedroom, they pass the deaf-mute in the hallway: "His face was in the ferocious repose that had fooled me during most of the car ride, but as he came closer to us in the hall, the mask reversed itself; he pantomimed to us both the very highest salutations and greetings. . . . It picked me up no end. 'What is he? Crazy?' the Matron of Honor said. I said I hoped so" (62). The deaf-mute's association with silence, poetry, and joy evokes a context in which Seymour becomes more approachable; his attributes symbolically express the nature of Seymour's unusualness.

While in the bedroom, Buddy sees Seymour's bag and notices his diary. To keep Edie from getting her hands on it, Buddy takes it. When he enters the bathroom, intending to place the diary in the hamper, he finds a message from Boo Boo written in soap on the mirror—a customary form of communication among the Glass siblings. In a playfully hyperbolic passage Buddy links Boo Boo's message with the deaf-mute's one-word poem: "It was a day, God knows, not only of rampant signs and symbols but of wildly extensive communication via the written word. If you jumped into crowded cars, Fate took circuitous pains, before you did any jumping, that you had a pad and pencil with you, just in case one of your fellow-passengers was a deaf-mute. If you slipped into bathrooms, you did well to look up to see if there were any little messages . . . posted high over the washbowl" (64). Boo Boo's "rampant" and "extensive" communication offers a private epithalamium, a celebration of marriage as a new order. She cites lines from Sappho: "Raise high the roof beam, carpenters. Like Ares comes the bridegroom, taller far than a tall man" (65). In wishing the couple a life of happiness in a spacious house, Boo Boo unifies poetic utterance and social context. Her note brings us closer to the insular Glass tribe and their tenuous negotiations between artistic expression and social engagement. We are getting closer to Seymour's interior world.

Like the parable, the deaf-mute's one-word poem, and the message in the mirror, Seymour's diary provides a textual counterpoint to Edie's reasonable denigration of Seymour's character. The purpose of the diary is not to explain or justify Seymour but to locate him within his appropriate aesthetic and spiritual framework. The diary offers the direct impress of Seymour's mind. His words frequently have the cryptic, haunting quality of a Zen koan: "I have no circulation, no pulse. Immobility is my home. The tempo of 'The Star-Spangled Banner' and I are in perfect understanding. To me, its rhythm is a romantic waltz" (66).

The diary reinforces the notion that Seymour and Muriel make an unlikely couple. In one entry, Seymour appears patronizing: "How I love and need her undiscriminating heart" (66–67). Later he writes, "She has a primal urge to play house permanently" (71). He meditates on her concern over her emotional fluctuations: "She worries over the way her love for me comes and goes, appears and disappears. She doubts its reality simply because it isn't as steadily pleasurable as a kitten. God knows it *is* sad. The human voice conspires to desecrate everything on earth" (67). Frequently Seymour's meditations consider the way in which everyday experience fails to imbue individuals with an elevated spiritual consciousness. Seymour's attempt to live out a sense of undiscriminating spiritual beneficence is precisely what removes him from other people.

Along with Mrs. Fedder's basic fear that Seymour is insane, she has three more specific apprehensions: "One, I withdraw from and fail to relate to people. Two, apparently there is something 'wrong' with me because I haven't seduced Muriel. Three, evidently Mrs. Fedder has been haunted for days by my remark at dinner one night that I'd like to be a dead cat" (70). This remark is not a "sophisticated" joke that no one gets but a reference to a Zen master's identification of a dead cat as the "most valuable thing in the world . . . because no one could put a price on it" (71).

Seymour's comments on Mrs. Fedder offer a parallel diagnosis to her comments on him. For all her dabbling in the arts, she is "deprived, for life, of any understanding or taste for the main current of poetry that flows through things, all things. She might as well be dead, and yet she goes on living" (72). Seymour concludes this meditation with a characteristically disjunctive thought: "I love her. I find her un-imaginably brave." The diary repeatedly demonstrates the incompati-bility between Seymour's quest for spiritual perfection and the conventional contexts of commonplace experiences. In fact, Seymour seems bemused over the way Mrs. Fedder's analyst advocates the "vir-tues of living the imperfect life, of accepting one's own and others' weaknesses" (74). This principle of self-acceptance informs Jungian psychotherapy. In this view, society can be understood as a confederacy of needy individuals. Seymour even agrees with Dr. Sims, "but only in theory. I'll champion indiscrimination till doomsday, on the ground that it leads to health and a kind of very real, enviable happiness. *Fol-lowed purely*, it's the way of the Tao, and undoubtedly the highest way."

What Seymour means by "indiscrimination" is not so much a blan-ket acceptance of individual idiosyncrasy as the capacity to perceive all entities without regard to hierarchy, classifications, or distinctions. Ego, then, asserts one's distance from a mystical state of selflessness. In discussing Jesus' capacity for discrimination, Zooey attacks Sey-mour's (and Franny's) desire to embrace all entities in terms of univer-sal equality (*FZ*, 164–65). To Seymour all actions have the same value; events in the phenomenal realm are thus illusory. Consequently, when Seymour writes of his intention to see a psychotherapist, he recognizes that it does not matter whether he sees one: "I can't see that I have anything to lose by seeing an analyst. . . . M. loves me, but she'll never feel really close to me, *familiar* with me, *frivolous* with me, till I'm slightly overhauled" (75).

Seymour's diary entries continually reinforce his dedication to mar-riage with Muriel.[73] The entries show no tendency toward failure of nerve; rather, Seymour laments that he and Muriel are not closer. In his theory of "indiscrimination" Muriel's differences from him become irrelevant. Seymour advocates, in essence, a transcendent connection whereby their souls are linked. The fact that they appear so unsuitable to each other in no way mitigates the strength of their spiritual bond. This is a concept that can never be reconciled with the conventional perspectives of Mrs. Fedder and her avatar, the matron of honor.

Having seen enough for one day, the matron of honor returns to the living room and announces that Seymour and Muriel have eloped: "The *groom's* no longer indis*posed* by *hap*piness" (85). She reports that "this *Sey*mour's promised to start going to an analyst and get himself straightened out. . . . Who knows? Maybe everything's gonna be hunky-dory" (87). Symbolically, Seymour's marriage seems to include a reconciliation with Charlotte. Muriel and Charlotte are certainly versions of each other. Indeed the photo of Charlotte reminds everyone of Muriel: "This child could *double* for Muriel at that age. But to a T" (83). Perhaps Seymour's marriage to Muriel compensates for his violent disfigurement of Charlotte.

This possibility, however, is belied by Buddy's alternative explanation. Salinger seems intent on undermining any sense of closure. After the Burwicks and Mrs. Silsburn leave, Buddy has "one remaining guest," the deaf-mute, and offers to explain Charlotte's injury to the man: "What happened was, she sat down in the middle of our driveway one morning to pet Boo Boo's cat, and Seymour threw a stone at her. He was twelve. . . . He threw it at her because she looked so beautiful. . . . Everybody knew that" (89). Buddy's words do not explain a thing. He immediately contradicts himself. As he notes, this explanation is a lie: "Charlotte never did understand why Seymour threw that stone at her." Since the old man has no idea what Buddy said anyway, the words are irrelevant.

Salinger ends the story not with the heightened promise symbolized by the wedding but with the cryptic and paradoxical contours of Seymour's story. Buddy's explanation is no explanation; he speaks but is not heard; he reads Seymour's last diary entry. While waiting for the clouds to lift so that he can fly in for the wedding, Seymour writes that he has "been reading a miscellany of Vedanta all day. Marriage partners are to serve each other. Elevate, help, teach, strengthen each other, but above all, *serve*" (91). Buddy then passes out from too much drink. When he awakens, the old man is gone, having left only his cigar butt. Buddy imagines mailing it to Seymour in a small box, "possibly with a blank sheet of paper enclosed, by way of explanation" (92). According

to Dennis L. O'Connor, "The blank paper symbolizes the 'inconclu-
sive' narrative, the unfulfilled possibilities of the wedding celebration,
and the range of suspended meanings that make this text so difficult
to interpret" (331). Like Buddy's remarks about Charlotte's injury, the
wedding gift explains nothing at all. We are left with an enigmatic sign,
unfilled space on a blank sheet of paper.

"Seymour: An Introduction": "A Thesaurus of Undetached Prefatory Remarks"

"Seymour: An Introduction" begins with epigrams from Kafka and
Kierkegaard that suggest an ideational matrix for the subsequent narrative. The citations from Kafka lament the playwright's failure to capture the actor's essence with the words that give the actor his being.
Once a performer assumes the role, he effectively escapes the artist's
rein. The text of *Hamlet*, for example, gives birth to an endless train
of Hamlets, each of whom is too rich in nuance to be contained by the
words he speaks: "The actors by their presence always convince me,
to my horror, that most of what I've written about them is false" (95).
Kafka's artist is caught between the ideal of "steadfast love" for his
creations and the actuality of his "varying ability" to express his creation in words. Kierkegaard extends this notion of an author's inevitable
failure. He posits the existence of an autonomous creative principle
that asserts its own desires beneath the guise of what seems to be the
writer's "clerical error."[74] Speaking "figuratively," Kierkegaard celebrates the spontaneous irruption of unconscious forces, a kind of self-
willed muse that has its say through so many "slip[s] of the pen." This
revolt against the writer is perhaps not an "error but in a far higher
sense . . . an essential part of the whole exposition."

Buddy Glass "reproduced these passages" to provide an introduction
to the *process* of writing his introduction of Seymour. Buddy associates
Seymour with Kafka, Kierkegaard, and van Gogh as preeminent practitioners of "modern artistic processes" (101). These four "Sick Men,"
as Buddy calls them, should not be categorized as "'classical' neurotic[s]" (103).[75] Instead each is sick because he sees too much: "I say
that the true artist-seer, the heavenly fool who can and does produce
beauty, is mainly dazzled to death by his own scruples, the blinding
shapes and colors of his own sacred human conscience" (105). The
suffering artist, then, "is at least being done in by the most stimulating

companion, disease or no, he has ever known" (103). Salinger thus links the problematic limitations of language with the mysterious nature of the strange, eccentric, or "sick" artist, a combination that leads Theodore L. Gross to see the diffuseness of Salinger's last published works as "clumsy temporizing before the central problem that Salinger has set for himself: the failure of the poet to survive in the modern world" (267).

At the very outset Buddy Glass confronts the necessary (and intrinsically self-defeating) paradox of his condition. The only way to introduce the late Seymour is to use language; the use of language by nature is doomed to fail. As Ihab Hassan argues, this introduction "betrays the desperate urge of rendering in words a superlative being, Seymour, who also happens to be a teacher and brother. The true aim of this work is less to describe Seymour, who beggars description, than to justify language which must, in the same breath, try and fail to encompass holiness" (1963, 13–14). A chief purpose of these "modern artistic processes" is the elaboration of an abiding futility, especially insofar as one may hope to get a true account of Seymour, or better yet, to come to hear the sound of Seymour's "cries of pain" (104). Buddy's induction contains a warning to any reader or critic who intends to approach Seymour armed with an explanatory paradigm. Buddy repudiates "the scholars, the biographers and especially the current ruling intellectual aristocracy educated in one or another of the big public psychoanalytical schools." Such paradigms impede one from a direct encounter with the "Sick Man." Understandably, Ian Hamilton, Salinger's most recent biographer, finds much amiss in these attitudes. He sees "Seymour" essentially as a one-way interview conducted from behind an impenetrable mask of fiction: "'Seymour' pretends to be a song of praise, and it is full of arch, self-deprecating charm, but the energy that keeps it going is essentially dour and retaliatory. J. D. Salinger may not give interviews, but here—uninvited—he is bending everybody's ear. Even poor Seymour's merits as a poet in the Oriental style are used chiefly as a means of drubbing the non-Oriental culture he is trapped in" (163).

Buddy's subject is a presentation not so much of Seymour as of the difficulty of apprehending the "true artist-seer." The form of "Seymour" might be understood as Buddy's fictional assay on the problem of composing an account of his late brother. As he does in "Raise High" and "Zooey," Buddy repudiates the offices of well-made fiction: "I'm anything but a short story writer where my brother is concerned. What

I *am,* I think, is a thesaurus of undetached prefatory remarks about him" (107). Buddy meanders on principle. He applies Kafka's observations on the limitations of language and Kierkegaard's sense of artistic truth through apparent accident. As James Lindquist (145), Ihab Hassan (1963), and Bernice and Sanford Goldstein suggest, "Seymour" presents Salinger's self-conscious depiction of the artistic process.[76] Buddy's "Introduction" records the improvisational unfolding of his thoughts. As he writes about Seymour, he presents his mind in the act of thinking. Thus he offers an "unpretentious bouquet of early blooming parentheses: (((())))" (98), a nonverbal sign of his compositional process, a series of digressions contained within his asides that provide the impetus for the next thought. Buddy's "inner, incessant elation" (119) impels this spontaneous display of memory and imagination. Given his zealous identification with his subject, he is "no longer in a position to look after the reader's most immediate want; namely, to see the author get the hell on with his story" (99). If the reader does not like it, Buddy suggests, he can leave.

Crucial to this "near-polemic" (103) in "enchanting semi-diary form" (192) is Buddy's insistence on offering his remarks in an ongoing narrative present. As with the preface to "Raise High" and "Zooey," Buddy conflates the narrative present and his experiential moment. The narrating and acting selves are one. The present tense records the turns of Buddy's mind as he thinks, while the past tense is reserved for anecdotal excursions on Seymour's life. Buddy repeatedly calls attention to the passage of time: "This is Thursday, and I'm back in my horrible chair." He comments on what he takes to be a just-completed stretch of inflated prose: "This sounds to me very suspiciously like a playbill note, but after that last theatrical paragraph I feel I have it coming to me. The time is three hours later. I fell asleep on the floor" (204). There is no question of striking out the offending passage. Revision is inimical to this narrative activity.

Buddy's sprawling improvisation complements Seymour's awesome dynamic force. The longer Buddy lives and the more time he spends on writing, the more Seymour grows in his mind. At one point Buddy takes two months' sick leave from his desk. By the time he returns he confronts a problem: "*He'd grown too much while I was away*" (151). Seymour is both absent (dead) brother and mythic (living) presence; he inhabits the nexus between natural and supernatural realms, and his philosophy is suitably a synthesis between Western and Eastern thought. Buddy consecrates, or canonizes, the absent presence:

"Surely he was all *real* things to us: our blue-striped unicorn, our dou-ble-lensed burning glass, our consultant genius, or portable con-science, our supercargo, and our one full poet. . . . [He] tallied with the classical conception, as I saw it, of a *mukta*, a ringding enlightened man, a God-knower. At any rate, his character lends itself to no legit-imate sort of narrative compactness that *I* know of" (106).

The main problem of approaching Seymour through Buddy's intro-duction is that Seymour in effect remains Buddy's creation. There is no authoritative ground beyond Buddy's exuberant testimony; "Sey-mour" remains the record of Buddy's mind in motion. This problem becomes most evident when Buddy discusses Seymour's poems.[77] On the one hand, Buddy identifies Seymour as one of the great poets of the century. In fact the "Introduction" constitutes a prolegomenon to the publication of 184 poems. Dutifully Buddy discusses Seymour's influences, most notably Chinese and Japanese verse. Seymour's fa-vored form—the haiku—provides a vehicle of religious enlightenment, especially in Seymour's preoccupation with evoking the intrinsic spir-ituality of all persons and things. The poet becomes a conduit for the spiritual world to express itself: "The material plainly chooses [the poet], not he it" (121). This kind of poetry eliminates the cult of per-sonality: "[O]ne pure poet's voice is absolutely the same as another's and at once absolutely distinctive and different" (122). As an artist, Seymour wanted to synthesize disparate cultural contexts. His adop-tion of Eastern forms does not exclude Irish, Jewish, and American influences. Buddy indeed sees Seymour as "this Semitic-Celtic Oriental."

On the other hand, while Buddy offers his sense of Seymour as poet, he never prints the poems themselves. What they are *like* is the subject of Buddy's rambling disquisition. What they *are* is currently unprinta-ble. Seymour's widow will not allow Buddy to excerpt the poems. As Ihab Hassan points out, "Needless to say, the poems were never pub-lished; they remain exquisite creations circumscribed by silence" (1963, 15). In the absence of the poems, Buddy orchestrates a frus-trating exercise in nondisclosure. At times his comments verge on tau-tology: "Within this six-line structure and these very odd harmonics, Seymour does with a poem, I think, exactly what he was meant to do with one" (128). What he was meant to do is never revealed. Instead Buddy offers plot summaries of his favorites, the last two pieces in the manuscript. In the penultimate poem an adulterous woman returns from her "tryst—in my mind, bleary and lipstick-smeared—to find a balloon on her bedspread" (129). The poem has few details. The final poem presents a "young suburban widower" sitting on his lawn looking at the full moon. A "bored white cat . . . comes up to him and rolls over, and he lets her bite his left hand as he looks at the moon." Buddy discusses the austerity of the poem and the way in which the details provide subjects for speculation. A poem, then, provides a point of departure and reference for the reader's speculation. This attribute is similar to Salinger's attachment to the open, often enigmatic ending. Many of the stories—and seemingly Seymour's poems—conclude with arresting dramatic scenes that invite meditation, precisely the intention of the Zen koan. Crucial to each situation is the unspoken, the suggestive, the mysterious. The invitation is for one to explore the implications of a carefully composed scene or concept.

Buddy recognizes that Seymour's art can never be separated from the fact of his suicide. In the introduction Buddy considers the nature of his reaction to the prospective onslaught of literary pilgrims. Publication of the poems will most certainly lead to inquiries regarding the biographical roots of literary art: "[A] good many people . . . respond with a special impetus, a zing . . . to artists and poets who . . . have something garishly Wrong with them as persons" (141). Buddy identifies the central questions revolving around Seymour Glass: Is he an artist of the first order? Is he a suicidal psychotic? Is he some combination of both? Buddy feels that his brother is "an unhealthy specimen" who is also a great poet. And perhaps it is the very imbalance—Seymour's dissociation from the everyday world of the Fedders—that creates the capacity for new vision.

The issue of Seymour's nature is not finally resolved. Rather, specific acts of simplistic diagnosis are exposed in the same way that psychological paradigms are mocked as inadequate. For example, the apparently "personal" or autobiographical poems are no reflection of Seymour's life. In fact the opposite is true: "[T]he more personal Seymour's poems appear to be, or *are*, the less revealing the content is of any known details of his actual daily life in this Western world. My brother, Waker, . . . contends . . . that Seymour, in many of his most effective poems, seems to be drawing on the ups and downs of former, singularly memorable existences in exurban Benares, feudal Japan, and metropolitan Atlantis" (133). The playfulness of this passage should not deflect one from appreciating how seriously Seymour and Buddy take the concept of reincarnation. The possibility that one's personal experience transcends the historical limits of one's current appearance and includes earlier lives mocks the reductive tendency of biographical and psychological criticism. The cumulative effect of Buddy's various introductory assays is to complicate Seymour's portrait.

Likewise, Buddy's decision to present an account of Seymour's facial and behavioral attributes underscores the improvisational nature of the "Introduction," offering a parody of mimesis. Buddy's attempt to describe Seymour's face accentuates the limitations of words. In seeking to "get a good likeness" Buddy must confront the problem of "which Seymour" to consider: "I get a vivid-type picture, all right, but in it he appears before me simultaneously at the ages of, approximately, eight, eighteen, and twenty-eight" (170–71). There is no single Seymour. Memory contains a range of images that belong to many times. Words freeze a subject and fix it into form. Buddy can render the *attempt* to present a face—he catalogs Seymour's hair, smile, ears, eyes, nose, skin—but no one face emerges. The attempt must fail. What *is* exposed is Buddy's playful sarcasm. He earnestly mocks the notion that words can accurately portray a reality: "Except for the eyes, and maybe (I say *maybe*) the nose, I'm tempted to pass up the rest of his face, and the hell with Comprehensiveness. I couldn't bear to be accused of leaving *nothing* to the reader's imagination" (175). Buddy's obsessive reflexivity undermines a reader's capacity to suspend disbelief in order to picture a face. One is left with the narrator's mockery and his insular engagement with the compositional process: "Hurrah. The nose is over. I'm going to bed" (178). The effect of presenting such a catalog is to lose the subject in the very accretion of expository detail. Buddy admits, "I see that I've discussed almost every feature of his face and haven't so much as touched on the *life* of it yet" (181). The "life" of Seymour remains elusive, and no amount of words can do anything more than make an introduction to the impossibility of making a truthful, accurate, detailed portrait.

Buddy could go on and on, just as he could have concluded his "Introduction" 30 or 50 pages earlier. In having dismissed the demands of crafting a well-made or mimetic story, Buddy gives the lie to premises that inform the practice of a great deal of literary exegesis, especially any approach, like New Criticism, that presupposes the internal consistency and coherence of literary artifacts. Salinger's "Seymour" is an experiment. Rather than being a story, it depicts a literary activity in which the mind making the words is literally the subject of the tale. Central to this process is the narrator's self-awareness of the artificiality of the literary endeavor. Consequently, Buddy asserts his discomfort with the need to conclude: "Fundamentally," he writes, "my mind has always balked at any kind of ending" (211). He claims to have destroyed a number of stories because they had "a Beginning, a Middle, and an End" (212). Years before he stopped attending because he "resented like hell filing out of the theatre just because some playwright was forever slamming down his silly curtain," an echo of sentiments expressed many years before in "Blue Melody": "A story never ends. The narrator is usually provided with a nice artistic spot for his voice to stop, but that's about all."[78] To Buddy a resounding conclusion—the car chase and shoot-out—is hackneyed artifice. What Buddy's narrative process most clearly celebrates is the randomness and vagaries of the creative imagination. There is no *ending* to Buddy's meditations on Seymour.

The occasion for writing the "Introduction" has led Buddy to make a series of notations, the effect of which is to affirm the continuing impress of Seymour in the life of Buddy. The "Introduction" simply ceases because Buddy realizes "my time is *up*." The writing of the piece merges with the imperative to go to school and teach: "[I]t's twenty to seven, and I have a nine-o'clock class." Along with affirming writing as a process, Buddy affirms his experiential life out in the world. His "description of Seymour" cannot come to an end without his "being conscious of the good, the real. . . . [A]nd I know . . . there is no single thing I do that is more important than going into that awful Room 307" (212–13). He embraces the notion that his students are his sisters: "They may shine with the misinformation of the ages, but they shine. This thought manages to stun me" (213).

The cessation of "Seymour" finds Buddy opening himself to the world. This moment is as moving as Holden Caulfield's realization at the end of *Catcher* that he misses everybody. The "end" of the story, as in "For Esmé," locates the narrator in that instant in which he is poised to take the next step. As Seymour "once said . . . all we do our whole lives is go from one little piece of Holy Ground to the next." Since all points or pieces along the way are equally holy, then it does not matter where Buddy stops writing. Buddy simply surrenders the literary process at this present time. His cessation, an arbitrary embrace of silence, celebrates the mind's capacity to negotiate tenuous passages between memory and the compositional moment, between the evocation of *what was* and the formulation in words of what might presently come to be.

"Hapworth 16, 1924":
"Continuing at Blissful Random . . ."

For the author of such stellar literary performances as "The Laughing Man," "For Esmé—with Love and Squalor," and *The Catcher in the Rye,* "Hapworth 16, 1924" offers a distressing coda: it is a rambling, 30,000-word preface to silence. Young Seymour Glass, age seven, writes a letter home from summer camp and offers a series of erudite, though gnarled, meditations: he discourses on his love for his parents; his "new and entirely trivial mastery of written construction";[79] his affection for the librarian, Miss Overman ("My God, please take the slight trouble to remember that this worthy woman and spinster has no comfortable home in the present century!" [33]); the activities of brother Buddy and such fellow campers as the afflicted Griffin Hammersmith ("his load in this appearance in the world is staggering" [34]); his precocious sexual yearning for a counselor, Mrs. Happy; and his offhanded, glib references to karma and reincarnation. Seymour is using his time at summer camp as a way of easing off; he is trying to decrease his mystical "glimpses" (38) into past lives. "Continuing at blissful random" (54), Seymour discusses his own poetry, gives sententious advice, and, most tediously, compiles an extensive reading list of books he wants his parents to procure.

"Hapworth" offers a challenge to critical assessment. Eberhard Alsen provides the most serious, incisive, and extended examination (78–95). He finds that "the meaning of 'Hapworth' . . . lies in Seymour's decision to withdraw from average humanity" (92). Anthony Quagliano discusses the letter within the "larger religious framework" of the Glass stories.[80] He argues that Salinger exploits the "syndrome of the cute child, then complicates it by insisting on a profound religious sensibility within his character" (36).

In "Hapworth" as in "Seymour," Salinger elaborates on the possibilities of art as process, the attempt to have the words on the page reflect the mind in motion. He provides a realistic depiction of creative consciousness, all the while that his informing principle—that his narrator is seven years old—makes any pretense at mimesis absurd. Seymour's meditations are a deadly drone of gushing earnestness. His recurrent exclamation "My God" punctuates his thoughts: "My God, think of the opportunities and thrusts that lie ahead when one knows without a shred of doubt how commonplace and normal one is at heart! . . . [W]ho can prevent us from doing a little good in this appearance?" (57).

Surely it would be possible to construe "Hapworth" as a joke, a hoax, or even, as I suggested earlier, an act of authorial contempt designed to deter hopeful (and unswervingly loyal) readers from desiring future productions. But in "Hapworth" Salinger seems serious. As with every other aspect of his professional career, Salinger makes no concessions. His 1965 conception of Seymour Glass calls for a brilliant seven-year-old engaged in a seemingly endless display of improvisational rumination. His intentions seem to demand that Seymour be unlike any imaginable child, that he be unique. Seymour is Salinger's saint, and "Hapworth" contains the young master's final words, words, words. In "Hapworth," Ian Hamilton observes, "the reader is blithely disregarded: 'Take it or leave it' is Salinger's unmistakable retort to any grumbles from the nonamateurs among his audience and he seems fairly certain (indeed *makes* certain) that most of them will leave it" (188). The concern for a readership is actually foreign to Salinger's "Hapworth": "The Glass family, has, in this last story, become Salinger's subject and his readership, his creatures and his companions. His life is finally made one with art" (Hamilton, 188).

It is remarkable, and perhaps ironically appropriate, that Salinger's last published fiction should, for one thing, appear in the *New Yorker* and, for another, be so utterly alien to the received sense of what the *New Yorker* story is supposed to be: urbane, pithy, wry, well made. One might only speculate on the editorial discussions that "Hapworth" elicited. Did anyone think it a successful work of fiction? Were the editors being loyal to one of their writers? Did they reach the consensus that anything by Salinger was sure to sell magazines? In any event the virtually unreadable "Hapworth 16, 1924" is Salinger's most recent, though perhaps not his last, published fiction. From any perspective the piece is an enigma, a fitting introduction to J. D. Salinger's extended, ongoing and, I hope, fruitful and happy hiatus.

Notes to Part 1

1. Richard Ford, "First Things First: One More Writer's Beginnings," *Harper's*, August 1988, 72.

2. See "Epilogue: A Salute to Whit Burnett, 1899–1972," in *Fiction Writer's Handbook*, ed. Hallie and Whit Burnett (New York: Harper & Row, 1975), 187–88. Salinger refers to his classroom experience as a "good and instructive and profitable year for me, on all counts, let me briefly say" (187).

3. See Ian Hamilton, *In Search of J. D. Salinger* (New York: Random House, 1988), 21–22 and 28–29—hereafter cited in text—for a discussion of Salinger's interest in the theater.

4. *Raise High the Roof Beam, Carpenters and Seymour: An Introduction* (New York: Bantam, 1965), 95; hereafter cited in the text. In "The Seymour Narratives" quotations appear without a prefix; other quotations are identified by *RH*.

5. "The Young Folks," *Story*, March–April 1940, 26; hereafter cited in text as "Young."

6. Warren French, *J. D. Salinger Revisited* (Boston: Twayne, 1988), 19; hereafter cited in text. See also Donald Barr, "Saints, Pilgrims and Artists," in *Salinger: A Critical and Personal Portrait*, ed. Henry Anatole Grunwald (New York: Harper & Row, 1962), 171—hereafter cited in text—for a brief discussion of "The Young Folks." Barr sees the story as "a sketch . . . of a girl trying too hard at a party, done in the slice-of-life fashion, its very point lying in its seeming pointlessness." This comment, however valid, reflects the generally dismissive attitude that the majority of commentators have taken toward most of the uncollected stories.

7. See Jack R. Sublette, *J. D. Salinger: An Annotated Bibliography, 1938–1981* (New York: Garland, 1984), 12; hereafter cited in text.

8. Lacey Fosburgh, "J. D. Salinger Speaks about His Silence," *New York Times*, 3 November 1974, 1, 69.

9. Arthur Mizener, "The Love Song of J. D. Salinger," in *Salinger: A Critical and Personal Portrait*, ed. Henry Anatole Grunwald (New York: Harper & Row, 1962), 24–25.

10. Bruce Bawer, "Salinger's Arrested Development," *New Criterion* 5 (September 1986): 37; hereafter cited in text.

11. Joseph Blotner and Frederick L. Gwynn, *The Fiction of J. D. Salinger* (Pittsburgh: University of Pittsburgh Press, 1958), 9–18; hereafter cited in text. See Ihab Hassan, "The Rare Quixotic Gesture," in *Salinger: A Critical and*

Personal Portrait, ed. Henry Anatole Grunwald (New York: Harper & Row, 1962), 143–44—hereafter cited in text—for a brief discussion of Salinger's "awareness of *craft*, of a structure that owes much less to Kipling than to Lardner." And for an account of Salinger's "astonishingly rapid advance in craft and deepening of thematic complexity," see James E. Miller, Jr., *J. D. Salinger* (Minneapolis: University of Minnesota Press, 1965), 7; hereafter cited in text.

12. Warren French, *J. D. Salinger* (Boston: Twayne, 1963; rev. ed. 1976), 36–46 (hereafter cited in text), and Hassan, 139–42; Miller identifies alienation as Salinger's central theme (20).

13. "Go See Eddie," *University of Kansas City Review* 7 (December 1940): 121; hereafter cited in text as "Eddie."

14. "The Long Debut of Lois Taggett," *Story*, September–October 1942, 228; hereafter cited in text as "Debut."

15. "Elaine," *Story*, March–April 1945, 38–39; hereafter cited in text as "Elaine."

16. Warren French indicates that this "tale suffers from serious structural problems" (1988, 20).

17. "The Varioni Brothers," *Saturday Evening Post*, 17 July 1943, 12; hereafter cited in text as "Varioni."

18. See Paul Levine, "J. D. Salinger: The Development of the Misfit Hero," *Twentieth Century Literature* 4 (October 1958): 92–99.

19. "The Heart of a Broken Story," *Esquire*, September 1941, 32; hereafter cited in text as "Heart."

20. John Skow, "Sonny: An Introduction," in *Salinger: A Critical and Personal Portrait*, ed. Henry Anatole Grunwald (New York: Harper & Row), 13–14.

21. See also Ian Hamilton, 85–93, for a further discussion of Salinger during the war.

22. "Soft-Boiled Sergeant," *Saturday Evening Post*, 26 February 1944, 18; hereafter cited in text as "Soft."

23. "Last Day of the Last Furlough," *Saturday Evening Post*, 15 July 1944, 26; hereafter cited in text as "Last Day."

24. "A Boy in France," *Saturday Evening Post*, 31 March 1945, 315; hereafter cited in text as "Boy."

25. "This Sandwich Has No Mayonnaise," *Esquire*, October 1946, 188; hereafter cited in the text as "Sandwich."

26. "The Stranger," *Collier's*, 1 December 1945, 18; hereafter cited in text as "Stranger."

27. *The Catcher in the Rye* (New York: Bantam, 1964), 115; hereafter cited in the text as *Catcher*. Publication data on the first editions of all of Salinger's works can be found in the Bibliography.

28. See French 1988, 34, for a discussion of the relationship between the early Holden Caulfield stories and *Catcher*.

29. "Slight Rebellion off Madison," *New Yorker,* 21 December 1946, 76; hereafter cited in text as "Slight."

30. "Both Parties Concerned," *Saturday Evening Post,* 25 February 1944, 14; hereafter cited in text as "Both."

31. "I'm Crazy," *Collier's,* 22 December 1945, 36; hereafter cited in text as "Crazy."

32. Ian Hamilton vents mean-spirited conjecture by attributing the polish of Salinger's *New Yorker* stories to "his editorial attendants": "It can be no accident that the slacknesses [*sic*] and vulgarities that disfigured even Salinger's best stories of the past decade contrived a sudden disappearance in this year. . . . *The Inverted Forest* is rambling, narcissistic, wasteful of its bewildered energy. 'Bananafish' is spare, teasingly mysterious, withheld. Salinger, it seems, had at last entered a world in which his own fastidiousness would be honored, and perhaps surpassed, by that of his editorial attendants" (105). The same case could be made (erroneously) to explain the stylistic disparity between Herman Melville's *Pierre* and his short story masterpiece, "Bartleby the Scrivener." Both works were composed within the same year. Hamilton's "it seems" and "perhaps" give him, it seems, license for unwarranted and invidious conjecture. There is no available evidence that Salinger's work was heavily edited. Every indication is that Salinger, as uncompromising as any person might want to be, would not stand for editorial dicing.

33. For other examinations of *Nine Stories* as a collection, see Paul Kirschner, "Salinger and His Society: The Pattern of *Nine Stories,*" *Literary Half-Yearly* 12 (Fall 1971): 51–60 and 14 (Fall 1973): 63–78 (hereafter cited in text); Howard M. Harper, Jr., "J. D. Salinger—through the Glasses Darkly," in his *Desperate Faith: A Study of Bellow, Salinger, Mailer, Baldwin, and Updike* (Chapel Hill: University of North Carolina Press, 1967), 71 (hereafter cited in text); Barr, 170; Helen Weinberg, "J. D. Salinger's Holden and Seymour and the Spiritual Activist Hero," in her *The New Novel in America* (Ithaca, N.Y.: Cornell University Press, 1970), 143 (hereafter cited in text); and William Wiegand, "Seventy-eight Bananas," in *Salinger: A Critical and Personal Portrait,* ed. Henry Anatole Grunwald (New York: Harper & Row, 1962), 127–29.

34. For discussions of Salinger's preoccupation with childhood, see Leslie A. Fiedler, "The Eye of Innocence: Some Notes on the Role of the Child in Literature," in his *No! in Thunder: Essays on Myth and Literature* (Boston: Beacon Press, 1960), 251–91; Bawer, 38–40; and French 1976, 36–46.

35. On Salinger's use of the epiphany, see Barr, 172–73, and see Sam S. Baskett, "The Splendid/Squalid World of J. D. Salinger," *Wisconsin Studies in Contemporary Literature* 4 (Winter 1963): 48–61; hereafter cited in text.

36. James Lundquist, *J. D. Salinger* (New York: Ungar, 1979), 74; hereafter cited in text. For accounts of Salinger's interest in Zen and Eastern religion, see Blotner and Gwynn, 73; Bernice and Sanford Goldstein, "Zen and *Nine Stories,*" *Modern Fiction Studies* 12 (Autumn 1966): 313–24 (hereafter cited

in text); Hassan, 152–53; Tom Davis, "J. D. Salinger: 'The Sound of One Hand Clapping,'" *Wisconsin Studies in Contemporary Literature* 4 (Winter 1963): 41–47; John Antico, "The Parody of J. D. Salinger: Esmé and the Fat Lady Exposed," *Modern Fiction Studies* 12 (Autumn 1966): 325–40; Klaus Karlstetter, "J. D. Salinger, R. W. Emerson, and the Perennial Philosophy," *Moderna Sprak* 63, no. 3 (Fall 1969): 224–36 (hereafter cited in text); James T. Livingston, "J. D. Salinger: The Artist's Struggle to Stand on Holy Ground," in *Adversity and Grace*, ed. Nathan A. Scott, Jr. (Chicago: University of Chicago Press, 1968): 113–32; and Eberhard Alsen, *Salinger's Glass Stories as a Composite Novel* (Troy, N.Y.: Whitston, 1983) (hereafter cited in text).

37. *Nine Stories* (New York: Bantam, 1964), 9; hereafter cited in text.

38. See Bawer for a recent discussion of Muriel as spiritually empty (40–41); see also Alsen, 13–16.

39. For a discussion of the relationship between "Bananafish" and Rilke, see Gary Lane, "Seymour's Suicide Again: A New Reading of J. D. Salinger's 'A Perfect Day for Bananafish,'" *Studies in Short Fiction* 10 (Winter 1973): 27–33.

40. T. S. Eliot, "The Waste Land," in *The Waste Land and Other Poems* (New York: Harcourt, Brace & World, 1934), 27.

41. Dallas E. Wiebe, "Salinger's 'A Perfect Day for Bananafish,'" *Explicator* 23 (September 1964): item 3. See also Frank Metcalf, "The Suicide of Salinger's Seymour Glass," *Studies in Short Fiction* 9 (Summer 1972): 243–46; John Russell, "Salinger's Feat," *Modern Fiction Studies* 12 (Autumn 1966): 299–311 (hereafter cited in text); and Karlstetter, 229–30.

42. James E. Bryan, "Salinger's Seymour's Suicide," *College English* 24 (December 1962): 226–29.

43. For discussions of Salinger's use of numbers, see Charles V. Genthe, "Six, Sex, Sick: Seymour, Some Comments," *Twentieth Century Literature* 10 (January 1965): 170–71, and David J. Piwinski, "Salinger's 'De Daumier-Smith's Blue Period': Pseudonym as Cryptogram," *Notes on Contemporary Literature* 15, no. 5 (October 1985): 3–4.

44. For commentary on the relationship between Eloise and Ramona, see Marianne Ahrne, "Experience and Attitude in *The Catcher in the Rye* and *Nine Stories*," *Moderna Sprak* 61, no. 3 (Fall 1967): 254, and Kirschner, 55.

45. For discussions of the Dufarges and the Laughing Man, see Kirschner, 59–60, and Edward Stone, "J. D. Salinger," in his *A Certain Morbidness: A View of American Literature* (Carbondale: Southern Illinois University Press, 1969), 130; hereafter cited in text.

46. Richard Allan Davison, "Salinger Criticism and 'The Laughing Man': A Case of Arrested Development," *Studies in Short Fiction* 18 (Winter 1981): 1–15; hereafter cited in text.

47. Irving Deer and John H. Randall III, "J. D. Salinger and the Reality beyond Words," *Lock Haven Review* 6 (Spring 1964): 19.

48. For commentary on the structure of "For Esmé" see Brother Fidelian Burke, F.S.C., "Salinger's 'Esmé': Some Matters of Balance," *Modern Fiction Studies* 12 (Autumn 1966): 341–47.

49. For a discussion of the narrator's relationship to his fellow soldiers, see John Wenke, "Sergeant X, Esmé, and the Meaning of Words," *Studies in Short Fiction* 18 (Summer 1981): 253–54.

50. For a discussion of Charles, see John Hermann, "J. D. Salinger: Hello Hello Hello," *College English* 22 (January 1961): 262–64.

51. For discussions of the identity of Sergeant X, see Tom Davis, "J. D. Salinger: The Identity of Sergeant X," *Western Humanities Review* 16 (Spring 1962): 181–83, and Robert M. Slabey, "Sergeant X and Seymour Glass," *Western Humanities Review* 16 (Autumn 1962): 376–77. Slabey proves that Sergeant X could not possibly be Seymour Glass.

52. John Russell, "Salinger, from Daumier to Smith," *Wisconsin Studies in Contemporary Literature* 4 (Winter 1963): 70–87.

53. The others include Miller, 25; Kirschner, 77; and Paul Elmen, "Twice-blessed Enamel Flowers: Reality in Contemporary Fiction," in *The Climate of Faith in Modern Literature*, ed. Nathan A. Scott, Jr. (New York: Seabury Press, 1964), 85.

54. For accounts of the story as parody, see Sally Bostwick, "Reality, Compassion, and Mysticism in the World of J. D. Salinger," *Midwest Review* 5 (Summer 1963): 30–43—hereafter cited in text—and Stone, 139.

55. See Alsen, 124–63, and William Bysshe Stein, "Salinger's 'Teddy': *Tat Tvam Asi* or That Thou Art," *Arizona Quarterly* 29 (Autumn 1973): 253–65.

56. John Updike, "Franny and Zooey," in *Salinger: A Critical and Personal Portrait*," ed. Henry Anatole Grunwald (New York: Harper & Row, 1962), 55; hereafter cited in text.

57. *Franny and Zooey* (New York: Bantam, 1964), 90; hereafter cited in the text. In "The Seymour Narratives" quotations from this text appear with the prefix *FZ*.

58. For discussions of the relationship between Salinger and Buddy, see Granville Hicks, "The Search for Wisdom," in *Salinger: A Critical and Personal Portrait*, ed. Henry Anatole Grunwald (New York: Harper & Row, 1962), 193–94—hereafter cited in text—and David Lodge, "Postmodernist Fiction," in his *The Modes of Modern Writing* (Ithaca, N.Y.: Cornell University Press, 1979), 241–42.

59. See dust jacket of *Franny and Zooey* (Boston: Little, Brown, 1961).

60. See Bernice and Sanford Goldstein, "Their self-consciousness is their burden, and they seek to rid themselves of it and to blend it into something else" (1966, 324). As my argument later in the text indicates, the Glass children contend most strenuously with their *failure* to escape the confinements of their minds.

61. G. E. Slethaug, "Form in Salinger's Shorter Fiction," *Canadian Review of American Studies* 3 (Spring 1972): 51.

62. See Alfred Kazin, "'Everybody's Favorite,'" in *Salinger: A Critical and Personal Portrait*, ed. Henry Anatole Grunwald (New York: Harper & Row, 1962), 43–52, and Bostwick, 39–40.

63. For a discussion of what he calls the "illness story," see Richard Ohmann, "The Shaping of a Canon: U.S. Fiction, 1960–1975," *Critical Inquiry* 10, no. 1 (September 1983): 199–223.

64. See George A. Panichas, "J. D. Salinger and the Russian Pilgrim," in his *The Reverent Discipline* (Knoxville: University of Tennessee Press, 1974), 292–305.

65. Herman Melville, *Typee*, ed. Harrison Hayford et al. (Evanston and Chicago: Northwestern University Press and the Newberry Library, 1968), xiii–xiv; Nathaniel Hawthorne, *The Scarlet Letter* (New York: Penguin, 1983), 36 (hereafter cited in text); Charles Dickens, *Bleak House*, ed. Morton Dauwen Zabel (Boston: Houghton Mifflin, 1956), xxxi–xxxii.

66. For a discussion of Salinger's "anti-form," see Ihab Hassan, "Almost the Voice of Silence: The Later Novelettes of J. D. Salinger," *Wisconsin Studies in Contemporary Literature* 4 (Winter 1963): 5–20; hereafter cited in text.

67. For discussions of the relationship between Zen and the Glasses, see Bernice and Sanford Goldstein, "Bunnies and Cobras: Zen Enlightenment in Salinger," *Discourse* 13 (Winter 1970), 101; Bernice and Sanford Goldstein, 1966, 314–15; and Russell, 308–11. Alsen provides the most extended, and incisive, discussion of this issue.

68. For discussions of Salinger and the issue of psychotherapy, see Philip Bufithis, "J. D. Salinger and the Psychiatrist," *West Virginia Bulletin: Philological Papers* 21 (December 1974): 67–77, and Sidney Finkelstein, "Cold War, Religious Revival, and Family Alienation: William Styron, J. D. Salinger, and Edward Albee," in his *Existentialism and Alienation in American Literature* (New York: International Publishers, 1965), 228–30, 232–33.

69. For selected discussions of Seymour's Fat Lady, see James Finn Cotter, "Religious Symbols in Salinger's Shorter Fiction," *Studies in Short Fiction* 15 (Spring 1978): 121–32; Bostwick, 36; Paul Phillips, "Salinger's *Franny and Zooey*," *Mainstream* 15 (January 1962): 38; Hassan, 13; and Miller, 35.

70. See dust jacket of *Raise High the Roof Beam, Carpenters and Seymour: An Introduction* (Boston: Little, Brown, 1963).

71. For discussions of the Taoist tale, see Bernice and Sanford Goldstein, "Some Zen References in Salinger," *Literature East and West* 15, no. 1 (March 1971): 84–85; Alsen, 41–46; and Dennis L. O'Connor, "J. D. Salinger's Religious Pluralism: The Example of *Raise High the Roof Beam, Carpenters*," *Southern Review* 20, no. 2 (April 1984): 316–32 (hereafter cited in text).

72. Theodore L. Gross, "Suicide and Survival in the Modern World," in

his *The Heroic Ideal in American Literature* (New York: Free Press, 1971), 267; hereafter cited in text.

73. See L. Moody Simms, Jr., "Seymour Glass: The Salingerian Hero as Vulgarian," *Notes on Contemporary Literature* 5 (November 1975): 6–8. Simms sees Seymour's marriage to Muriel as his attempt "to abandon his personal standards and immerse himself totally in Vulgarian society." This view does not contend with Seymour's concept of "indiscrimination."

74. See William Wiegand, "Salinger and Kierkegaard," *Minnesota Review* 5 (May–July 1965): 137–56.

75. For discussions of Seymour as saint, see Alsen, 165; Baskett, 58; and Hicks, 194.

76. Bernice and Sanford Goldstein, "'Seymour: an Introduction'—Writing as Discovery," *Studies in Short Fiction* 7 (Spring 1970): 248–56; see also Weinberg, 147.

77. See Bernice and Sanford Goldstein, "Seymour's Poems," *Literature East and West* 17 (June–September–December 1973): 335–48.

78. "Blue Melody," *Cosmopolitan*, September 1948, 118.

79. "Hapworth 16, 1924," *New Yorker*, 19 June 1965, 32; hereafter cited in text.

80. Anthony Quagliano, "'Hapworth 16, 1924': A Problem in Hagiography," *University of Dayton Review* 8 (Fall 1971): 35–43; hereafter cited in text.

Part 2

THE WRITER

Introduction

J. D. Salinger moved to Cornish, New Hampshire, in 1953. He still lives there and he still refuses, in Nathaniel Hawthorne's fine phrase, "to open an intercourse with the world." Given his repudiation of celebrity status, it is ironic that his legal actions to safeguard his privacy have in themselves become news. The same can be said for more pedestrian acts. Every now and then some snoop, either professional or amateur, stakes out Salinger's environs. In 1988 the scowling J. D. Salinger was photographed pushing a shopping cart outside his local supermarket. The shopping cart contained a number of brown paper bags. This was news. The photo appeared in *Time* magazine's "People" section.

Part 2, "The Writer," would normally reprint materials on the subject's views of the craft of writing. In Salinger's case no appropriate—and publishable—materials exist. Although some of his letters are available for public inspection, Salinger will not allow them to be reprinted. He has also made it known that he does not wish to give interviews, a matter that is his right, not his privilege. For the record, I made no attempt to solicit an interview from Salinger or to photograph him buying a newspaper. I make this statement not from any sense of self-righteousness but simply from the belief that human respect requires one to observe clearly demarcated limits. Nevertheless, Salinger has left on record a substantial body of work: no one forced him to publish his fiction over a 25-year period. It is this part of his life—the life that is the work—that remains open to scrutiny by professional and amateur readers.

Because of Salinger's reclusion, I have solicited for this volume an original essay on the relationship among the public life, the craft, and the legend. Joseph Wenke's essay "Biographical Reflections on J. D. Salinger" explores the intersections of biography and art, considering the odd disjunctions that arise from Salinger's refusal to accept celebrity status. Currently an executive speech writer for IBM, Joseph Wenke has published a book on the political and mythical contexts of

Part 2

Norman Mailer's work (*Mailer's America*, 1987) and a number of articles on modern culture, especially the Beat Generation. I thought it would prove interesting to have someone who has written extensively on Norman Mailer, arguably America's most public writer, examine the case of J. D. Salinger, arguably America's most private well-known writer.

Biographical Reflections on
J. D. Salinger

Joseph Wenke

The irony of J. D. Salinger's life is that his legend was made by reclusion. Curiosity may be older than human nature itself, with genetic roots trailing back as far as the Cambrian explosion of life. But our electronic culture has taken this prehistoric desire to extremes. The instinctual urge to know what is private and hidden has become an obsession. And that obsession has spawned an industry of exposure that shapes the content and style of much of our communications media.

Supermarket tabloids, shock radio, TV talk shows, biographies that smear the reputations of their posthumous subjects—they're all there because we want them to be there. We've created the market for them, and now they in turn influence our values and beliefs, producing finally a tabloid mentality that seeks to abolish privacy while accepting without question the legitimacy of all forms of personal investigation.

Today's tabloid mentality may be a relatively recent phenomenon, but it is the result of a cultural process that has been going full throttle since at least the 1950s, when the mass media really began to take hold. An unexamined tenet of this mentality is that public personalities are not entitled to private lives. It is from this attitude that J. D. Salinger was trying to escape by seeking refuge in Cornish, New Hampshire, in the early fifties. And it is now clear, in retrospect, that he never really had a chance of getting away.

Over the years, Salinger has been approached by a host of curiosity seekers, misguided admirers, quasi-journalists, and even a few serious biographical investigators. And so he has hardly kept the world away from his door. But he *has* succeeded in shutting off the flow of information about his life, even if in doing so he has helped create and perpetuate the Salinger legend. After all these years and after all the attempts to penetrate his private life, we know very little about him.

This essay was written specifically for this volume and is published here for the first time by permission of the author.

121

The salient facts are few. Indeed, when one combs the public record, one finds little that is remarkable—except for the writings.

We do know the date Jerome David Salinger was born—1 January 1919. But we know next to nothing about his immediate family. And the facts that have been established are almost comic in their superficiality and insignificance. For example, we know that Salinger's father, Sol, was a Jewish importer of European hams. Salinger's mother was a gentile—Scotch-Irish—and her maiden name was Marie Jillich. After she married Sol, she changed her name to Miriam. Salinger's only sibling, Doris, is eight years older than he. She has retired after working as a buyer at Bloomingdale's in New York City. And she gives no interviews.

We know about as much of Salinger's childhood as we do of Shakespeare's and Jesus' lives as young boys. Accordingly, would-be Freudian biographers had better beware—there is simply nothing to analyze. The absence of information on Salinger's childhood presents an insuperable barrier to any serious Salinger biographer. In his review of Ian Hamilton's biography of Salinger, Bruce Bawer criticized Hamilton for coming up with little biographical material on Salinger before the age of 15. After recounting the crumbs of information that Hamilton had collected, Bawer capped his criticism with the following flourish: "And that, essentially, is all that Hamilton gives us on the childhood of a writer whose fiction is enigmatically obsessed with the theme of childhood—whose entire *oeuvre* cries out for a biographer able to shed some light on the reasons for its strange fixation."[1]

Bawer could hardly have done any better, but he does make a critical point. Setting aside the unkind judgment that Salinger's interest in childhood is a "strange fixation," it is undeniably true that Salinger's published work does focus to a great extent on childhood and adolescence. Since it seems virtually impossible to uncover anything important about Salinger's own youth, the act of literary biography is doomed to be derailed before it even gets out of the station.

Of course, the biographer's task hardly eases as Salinger gets older. No single period of his life is particularly well documented, and the facts we do have reveal little of the inner man, except in the broadest terms. For instance, of Salinger's adolescence we know that he attended the McBurney School in Manhattan from 1932 to 1934, when, at the age of 15, he transferred to Valley Forge Military Academy in Pennsylvania. School records show that Salinger was a relatively poor student at McBurney and a slightly above-average one at Valley Forge (his IQ was 115; his final grades in June 1936 ranged from 76 to 88) and that he was also literary editor of *Crossed Sabres*, the Valley Forge yearbook.

A number of critics have seized upon Valley Forge as an autobiographical model for Pencey Prep, Holden Caulfield's school in *The Catcher in the Rye*. To support this theory, Hamilton establishes some parallels. For example, while at Valley Forge, Salinger reportedly used the phrase "a prince of a guy" to describe people he didn't like—and so does Holden Caulfield. Then too, apparently a boy at Valley Forge fell to his death from a dormitory window, and, of course, James Castle in *The Catcher in the Rye* is killed as a result of falling or jumping from a window to escape a beating from a group of fellow students.

There are other cross-references as well, but the point is that superficial similarities such as these do not really mean very much. Certainly Salinger's fiction encourages autobiographical interpretation. It carries a burden of psychic agitation that reflects the deep emotional involvement of the author with his characters and themes. And Salinger did state in a 1953 interview with Shirley Blaney, a Windsor, Vermont, high school girl, that his "boyhood was very much the same as [Holden Caulfield's], and it was a great relief telling people about it."[2] When asked about this comment some 28 years later in a conversation with Betty Eppes, a reporter for the Baton Rouge *Advocate* who had traveled to Salinger country in the hope of having just such an encounter, Salinger became upset. According to Eppes, Salinger "seemed to be made very uncomfortable" by the question and said "I don't know . . . I don't know. I've just let it all go. I don't know about Holden any more."[3]

Whatever we make of these stray comments and however strongly we believe that Salinger's fiction is essentially autobiographical, the fact remains that we cannot go very far with an autobiographical interpretation of Salinger's work without indulging in speculation. The problem quite simply is that we know so much more about Salinger's characters than we do about him. Any single episode of *The Catcher in the Rye* tells us more about Holden Caulfield than we have ever learned about Salinger from all the published biographical sources combined. We can discover, for example, that in 1937 he traveled to Vienna and Bydgoszcz, Poland, to improve his foreign language skills and learn the ham exporting business. And we can note that in 1938 he attended Ursinus College for a total of nine weeks. But what have we really learned that helps us better understand Salinger the man? What do we glean from these nondescript life experiences that illuminates the source and the nature of Salinger's art and helps us gauge the relationship between Salinger and his characters?

We do know, of course, the kind of literary career that Salinger was building for himself throughout the 1940s, before the success of *The Catcher in the Rye* launched him into a whole new realm of notoriety. He was establishing himself as a successful professional short story writer for the so-called slicks, relatively well-paying mass market magazines like *Collier's*, *Esquire*, and the *Saturday Evening Post*.

In 1939 he attended a Columbia University short story–writing class taught by Whit Burnett, editor of *Story* magazine, which provided an outlet for such promising young writers as Norman Mailer, Joseph Heller, Truman Capote—and J. D. Salinger. "The Young Folks," Salinger's first published short story, appeared in *Story* in 1940. Over the next year or so, Salinger published stories in the *University of Kansas City Review*, a prestigious academic quarterly, as well as in *Collier's* and *Esquire*. He also sold "A Slight Rebellion off Madison," his first Holden Caulfield story, to the *New Yorker*, but its publication was delayed until after the war.

In 1942 Salinger was drafted into the army, but not even World War II could deter him from pursuing his writing career. He became a staff sergeant, wrote romantic letters to Oona O'Neill (Eugene O'Neill's daughter and later Charlie Chaplin's wife), served in the Army Intelligence Corps, landed on Utah Beach on D day, met Ernest Hemingway, married a French doctor named Sylvia (surname unknown)—and, most important, continued writing and publishing stories. Three of Salinger's wartime stories appeared in 1944 in the *Saturday Evening Post*, including "Last Day of the Last Furlough," in which Holden Caulfield is mentioned as a young soldier missing in action. The story also features Holden's brother, Vincent, and the army number of the main character, Babe Gladwaller, is, according to Ian Hamilton, the same as Salinger's. In 1945 a number of other stories appeared with these characters, and "I'm Crazy" in *Collier's* was the first published story containing material later to be included in *The Catcher in the Rye*.

Salinger was discharged from the army when the war ended, but he remained in Europe, working as a civilian for the Department of Defense until May 1946, when he returned to New York City. His wife accompanied him but soon returned to France and ended the marriage. That same year, "A Slight Rebellion off Madison" finally appeared in the *New Yorker*. There was also reportedly a novella about Holden

Caulfield that was accepted for publication but then withdrawn by Salinger.

The year 1948 was Salinger's breakthrough year as a short story writer. In January he published "A Perfect Day for Bananafish," his first Seymour Glass story, in the *New Yorker.* Two other *New Yorker* stories quickly followed—in March, "Uncle Wiggily in Connecticut" and in June, "Just before the War with the Eskimos." These stories mark the true beginning of Salinger's close relationship with the magazine. Indeed, from this point on he would publish his short fiction almost exclusively in the *New Yorker,* the most prestigious forum of the day. Most important, however, these stories represent a new degree of maturity and control in Salinger's writing.

At about this time Salinger had a rather unfortunate encounter with Hollywood. Darryl Zanuck bought the motion picture rights to "Uncle Wiggily in Connecticut" and turned it into the horrendous 1950 tearjerker *My Foolish Heart,* starring Susan Hayward, who was nominated for an Academy Award for her portrayal of Eloise. Needless to say, Salinger never again sold the rights to any of his works.

On a much more positive note, Salinger's first appearance in print in the 1950s was a memorable one. In April 1950 he published in the *New Yorker* what is perhaps his finest short story, "For Esmé—with Love and Squalor," deft in its characterization and remarkably poignant. This was his last published story with a wartime setting and theme and his last appearance in print before the publication of *The Catcher in the Rye.*

At this point Salinger had indeed established himself as a writer. At only 31 he had a solid relationship with the *New Yorker,* had published a handful of very accomplished stories, and was attracting attention in New York literary circles. He was, in short, a success but by no means famous and certainly unprepared for the notoriety that was soon to follow.

As an indication of the stir Salinger created among New York publishers, in 1949 Robert Giroux, then an editor at Harcourt Brace, wrote him in care of the *New Yorker* to find out if he was writing a novel and to express interest in publishing his stories. Salinger failed to respond to the letter for months. But one day he suddenly appeared at Giroux's office. In a letter to Ian Hamilton, Giroux recalled the encounter.

> A tall, sad-looking young man with a long face and deep-set black
> eyes walked in, saying, "It's not my stories that should be published

first, but the novel I'm working on." I said, "Do you want to sit behind this desk? You sound just like a publisher."

He said, "No, you can do the stories later if you want, but I think my novel about this kid in New York during the Christmas holidays should come out first."[4]

Giroux immediately offered to publish Salinger's work, and the agreement was confirmed with a handshake.

The novel about the "kid in New York" had been gestating for many years, but Salinger was now finally at the point of working on it continuously and seeing it through to completion. A year after meeting Giroux, Salinger sent him the manuscript. Giroux thought the book "remarkable" and "considered [himself] lucky to be its editor" (Hamilton, 114). But apparently others at Harcourt Brace failed to share Giroux's admiration or understanding of the book. Salinger had a falling-out with Harcourt Brace and withdrew his manuscript. *The Catcher in the Rye* was finally published by Little, Brown in July 1951.

Salinger, however, again found himself at odds with his publisher. He objected to any attempt at publicizing the book or making it available to the press to review, and he insisted that his photograph be removed from the cover. (The photo did appear in the American *Catcher* but not in the British.) Salinger did agree, however, to being interviewed by William Maxwell, a *New Yorker* colleague, for the book's appearance as a main Book-of-the-Month Club selection. In the interview Salinger revealed some of his feelings about writing: "I think writing is a hard life," he said. "But it's brought me enough happiness that I don't think I'd ever deliberately dissuade anybody (if he had talent) from taking it up. The compensations are few, but when they come, if they come, they're very beautiful."[5]

The reviews of *The Catcher in the Rye* were for the most part very positive, with some hailing its brilliance and originality. The book was soon a best-seller, peaking at number 4 on the *New York Times* best-seller list and staying on the list for seven months. But the initial reception of *The Catcher in the Rye* hardly suggested the almost mythical dimensions of the book's ultimate popularity. As the first wave of attention subsided, Salinger breathed a sigh of relief. He told the *Saturday Review,* "I feel tremendously relieved that the season for success of *The Catcher in the Rye* is over. I enjoyed a small part of it, but most of it I found hectic and professionally and personally demoralizing. Let's say I'm getting good and sick of bumping into that blown-up photograph of my face on the back of the dust-jacket."[6]

We might say that Salinger has been trying to avoid "bumping into that blown-up photograph" ever since. But one thing was unavoidable: though he may not have wanted to believe it, his life was forever changed. With the publication of *The Catcher in the Rye,* J. D. Salinger had crossed the great divide between private person and public personality. And try as he might, he could never return to being a completely private person.

At about this time, Salinger was becoming increasingly interested in a form of Hinduism that had been taught by the nineteenth-century Indian mystic Sri Ramakrishna. Salinger began formal studies under Swami Nikhilananda at the Ramakrishna Vivekananda Center in New York City in 1952 and reportedly is still associated with the center and attends seminars and lectures.

On 1 January 1953—his thirty-fourth birthday—Salinger moved to Cornish, New Hampshire, a move that effectively marks the beginning of his legendary reclusion. His new accommodations were sufficiently secluded and austere to meet even the strictest hermitic standards. His cottage, across the Connecticut River from Windsor, Vermont, was situated on 90 acres of land and had no heat, no electricity, and no running water.

Soon after arriving in Cornish, Salinger befriended a number of high school students. The friendship led to the aforementioned interview with Shirley Blaney, which was supposed to be printed on the high school page of the *Claremont* (New Hampshire) *Daily Eagle.* The interview appeared, however, on the front page of the newspaper. As one might expect, Salinger objected and apparently broke off his friendship with the high school students as a result. Salinger has never granted another interview, unless one counts a telephone conversation he initiated with a San Francisco staffer for the *New York Times* to protest the pirated publication of his uncollected stories in 1974.

Very little is known about Salinger's personal life from this point on beyond a few basic facts. In February 1955 he married Claire Douglas, a 19-year-old Radcliffe student. In December a daughter, Margaret Ann, was born; in February 1960, a son, Matthew, was born; and in 1967 Claire and J. D. Salinger were divorced.

What we do know, of course, is the record of his publications. In April 1953 *Nine Stories* was published by Little, Brown. The book collects the best of Salinger's short fiction and includes all of his *New Yorker* stories from 1948 to 1953, as well as "Down at the Dinghy," first published in *Harper's* in 1949, and "De Daumier-Smith's Blue Period," which appeared in the London *World Review* in 1952. The volume was favorably reviewed and sold well, peaking at number 9 on the *New York Times* best-seller list.

All of Salinger's remaining periodical publications appeared in the *New Yorker*: "Franny" and "Raise High the Roof Beam, Carpenters" in 1955, "Zooey" in 1957, and "Seymour: An Introduction" in 1959.

Franny and Zooey, published by Little, Brown in 1961, was an immediate success, going all the way to number 1 on the *New York Times* best-seller list and staying there for six months. On the book's dust-jacket, Salinger describes "Franny" and "Zooey" as

> early, critical entries in a narrative series I'm doing about a family of settlers in twentieth-century New York, the Glasses. It is a long-term project, patently an ambitious one, and there is a real-enough danger, I suppose, that sooner or later I'll bog down, perhaps disappear entirely, in my own methods, locutions, and mannerisms. On the whole, though, I'm very hopeful. I love working on these Glass stories, I've been waiting for them most of my life, and I think I have fairly decent, monomaniacal plans to finish them with due care and all-available skill.
>
> A couple of stories in the series besides FRANNY and ZOOEY have already been published in the *New Yorker*, and some new material is scheduled to appear there soon or Soon. I have a great deal of thoroughly unscheduled material on paper, too, but I expect to be fussing with it, to use a popular trade term, for some time to come.

In 1963 *Raise High the Roof Beam, Carpenters and Seymour: An Introduction*, the other "stories in the series" previously published in the *New Yorker*, were published in book form by Little, Brown. On the dust-jacket Salinger again refers to his Glass family saga as a work in progress: "I have several new Glass stories coming along—waxing, dilating—each in its own way." Unfortunately, we have not been privileged to read any of these stories, with the exception of "Hapworth 16, 1924," which appeared in the *New Yorker* in 1965. And it remains to this day Salinger's last appearance in print.

Over the past quarter-century Salinger has surfaced only on rare occasions. In 1974 pirated editions of Salinger's uncollected stories began showing up in bookstores in San Francisco, New York, and Chicago. Reportedly, the books were sold to these stores by a number of different men, all of whom identified themselves as John Greenberg from Berkeley, California.

To protest the illegal publication of his work, Salinger called the San Francisco bureau of the *New York Times* and spoke for almost a half-hour to correspondent Lacey Fosburgh. In the course of the conversation, Salinger stated that "there is a marvelous peace in not publishing. It's peaceful. Still. Publishing is a terrible invasion of my privacy. I like to write. I love to write. But I write just for myself and my own pleasure."[7]

Salinger described the pirating of his stories as "an illicit act" and went on to say, "I'm still trying to protect what privacy I have left" (1). When asked if he expected "to publish another work soon," Salinger replied, "I really don't know how soon." He confirmed that he continued to write daily and said,

> I don't necessarily intend to publish posthumously, but I do like to write for myself. I pay for this kind of attitude. I'm known as a strange, aloof kind of man. But all I'm doing is trying to protect myself and my work.
>
> I just want all this to stop. It's intrusive. I've survived a lot of things, and I'll probably survive this. (69)

He subsequently sued, on the basis of copyright infringement, "John Greenberg" and the bookstores that sold the books. The bookstores paid Salinger damages, but none of the various "John Greenbergs" has ever been found.

In December 1980 Salinger and *The Catcher in the Rye* were in the news in connection with the murder of John Lennon. Mark David Chapman, Lennon's murderer, was a devotee of Holden Caulfield. He even had a copy of *The Catcher in the Rye* with him when he killed Lennon. After shooting Lennon five times in the back, Chapman sat down, pulled out the book, and began reading it while he waited for the police to arrive. Apparently Chapman's interpretation of Holden Caulfield's view of "phonies" and Chapman's belief that Lennon was somehow a phony influenced his decision to kill the former Beatle.

In September 1986 J. D. Salinger filed suit to prevent the publication of Ian Hamilton's unauthorized biography, *J. D. Salinger: A Writing Life*, objecting to the use of quotations from his unpublished letters and claiming copyright infringement. In October a New York district court issued a temporary restraining order. As part of his deposition, Salinger reconfirmed that he has continued writing fiction. When asked whether he had "written any full-length works of fiction during the past twenty years," Salinger stated, "It's very difficult to answer. I don't write that way. I just start writing fiction and see what happens to it." In response to further prodding to describe his "literary efforts," he said, "Just a work of fiction. That's all. That's the only description I can really give it. . . . It's almost impossible to define. I work with characters, and as they develop, I just go from there" (Hamilton, 202).

In October 1987 the U.S. Supreme Court refused to review lower-court decisions to bar the publication of Hamilton's book, thereby upholding those decisions. Subsequently, Hamilton revised his book and published the new, censored version under the title *In Search of J. D. Salinger.*

And that is where we stand today. Salinger continues to protect his privacy, and we assume that he continues to write while refusing to publish. Many people continue to care very much about the man and his work because Salinger is that rare human being who has been able to touch other lives through the power of his imagination. People identify with his writing in a very personal way, for they believe that reading it has somehow changed their lives. They feel that his work matters.

Salinger has established a unique bond with his readership, one that survives his decision to stop publishing. It is a bond that will continue to survive so long as there are readers who are open to change and alive to the imagination of J. D. Salinger.

Notes

1. Bruce Bawer, "Salinger's Arrested Development," *New Criterion* 5 (September 1986): 35.

2. Shirley Blaney, "Twin State Telescope," *Claremont* (New Hampshire) *Daily Eagle*, 13 November 1953, 1.

3. Betty Eppes, "What I Did Last Summer," *Paris Review* 23 (Summer 1981): 232.

4. Ian Hamilton, *In Search of J. D. Salinger* (New York: Random House, 1988), 109; hereafter cited in the text.

5. William Maxwell, "J. D. Salinger," *Book-of-the-Month Club News*, July 1951, 5–6.

6. Eloise Perry Hazard, "Eight Fiction Finds," *Saturday Review*, 16 February 1952, 16.

7. Lacey Fosburgh, "J. D. Salinger Speaks about His Silence," *New York Times*, 3 November 1974, 1.

Part 3

THE CRITICS

Introduction

The following discussions of the works of J. D. Salinger were selected from an extensive body of secondary materials. These approaches to Salinger include literary exegesis (Miller), cultural analysis (Gross, French), source study (Panichas, the Goldsteins), and biographical criticism (Bawer). These excerpts indicate the lively and serious nature of Salinger criticism. I have allotted most space to the taxing questions regarding the putative unity of *Nine Stories* and the religious preoccupations of the later fiction, especially Salinger's interest in Eastern religion and philosophy.

Theodore L. Gross

We might begin by citing Salinger's compassion for the victims and fallen figures of an urban America; his self-conscious, chastening wit; or his remarkable ability to illuminate character through the finest detail. But the deeper, more permanent attraction of Salinger's work must have something to do with his treatment of suicide and survival, his attempt to suggest a mode of survival in this world that is not without meaning and a little dignity. Suicide, we realize, as we trace the development of Salinger's fiction from "A Perfect Day for Banana Fish" to *Seymour, an Introduction* and *Hapworth 16, 1924* haunts his characters; and it becomes more self-conscious, more present, as he draws increasingly closer to Seymour Glass, signifying, in the case of the Glass family, not only the tragic death of an ideal man but the suicide of the poet and the consequent failure of art to survive in the modern world. The act of suicide—at times it seems the *only act* in all of Salinger's fiction—occurs in 1948, when Salinger first begins to write with a clarity of focus and with real efficacy; the rest is a painstaking and elaborate account of how individuals seek to forsake madness by understanding death and suicide, how they manage to survive in the world without yielding to an ultimate act of despair and yet, as Buddy Glass puts it, without "going astray in any cheap way."

Whatever else we may say of him, Seymour Glass is a hero tenaciously committed to the ideal of art—he is the artist as hero. Apparently he could not modify his idealism when the authority of the real world encroached; suicide tore him away from the unbearable. But Seymour's suicide has allowed the other Glass children—particularly Buddy Glass—to survive; and in that sense it has not been without purpose.

In Salinger's fiction one feels a persistent idealism despite the profound distrust of all those forms of authority that contribute to con-

From *The Heroic Ideal in American Literature* by Theodore L. Gross (New York: Free Press, 1971), 263–65. © 1971 by Theodore L. Gross. Reprinted by permission of the Free Press, a division of Macmillan, Inc.

formity of mind and spirit. Indeed the struggle between idealism and authority causes the special tension of Salinger's work; it is a struggle that drives the hero to the point of madness and suicide. These concerns are evident in Salinger's early work as the idealist searches for a form of compassion that is all but impossible to realize, as his sanity is threatened by the trivial vanities of other people. . . .

In the tales that Salinger reprinted in *Nine Stories*, the victimized figures are at times filled with an anxiety that approaches madness, or, at other times, are driven to suicide itself. "A Perfect Day for Banana Fish" sets the mood of the collection and introduces Seymour Glass, the central character of Salinger's fiction, committing the central act of that fiction. His suicide in the story stems from a conflict with his vapid wife that comes at the climax, as we see in his later appearances, of an ideological conflict with a world in which his extraordinary, poetic, and ideal character can find no suitable place. In "A Perfect Day for Banana Fish," poetry assumes only a suggestive form in the myth of the banana fish that Seymour tells to the girl on the beach; the power of the story, nevertheless, resides in the implied collision of the poet and the actual world. Seymour's suicide initiates the morbid tone of *Nine Stories:* "Uncle Wiggily in Connecticut," "For Ésme With Love and Squalor," and "Teddy" share its mood of anxiety and terror, its sense of proximate madness; other stories—"Just Before the War With the Eskimos" and "Pretty Mouth and Green My Eyes"—also treat of aberration and neurosis. But it is not really until the publication of *Franny and Zooey* that Salinger's central ideas assume a clear pattern and that Salinger begins an elaborate, painstaking examination of the conflict between art and life, between the poetic vision and the vanity of existence, a conflict which Seymour himself could not resolve but which the other creative members of the Glass family—writers, actors, entertainers—grow to understand as they explore the meaning of Seymour's ideas and, ultimately, of Seymour's suicide.

James E. Miller, Jr.

The chasteness of the title *Nine Stories* (1953) is in line with the severity of the selection. The stories Salinger chose are late stories, published between 1948 and 1953—all, with two exceptions, in the *New Yorker*. Although the tales in *Nine Stories* are arranged in the order of their publication . . . , it is illuminating to look at them in a series of thematic groupings. Before rearranging the order, however, it is useful to note that the opening and closing stories of the volume portray violent deaths, the first (Seymour Glass's) a certain suicide, the second (Teddy's) a foreseen "accident." It is possible that the nature of the one death may help in understanding the other. Indeed, there are thematic echoes and reverberations throughout *Nine Stories* which give the volume a singleness of impact which belies its multiplicity.

The dominant theme which recurs, in richly varied thematic contexts, is alienation, an alienation which may conclude in some kind of reconciliation or accommodation, but which may also result in distortion of the soul, bitterness, nausea, and the ultimate withdrawal into death. The causes of the alienation are frequently obscure but always complex. Sometimes society seems at fault, in the horrors of racial prejudice or the horrors of war. But sometimes the fault seems to lie in a failure of personal relationships—the filament (of Whitman's spider) is launched, but does not catch; or caught, does not hold. Sometimes, however, the cause of alienation lies deeply within, in a turbulence of the spirit—plunging the individual into a dark night of the soul, or dazzling him in the ecstasy of a vision of mystical union—two radically different states that mystics have always found in close conjunction.

"Down at the Dinghy" (which holds the center position in *Nine Stories*) is the single story in the volume dealing directly with a social issue—racial prejudice; a young boy, four-year-old Lionel Tannenbaum, has heard a housekeeper call his father a "kike," and has run

From *J. D. Salinger* by James E. Miller, Jr. (Minneapolis: University of Minnesota Pamphlet Series, 1965), 19–27. © 1965 by the University of Minnesota. Reprinted by permission of the University of Minnesota Press.

136

away to the family dinghy, from which his mother (who is, incidentally, Boo Boo Glass) finally coaxes him—discovering, ironically, that he thought a kike "one of those things that go up in the *air*" (a kite).

Several stories are tales of estrangement in love, both premarital and marital. Perhaps the most optimistic of these is "Just before the War with the Eskimos": a sensitive, perceptive young man (Franklin Graff) who has been kept out of the war—and somewhat out of life—because of a bad "ticker," has drifted into an unwholesome relationship with what appears to be a homosexual; when Ginnie Mannox comes home with his sister one day, the young man launches forth a filament that appears to catch (he had written eight letters to Ginnie's sister that went unanswered), and she accepts his zany offer of a leftover chicken sandwich and leaves determined to come back. "The Laughing Man" describes the sad end rather than the happy beginning of a relationship: John Gedsudski, a young law student, is in charge of a group of young boys (the Comanches), and keeps them entertained between ballgames by narrating an endless tale about a kind of deformed Robin Hood (with a "hairless, pecan-shaped head and a face that featured . . . . an enormous oval cavity below the nose"); when the young man's relationship with Mary Hudson blossoms, and she even participates in the ballgames, the plot of his tale proliferates with great energy and gusto, but when they quarrel and part (no cause is given), he bitterly describes the brutal captivity and death of his "laughing man," unforgettably shocking his young Comanches.

Two stories describe marital estrangement and betrayal. "Uncle Wiggily in Connecticut" portrays a gray flannel world in which a suburban housewife, Eloise, drinking with an old school chum, gradually reveals the hidden source of her antagonism toward her daughter (who has a naughty imaginary playmate) and her indifference toward her husband: she recalls with alcoholic vividness her old love (his name is Walt Glass) killed during the war in Japan by the absurd explosion of a toy Japanese stove. "Pretty Mouth and Green My Eyes" is an urbanized tale of the managerial set and consists of two telephone conversations that take place after a cocktail party, initiated each time by a junior executive to a superior in the same firm, the first to inquire whether the older man saw the younger's wife leave the party, the second to explain that the wife has just come home; but the irony is that the wife is in bed with the older man even as he takes the two calls.

But Salinger's best stories portray an alienation more profound and

137

more unsettling than that produced by the shock of racial prejudice or the shock of the failure of love. The most celebrated example of this more ambiguous alienation is found in "For Esmé—with Love and Squalor," a tale of war and spiritual crisis told by the protagonist some six healing years after the searing events. But the events remain so vividly painful that the narrator must envelop them in anonymity and must remove them from himself by placing them in the third person. In England during the war, in training for duty in Europe, the narrator meets and has tea with thirteen-year-old Esmé and her five-year-old brother Charles, and discovers a moment of human warmth and sanity to relieve the dreariness and insanity of camp life in wartime. Esmé is all the more endearing for the mature role she has bravely assumed in her family after the death of her father, slain in North Africa. The scene shifts to occupied Bavaria after five campaigns (and V-E Day), and the narration suddenly shifts into the third person. Sergeant X, feeling "his mind dislodge itself and teeter, like insecure luggage on an overhead rack," picks up from the table a book by Goebbels entitled *Die Zeit Ohne Beispiel* ("The Unprecedented Era"), once owned by a low-ranking Nazi that X himself had arrested, and finds written in it, "Dear God, life is hell." Sergeant X writes under this inscription a quotation from Dostoevski: "Fathers and teachers, I ponder 'What is hell?' I maintain that it is the suffering of being unable to love."

It is precisely this hell that Sergeant X is experiencing, as is immediately demonstrated by the intrusion of his companion on the five campaigns, Corporal Z, an insensitive, vacuous individual whose very physical presence—belches, brick-red slicked-down hair, overdecorated uniform, and all—is overwhelming. Corporal Z's brutalized, dehumanized conversation at this moment of spiritual crisis, especially his casual recollection of the cat he cruelly and meaninglessly shot while with his buddy during a moment of battle tension, triggers the revulsion in Sergeant X that causes him immediately to vomit. But a sickness of the soul—the sickness of being unable to love—cannot be regurgitated. Left alone, Sergeant X aimlessly looks through his mail and finds a package that turns out to contain a letter from Esmé together with her father's watch which she had been wearing on their first and only encounter. The letter and watch are like a fresh breeze that blows through and cleanses the sickroom of the soul. They provide an illumination that renews and refreshes Sergeant X's darkened spirit, as he once again—in the presence, however remote, of such innocent affection—feels himself able to love. He had, perhaps, in his nausea at humanity, been near suicide; the watch that Esmé sent him restored to him a reservoir of time that he had been on the verge of losing forever.

"De Daumier-Smith's Blue Period" tells the story of a young man, at loose ends with life, who obtains a job as an instructor at a Canadian correspondence art school, run by a Japanese man and his wife; among his mediocre students is a talented nun who attracts his attention and to whom he writes a long, almost intimate letter, which precipitates the nun's withdrawal from the course; shortly after, the school is closed down for being improperly licensed and De Daumier-Smith returns to his former life to pick up the threads he had cut. Of course, the story is much more than this bare outline shows. The episode is the crucial, formative experience in the protagonist's life, but it is, fundamentally, an experience of the spirit. The young man, who narrates his own story, is a kind of Ishmael at the beginning, his mother dead, his step-father providing a tenuous hotel existence in New York; he is sickened by the multitudes of people in the city, prays to be alone, and suddenly discovers that everything he touches turns to "solid loneliness." It is out of a mixture of frustration and desperation that he applies for the art school job in Canada under the fantastic name of De Daumier-Smith—in search of a new identity.

The thematic focal point of the story is an orthopedic appliances shop underneath the second-floor art school. There two incidents occur, one "hideous" (a dark night), the other "transcendent" (an illumination), that determine the fate of the narrator. After he has mailed his long, adulatory letter to the nun about her work, even suggesting that he visit her, and is living in a kind of exalted anticipation of her reply, he pauses one evening before the window of the shop and is inexpicably plunged into gloom: "The thought was forced on me that no matter how coolly or sensibly or gracefully I might one day learn to live my life, I would always at best be a visitor in a garden of enamel urinals and bedpans, with a sightless, wooden dummy-deity standing by in a marked-down rupture truss." The thought is unendurable, and De Daumier-Smith rushes off to bed and forces his mind to envision a visit with the nun at her convent, in a relationship "without sin" but in a purity of image "too ecstatic to hold in place."

After receiving word that the nun has been withdrawn from the art course, De Daumier-Smith is depressed, angrily writes letters dismissing his other students, and goes out for a walk—only to pause once again before the terrible window. This time there is a girl in a "green, yellow and lavender" dress in the window changing the truss on the wooden dummy; when she sees the narrator, she becomes flustered, starts to exit, and falls on her bottom (recalling the "buttocks to buttocks" bus scene in New York earlier in the story). As De Daumier-Smith reaches out to help her, his fingers are stopped by the glass of the window—and the "Experience" occurs: "Suddenly . . . the sun came up and sped toward the bridge of my nose at the rate of ninety-three million miles a second. Blinded and very frightened—I had to put my hand on the glass to keep my balance. The thing lasted for no more than a few seconds. When I got my sight back, the girl had gone from the window, leaving behind her a shimmering field of exquisite, twice-blessed, enamel flowers." In spite of the narrator's protests, the incident has all the elements of some kind of "genuine mysticism." De Daumier-Smith's mystic response to the girl in the window is reminiscent of Stephen Dedalus' reaction to his glimpse of the wading girl in *A Portrait of the Artist as a Young Man*—a glimpse that deflected him from priesthood and sent him out to encounter the world. The narrator, in returning to his former life, is symbolically rejoining the human race; he has made the decision to become more than just a "visitor" in the physical universe.

In "Teddy," Salinger carries experimentation in mystical fiction about as far as it can be carried without entering the realm of fantasy, and even in "Teddy" there are elements of the fantastic. Ten-year-old Theodore McArdle, on an ocean voyage with his irritable, quarreling parents and his six-year-old sister (who, he says, doesn't like him), is gradually revealed to us as the most remarkable child in Salinger's large gallery of remarkable children. He holds the Vedantic theory of reincarnation, and believes that in his last incarnation he was "making very nice spiritual advancement." He had his first mystical experience at an early age: "I was six when I saw that everything was God, and my hair stood up . . . It was on a Sunday, I remember. My sister was only a very tiny child then, and she was drinking her milk, and all of a sudden I saw that *she* was God and the *milk* was God. I mean, all she was doing was pouring God into God, if you know what I mean." But perhaps Teddy's most marvelous gift is his intuitive grasp of the future—not clairvoyance, but a sense of the need for increased awareness or concern at certain potentially hazardous times. He writes in his diary: "It will either happen today or February 14, 1958 when I am sixteen. It is ridiculous to mention even." The reference, we find out later, is to his own death. In his final conversation with a fellow passenger, the teacher Bob Nicholson, he says that death is a minor matter, really ("All you do is get the heck out of your body when you die"), and that it could happen to him that very day—say, for example, if he went down to the swimming pool, found it empty, and was pushed in by his small sister (who, after all, "hasn't been a human being for very many lives"). As events turn out, this is precisely what happens, as Nicholson realizes on his way following Teddy down to the pool—when he suddenly hears the piercing scream of Teddy's sister, no doubt hysterical in fear and horror at what she has done.

If we accept the world created by Salinger in this story, we do not mourn for Teddy, but recognize that he is on his way to another incarnation, and closer in the cycle that will bring him to the final and permanent meditation with God. In the story, Salinger was probably experimenting with rather than expressing belief, and the tale should be accepted in that spirit. More important, however, than Teddy's gift of intuitive foresight are his desire for meditation, his dislike of sentimentality, and his distaste for logic. It is through periodical retreat and meditation that he is able to achieve his remarkable knowledge—or make "spiritual advancement." Poetry and love are too frequently destroyed by sentimentality; thus Teddy prefers Japanese poetry ("'Nothing in the voice of the cicada intimates how soon it will die'"), and thus he loves God ("If *I* were God, I certainly wouldn't want people to love me sentimentally"). Adam brought logic into the world by his eating of the apple, and man has been an apple-eater ever since; man must "vomit" up this "logic and intellectual stuff" if he ever wants "to see things as they really are" (the language here—especially the image of vomiting—is revealing as it relates to the recurring nausea in Salinger's heroes). After man has emptied himself of the "intellectual stuff," he might, through meditation, be able to get back the conscious knowledge that he has somehow lost. ("I grew my own body. . . . Nobody else did it for me. So if I grew it, I must have known *how* to grow it. Unconsciously, at least. I may have lost the *con*scious knowledge of how to grow it sometime in the last few hundred thousand years, but the knowledge is still *there* . . .") Whatever we may think of Teddy—and I think that we must accept him (if necessary through willing suspension of disbelief) as a genuine mystic, spiritually advanced far beyond the general level of this world, operating on the very highest levels of cosmic consciousness—it is clear that he is too much for this world to contain. Like Melville's Billy Budd with his colossal innocence, Teddy with his staggering spirituality must die, as he himself seems to understand, before he unsettles society from its foundations.

James Lundquist

It is in *Nine Stories* . . . that Zen is most pointedly being used as a conceptualizing force for Salinger's fiction, and the puzzle that we are presented with before we can even start reading the stories is this one: "We know the sound of two hands clapping. But what is the sound of one hand clapping?" This, of course, is one of the most famous Zen *koan*, originated by Hakuin (1685–1768), generally acknowledged as the greatest of the Zen masters. The word *Zen* means thinking, meditation, to see, to contemplate, and the *koan* is central to the Zen process. Zen is an anti-rational Buddhist sect that developed in India and that later became widespread in Japan; it differs from most of the other Buddhist sects in seeking enlightenment through introspection and intuition rather than in (Pali) scripture. Accordingly, Hakuin devised his famous *koan*, Heinrich Dumoulin explains in his *History of Zen Buddhism*, as "a problem which he believed would penetrate into one's consciousness with incomparable sharpness and would readily lead to the awakening of doubt and to progress in the exercises."[1] The "exercises," which are to a great extent the work of Hakuin, involve passing six series of tests involving five groups of *koan* and a sixth stage devoted to a study of the Buddhist precepts and the regulations of the monk's life as described in the light of Zen understanding. The *koan* Salinger cites is a preliminary *Hosshin* or first-level type, and its purpose is to profoundly acquaint the student with a way of thinking, a way of apprehending the nature of the self that is actually based on a theory of knowledge or what can be known.

Zen is the product of Oriental ways of thinking that do present some problems for the Western mind. This is because Westerners have generally taken what a Zen master would call a restricted view of human knowledge, what would be termed "conventional knowledge" or the assumption that we do not know anything unless we can put it in words

From *J. D. Salinger* by James Lundquist (New York: Ungar, 1979), "Zen Art and *Nine Stories*," 74–79. © 1979 by the Frederick Ungar Publishing Co. Reprinted by permission of the publisher.

or contain it within some systems of conventional signs (the notations of mathematics or music, for example). Conventional knowledge is a system of abstractions, consisting of signs and symbols in which things and events are reduced to their general outlines so that they can be comprehended one at a time. But we live in a universe that does not conform to this system, a universe in which things are happening altogether-at-once and whose reality escapes perfect definition through abstract terms. How then do we come to a better awareness of this "real" universe?

The Zen answer would be that we already know it without knowing it, and that what we call conscious, ordering thought is but a small function of our total consciousness. For instance, we have the notion of "controlling" our lives by adopting a role (doctor, carpenter, even priest), but life itself does not proceed in such a transparently artificial and cumbersome fashion. Our own organisms, for example, could not live for a minute if we had to take thought of every breath, every beat of the heart, every neural impulse. Yet we tend to hold to a conventional view of ourselves, even thinking about ourselves as a history consisting of selected memories, instead of the truer (in the Buddhist sense) realization that we each are simply what we are doing now.

This emphasis on coming to terms with the spontaneity of the self also suggests an idea of restoring our original nature or returning to a state in which the spontaneous rather than the conventional indeed seemed most natural—to childhood. The peculiar naturalness and un-self-consciousness of children is gradually eliminated by conventional education through which the child is taught not only what words are to stand for what things, but also the way his culture has arbitrarily agreed to divide things from each other. The function of Zen is to undo the inevitable "damage" of this discipline, to encourage a state of wholeness in which the mind functions freely and easily and spontaneously. The *koan* is the method by which the Zen master "instructs" the student away from conventional knowledge and reliance on wrong-thinking.

The student begins with one assumption—that the "Buddha nature" is within oneself and is not to be sought outside. He does not have to journey to India to find it. The master then asks the student a question, presents him with a *koan*, and tells him to return when he has discovered the answer, and to give some proof of his discovery. In addition to the "one-hand" *koan*, the "original face" *koan* is among the first to be presented, and perhaps makes for a better example of what the stratagem involves. The "original face" *koan* poses this question of the student: What was your "original face," your basic nature, before your father and mother conceived you? The student's first impulse is to try to respond with philosophical and wordy answers. He may, using conventional reasoning, speculate on the origin of his *ego* and try to explain what is meant by the term. But the master has no patience with this—he wants to be "shown." The student then might bring in "specimens of reality" such as a rock and try to explain that before he was conceived he was like the object, undesigned, without consciousness. The master rejects all such approaches, and the student winds up at his wits' end, which is where he should be because he "knows that he does not know."

It is at this point that the mystery of Zen begins. The *koan* method is a process designed to produce *satori* or spontaneous comprehension of and communion with the true reality of self and nature and cannot be adequately described through words. It is, after all, a way of penetrating the fog of abstraction and therefore cannot be explained through further abstraction. But what happens is something like this—the student at last reaches the point of feeling utterly stupid. The metaphor that is often used in reference to this state is that of a huge block of ice in which the student is unable to move or think. He knows absolutely nothing; everything is as incomprehensible as "the sound of one hand." But then, after an undetermined time, there comes a moment when the ice suddenly melts. The problem of who he is becomes absurd; from the beginning, the question meant nothing. The knot has vanished because the abstraction of the mind seeking to know the mind has been defeated—no longer exists. When the student has reached this stage of liberation, the master knows that his training can now begin because it has (Zen relishes paradoxes) been finished.

The student, through continued practice, has an unobstructed mind into which the subsequent *koan* descend and are "solved" ("realized" might be a better word, although it too is inadequate). As the student finishes with each *koan*, the master usually requires that he present a verse from the *Zenrin Kushu*, an anthology of some five-thousand two-line poems, compiled by Toyo Eicho (1429–1504), or from some other book which expresses the point of the *koan* just solved. This is a practice that brings us directly back to *Nine Stories*, for each of the stories can be seen as a "verse" serving to comment on the *koan* with which the book begins. And just as the Zen "work" for the student involves alternating a crucial *koan* with subsidiary ones that explore the implications of the former, each story presents puzzles of its own that give us a working acquaintance with the Buddhist view of the universe.

What then is the point of the "one-hand" *koan*? It leads us through a series of questions. Can you hear something that is not making any noise? Can you get any sound out of a hand that has nothing to hit against? Can you obtain any knowledge of your own real nature—can the mind hit against itself? It is this final question that Salinger comes down to in his stories as he presents characters who achieve or fail to achieve *satori*, who either do or do not achieve a sudden and intuitive way of seeing into themselves. And for those who do solve the *koan* that is crucial to their awakening, what happens is described by Dumoulin this way: "He who lifts one hand and while listening quietly can hear a sound which no ears hear, can surpass all conscious knowledge. He can leave the world of distinctions behind him; he may cross the ocean of the *karma* of rebirths, and he may break through the darkness of ignorance. In the enlightenment he attains to unlimited freedom" (172).

To the western mind, this unlimited freedom is most easily symbolized in children, and this, of course, is why Salinger relies on the child as symbol so often in *Nine Stories*. Sybil of "A Perfect Day for Bananafish," Ramona of "Uncle Wiggily in Connecticut," Esmé in "For Esmé—With Love and Squalor," and even the outrageously precocious "Teddy" of the story bearing his name all embody, to one degree or another, the state of enlightenment against which Salinger posits the inadequate conventional wisdom of the adults who populate their world. To become like children, his adult characters must struggle with the *koan* paradox until their minds are literally dragged to the edge of Holden Caulfield's "crazy cliff" and beyond. The same thing happens to us as we read Salinger. His stories often end in a puzzling way, often with lines that at first seem to make no sense and we are forced to ask what happened, what does this mean. As we try to answer such questions, we find ourselves in the same dilemma as the student of Zen and come to realize that we are dealing with a stern taskmaster who is trying to guide us toward the Way, who is trying to get us to vomit up the apple of logic.

Note

1. Heinrich Dumoulin, *History of Zen Buddhism*, cited by Bernice and Sanford Goldstein, "Zen and Nine Stories," *Renascence* 22 (1970): 172.

Bruce Bawer

Like many other Beat and hippie-era American children in search of pure and sweet and simple keys to the cosmos, Salinger was, it is clear, drawn all too easily into the black hole of Oriental mysticism, where Western systems of aesthetic valuation have no place and where a Seymour Glass—child prodigy, Oriental poet, spiritual *Übermensch*, and tragiheroic suicide—could evolve post-haste into an all but godlike symbol, the typical Salinger protagonist taken to its illogical extreme. So fascinated did Salinger become with the idea of Seymour that he lost all interest in plot, pace, characterization, conflict, and other such irrelevancies; far from being recognizable works of contemporary American fiction directed at a literary audience, his last two published prose pieces are, rather, letters to himself—gospels, as it were, about the Glass family, that private pantheon of eternally puerile Olympians.

To be sure, generations of celebrated American writers have been nearly as devoted as Salinger to the theme of innocence and experience, to the exploration of characters who are extraordinarily pure in soul or who refuse to accept adulthood or whose characteristically American guilelessness is contrasted tellingly and tragically with the sophistication and corruption of Europe. One thinks—to select only a few representative names—of Melville's Billy Budd, Twain's Huckleberry Finn, James's Daisy Miller. (The writer as a child of sorts has also, in this century at least, become a peculiar American institution: one thinks of Fitzgerald, Hemingway, Mailer.) Leslie Fiedler wrote an entire book, *Love and Death in the American Novel*, demonstrating that the protagonists of American fiction since the time of Cooper had, to an extent unprecedented in Western literature, been notable for their aversion to adult relationships and responsibilities. But the writers—at least the greatest writers—of the works in question did not themselves *endorse* their characters' childish aversions; they did not see those characters' immature behavior as marks of superiority.

From "Salinger's Arrested Development," *New Criterion* 5 (September 1986): 34–47.
© 1986 by Bruce Bawer. Reprinted by permission of the author.

And that is where J. D. Salinger is different. For, despite its many virtues, its frequent charm and felicity of style, the bulk of Salinger's fiction is seriously weakened by the fact that he is congenitally less interested in getting to the bottom of his characters' emotionally retarded behavior than he is in celebrating it; less interested in creating a credible fictional universe than in sequestering himself within a private, privileged nursery with his child-heroes and childish heroes, a place from which he can look down upon those numberless masses who are not only less sensitive and intelligent, but less beautiful, sophisticated, and wealthy, than his protagonists. (And who, incidentally, unlike most of his central characters, neither have a connection to show business nor look down upon it as fervently as Salinger thinks they should.) For all his supposed spiritual enlightenment, then, Salinger manifestly remained, throughout his public writing career, as snobbish as he had been at military school and college. It is dismaying, but should not be surprising, that so contemptuous a man, however considerable his talent, was unable to produce a more consequential body of work than that which he has bequeathed us. Nor, alas—given the current literary climate, in which cultish devotions and sentimental attachments often count as strongly as sensible critical evaluation in the making of a literary reputation—is it surprising that the immense esteem in which Salinger is held by literate Americans should continue to stand in such remarkable disproportion to the actual level of his literary achievement.

Edward Stone

"De Daumier-Smith's Blue Period" is a phase in the young life of the painter-teacher who tells the story. It is one that he enters and from which he emerges toward the end of the story. Our concern is with the reason why the Blue Period began, then why it ended; with the factors or events causing it and then those which are responsible for his outgrowing it. Here we become aware of a variety of correspondences to Salinger's story, two of which are important to our understanding of it: one of these is from German poetry and the other, from French painting. Even with this awareness, the full intent of "De Daumier-Smith's Blue Period" may evade us, its underlying sentiment being carefully restrained—even mocked good-naturedly—perhaps in an attempt to avoid mawkishness. And understandably, if so. For what Salinger has written is an intimate confession of the irrational conduct that grief at his mother's death caused in a young man of nineteen in the year 1939.

The story opens with the removal, resulting from her death, of her son and her husband (but the son's stepfather) from Paris back to New York. The young man (his name is probably John Smith, but we are never told) reacts by rejecting both New York and stepfather. He chafes at the enforced intimacy of the room they share at the Ritz, at his dependence on the stepfather for everything. His other rejection takes the form of revulsion at the crudity and commercialism of the culture of his new home, New York City (in which he spent the first ten years of his life), and a steadfast devotion to the charm of the old one, France. This latter brings about an early departure from both stepfather and step-country. Off the young man goes to the only French civilization he is in a position to afford, Montreal. The term by which, years later, he describes his mental condition at this point in his life is applied indirectly, but it is borrowed directly from psychiatry: it is trauma.

From *A Certain Morbidness: A View of American Literature* by Edward Stone (Carbondale: Southern Illinois University Press, 1969), 121–24, 132–34. © 1969 by Southern Illinois University Press. Reprinted by permission.

He has been accepted as an instructor in a correspondence school of art in Montreal run by a Japanese couple for students that none of them ever see. This provides a complete suspension of reality for young Smith, who has arrived affecting a completely new identity (dress, name, age, and so on) and who has chosen this way of living as necessary to sustain his illusion. (What other measures he takes we shall see shortly.)

At first, disillusion threatens. The Yoshotos treat him with mysterious impersonality; his quarters border on primitiveness; and they give him no work to do worthy of his talents. Then, as he is accepted and given pupils of his own, he recovers his peace of mind. Even the ineptitude of his first pupils does not dismay him, for among them is one, Sister Irma, whose work, untutored though it is, reveals a talent that excites him. He pours out professional advice (and makes personal advances) to her in his letter. But this dear relationship with the correspondence student is abruptly ended by a note from the father superior canceling her enrollment in the course.

Before and after this setback, he has a most unusual experience. This is the crisis toward which his frame of mind has been impelling him. When it is over, the story ends quickly. What happens is that he has a vision: first, a foreshadowing, then a veritable initiation. Both occur in front of the window of an orthopedics appliance store, above which the art institute has its quarters. Although he both does and does not invest this vision with the importance of an epiphany or religious revelation, that is actually what it is, incongruity, comedy, and all.

In the experience that foreshadows his initiation, a "hideous" intuition visits him while he is still in a state of excitement and expectation about the reply awaited from Sister Irma. He looks at the display in the window and thinks that "no matter how coolly or sensibly or gracefully I might one day learn to live my life, I would always at best be a visitor in a garden of enamel urinals and bedpans, with a sightless, wooden dummy-deity standing by in a marked-down rupture truss."

As for the vision itself that comes later, his commentary on it both deprecates and aggrandizes it. Disclaimer and all, he devotes a fairly substantial paragraph entirely to preparing the reader for it. While not "even a border-line case . . . of genuine mysticism," still it is "extremely out of the way," is "extraordinary," and "quite transcendent." This time he actually sees a visitor in the garden of enamel urinals and bedpans, tending the wooden dummy. His presence and friendly gesture discompose the young woman. She falls, but then recovers and resumes her work. At this point, the young man experiences a blinding sensation that dizzies him. When he can see again, the girl is gone and the vision is over, but not its effects.

This much of the story we perceive, however indistinctly, by ourselves. But the crucial vision that brings about this change of affairs will continue to seem unaccountably incongruous in its seriousness, even intensity, in a story characteristically self-mocking, even comical, if we do not recognize it for what it appears to be: a burlesque, possibly even of two famous visions, one ancient, the other modern, and both intensely religious. . . .

Being an art enthusiast, he naturally finds himself drawn to and identifying himself with the greatest period of Picasso's life, the Blue Period ("the glory, long forfeited, that had been his"). He develops a passion for blue. The suit which he puts on for the opening day of the art school is blue: he thinks the color "appropriate for an instructor" of art. Of all the many water colors of Yoshoto the one he still dreams of today is an exciting tour de force of blue: "white geese flying through an extremely pale-blue sky, with . . . the blueness of the sky, or an ethos of the blueness of the sky, reflected in the bird's feathers." (This impression is precisely like the one the faded autumn blossoms have on Rilke in "Blue Hydrangeas": they have no blue of their own, but reflect and mirror the blue of the sky.) He is struck by the contents of the nun's envelope, by one painting in particular. Where Picasso had first displayed his grief by painting a large burial scene of his friend Casagemas, the suicide, Sister Irma had painted a large burial scene of Christ. Equally important is a detail in this painting that the young man cites three times, a detail straight out of Picasso's famous Blue Period: a prostitute, Mary Magdalene, and a prostitute, moreover, dressed in a "blue outfit." In all of this, I think, the young man recognizes not only Picasso but himself: another possibly young person crushed by the crass burdens of daily existence (Sister Irma spends her convent life teaching cooking, as well as drawing, and to children, at that) and finding release for her spirit by expressing herself in funerals, prostitutes, and blue. She and he even have both been oppressed by a man with the same name: just as a Zimmerman was the dentist who had pulled eight of the disguised-name young instructor's teeth, so a Zimmerman was the Father who directed the life of a woman of concealed age and appearance and of real talent. This would explain why he is excited by her work and alternates technical advice with questions about her life and proposals for a meeting. These latter concerns betray

151

his inner motives (as he eventually realizes): mixed with his dispassionate and professional attitude is a distinctly erotic one, which he as much as tells us in his well-related love fantasy. Thus, his discomfiture when he reads Father Zimmerman's letter canceling Sister Irma's enrollment, and his rediscovery of himself, made possible by the blinding experience before the shopwindow, discussed above.

As a result, he knows that his actions since returning from France have all been a madness arising from unbearable grief. Invited or not, disillusions knock at our door, and we cannot stay in the dark. Although he had tried to spiritualize his intentions toward the nun (by visualizing himself as "the Peter Abelard-type man"), his intentions all along had been erotic. So now he renounces them and demonstrates his renunciation of hypocrisy as well by giving himself over freely to the vulgar pastime of contemplating girls in shorts on the beach. "It was Freud who defined neurosis as 'abnormal attachment to the past' and who urged what Philip Rieff calls an 'ideal contemporaneity' as the measure of health."[1] And his rejoining of the present and of actuality is demonstrated also by his returning to the United States to do his ogling. He has outlived his Blue Period—his grief at his mother's death—his hatred of the country he has had to return to, and his idealization of his natural feelings toward women.

In so doing, he is renouncing the poseur as he is outliving grief. He who had been in love with his dead mother is acknowledging woman alive (not dead or cloistered). Now that the Blue Period is over, he and we can see it as a passing phase. With him, as with his beloved Picasso (whose well-known, public plight thus illuminates the young man's private plight), grief at the death of a loved one at last wears out. Recovering, he proceeds to the Period of life and love and the flesh as it really is—Rose.

Note

1. Frederick C. Crews, *The Sins of the Fathers: Hawthorne's Psychological Themes* (New York: Oxford University Press, 1966), 265.

Warren French

Salinger did not settle on this final direction for his story-telling at once. Readers could find no indication that "Franny," which appeared in the *New Yorker* of 29 January 1955, had any relationship to the two earlier stories, "A Perfect Day for Bananafish" and "Down at the Dinghy," which featured members of the Glass family. Rather readers were somewhat scandalized to find that Salinger had left innocent children behind and was apparently writing about a distraught college girl who was experiencing a bout of morning sickness while visiting during a football weekend at an Ivy League college the arrogant boyfriend who was the father of her unborn child.

Almost two and one-half years passed before the title character of this earlier story was identified as Franny Glass, the youngest of Seymour's six siblings. It was also made clear that this Franny Glass was not pregnant during the morning episode with the boyfriend, but was, as sympathetic readers had thought all along, suffering a nervous breakdown resulting from a spiritual crisis.

But had the girl in the earlier story always been Franny Glass? Her last name was never mentioned in the story; some brothers were mentioned as having come to see her in a play, but they were not named. Franny Glass had appeared in November 1955 in "Raise High the Roof Beam, Carpenters," but she was not specifically identified as the girl from the earlier story, though readers probably took for granted that she was, because she would have been about the right age (Franny Glass is identified as eight in May 1942 in "Raise High the Roof Beam, Carpenters"). When "Zooey" in 1957 continued the story of "Franny" as that of Franny Glass, readers just assumed that this was what Salinger had had in mind all along.

John Updike cast doubts upon this easy assumption when he reviewed *Franny and Zooey*, the volume into which the two stories were

From *J. D. Salinger Revisited* by Warren French (Boston: Twayne, 1988), "Franny," 89–93. © 1988 by Twayne Publishers, a division of G. K. Hall & Co. Reprinted by permission of the publisher.

collected in 1961, for the *New York Times Book Review,* but enthusiasts were too excited to pay attention to cavilers; during the first months after publication they made it Salinger's best-selling book.

Updike flatly asserts that the two Frannies were not the same girl. The first he describes as "a pretty college girl passing through a plausible moment of disgust," who comes from a family of "standard upper-middle class gentry" in "what is recognizably our world."[1] The second he describes as one of the "dream world" children of the vaudeville team of Gallagher and Glass. Updike seizes on a key discrepancy that Salinger tried rather clumsily to cover up in the second story. In "Franny," the title character borrows a book called *The Way of a Pilgrim* from the college library on the recommendation of the professor from whom she is taking a religion survey.[2] In "Zooey," her brother identifies the book she is carrying to their mother as *The Pilgrim Continues His Way,* a sequel to the other, both of which Franny got from Seymour's old room where they had been sitting on his desk for as long as Zooey can remember. Salinger does have mother Bessie Glass explain that boyfriend Lane Coutell had said that Franny got it from the college library, and it is plausible that Franny might not have wanted to reveal its actual source to the skeptical Lane. Updike is on quite firm ground when he wonders, however, "how a girl raised in a home where Buddhism and crisis theology were table talk could have postponed her own crisis so long, and, when it came, be so disarmed by it." Eberhard Alsen also questions whether a girl who had "received religious training in Seymour's 'home seminars' for many years" would have taken an introductory religion course in college.[3] Certainly the girl in the first story does not sound like a hardened veteran of the radio quiz program, "It's a Wise Child," on which sister Boo Boo reports that at eight she could stand her ground against an obtuse announcer ("Raise High the Roof Beam, Carpenters" [10]).

I do not agree with Alsen, however, that the story was written before "Teddy." Salinger's former wife Claire's brother has said that she was "hung on the Jesus Prayer," and Salinger did not meet her until after "Teddy" was published.[4] It seems entirely plausible that Salinger had seized upon the idea of a college girl's spiritual crisis as the basis for a contrasting companion piece to "Teddy" in a new series of stories about the difficulties of living a spiritual life in an egotistic society. In contrast to Teddy, whose spiritual quest ended in his departing this world, Franny becomes a pilgrim, humbly trying to preserve by praying without ceasing her spiritual integrity in spite of the obstacles posed by her supercilious and self-promoting boy friend, who disappears after a few frantic phone calls in "Zooey." Franny (whoever she may be) and Lane Coutell serve as excellent allegorical representations of the sacred and profane unhappily coupled. In any event, the story launched Salinger on a new cycle, one that resembled French filmmaker Eric Rohmer's later sequence of moral fables, including *My Night at Maud's* and *Claire's Knee*, although one wonders, as Updike also did, what even the original Franny and Lane could have seen in each other.

Read as the isolated story it may originally have been, "Franny" today does not stand up very well. Most readers have probably come to regard it as a necessary prologue to "Zooey," which carries us deeply into the history of the Glass family and Salinger's theories of artistic integrity. By itself, the story strains credibility. The leering and self-congratulating Lane is too much a caricature of the "section man" at an Ivy League college; he seems to have been too spitefully prompted to suggest compassionate detachment on the author's part. Franny, on the other hand, is just too much of a nervous wreck to have ever continued at one of the "seven sisters," even if she had survived the selection procedures of what now seems an undemanding time. It is easy to see why the first readers of the tale suspected Franny was pregnant; Lane is so insensitive to her condition and so intent on bedding her down, while her hysteria seems totally incommensurate to Lane's affectations that one cannot take it seriously unless Franny is truly "in trouble" in the sense intended in those days of curfews when *New Yorker* readers would have swooned at the thought of co-ed dormitories. (We need to be reminded today that in 1953 the use of the word *virgin* in Otto Preminger's lightweight comedy film *The Moon Is Blue* brought down thunderous condemnation from pulpits all over the nation.)

Properly attuned readers in those days, however, could share Franny's spiritual crisis. Salinger had a rich territory largely to himself. Eastern religious thought had, of course, attracted avant-garde Americans since the days of the transcendentalists in the nineteenth century, but the resolution of spiritual dilemmas that made Somerset Maugham's *The Razor's Edge* a best-seller in 1944 was still a somewhat suspect novelty even in trendy Manhattan. Enthusiasm for the swamis Salinger began to consult in the 1950s was just beginning to filter up from the underground (Allen Ginsberg's *Howl* was first delivered just a month before "Raise High the Roof Beam, Carpenters" appeared); and the

Maharishi's mass marketing of transcendental meditation was almost a decade in the future, when it received a temporary assist from the Beatles.

New Yorker readers could share Franny's histrionic response to the dehumanizing ego, ego, ego of Madison Avenue's hollow men in gray flannel suits. Since then, however, readers have taken the road to minimalism after surviving the fragmentation of the meditation movement, the airport encounters with agents of the Hare Krishna, the rise and fall of the Bhagwam, the wedding of spirituality with high finance by Dr. Moon, and the campaigns of the native "Jesusfreaks" and television evangelists, with their "cash for God's sake" appeals, climaxing in the self-consuming holocaust at Jonestown. Lane's diffident skepticism and Franny's angst are less heart-rending today than when Salinger's "amateur readers" (see the dedication to his last book) were dazedly emerging from the convulsive dying days of McCarthyism.

Allen Ginsberg's *Howl* remains a much more powerful battlecry from a generation that had seen its "best minds destroyed" than Franny's vaporizings, and Lane's arch posturings now seem a trivial threat to humanism compared to the secret activities that we know now were then under way at our major universities. The road to the Orient— whether taken for our disastrous military adventure or a search for sentimental spirituality—has not proved a rewarding one for American pilgrims. "Franny" is today, much more than *Catcher in the Rye* or most of Salinger's nine stories, a period piece, reminding us of a time when perhaps the ultimate American failure resulted from an attempt to confront too much insensibility with too much sensibility.

Notes

1. John Updike, "Anxious Days for the Glass Family," *New York Times Book Review*, 17 September 1961, rpt. in *Salinger: A Critical and Personal Portrait*, ed. Henry Anatole Grunwald (New York: Harper & Row, 1962), 53–55.

2. J. D. Salinger, *Franny and Zooey* (Boston: Little, Brown, 1961), 32.

3. Eberhard Alsen, *Salinger's Glass Stories as a Composite Novel* (Troy, N.Y.: Whitston, 1983), follows Updike in summing up the evidence that "Franny" was written before Salinger's plan for the Glass family series had taken shape (21).

4. [Jack Skow,] "Sonny: An Introduction," *Time*, 15 September 1961, 89.

George Panichas

Critical estimates of J. D. Salinger's *Franny and Zooey* invariably contain references to the profound influence made on Franny Glass by a little book of Russian Orthodox spirituality, *The Way of a Pilgrim*.[1] It is obvious that Salinger attaches much significance to this work of Russian piety, as is clearly registered in his depiction of Franny's response to the book. This influence, however, does not necessarily prove distinct structural affinities or parallels, but rather reveals a sensitive recognition on Salinger's part of the moving spirit and message of *The Way of a Pilgrim*. That is to say, Salinger, in showing the influence of this book on Franny, confesses at the same time a decidedly sympathetic and intuitive understanding of the Russian work. He seems to have found in it what might be called a transcending religious meaning and experience; and in his characterization of Franny he re-creates the form, direction, and power of such an experience. *Franny and Zooey* is, then, another example of how modern fiction can affirm the divinity of all men.

The difficulties and the doubts that Salinger must have experienced in order to achieve a positive realization of *The Way of a Pilgrim* are readily seen at the beginning of *Franny and Zooey*, where allusions to the Russian book are couched in obscure, even suspicious terms. Like Franny, Salinger seems at first somewhat ashamed of the "small pea-green clothbound book," which Lane Coutell notices Franny carrying in her left hand when he meets her on the station platform. She has come to join him for "the weekend of the Yale game." He questions her about the book, but she avoids discussing it and quickly stuffs it into her handbag. Yet, by the end of Salinger's book, *The Way of a Pilgrim* is freed from this preliminary obscurity and suspicion. Gradually, its title and content are referred to freely and fearlessly, and its

From *The Reverent Discipline: Essays on Literary Criticism and Culture* by George Panichas (Knoxville: University of Tennessee Press, 1974), "J. D. Salinger and the Russian Pilgrim," 292–94. © 1974 by the University of Tennessee Press. Reprinted by permission of the author.

growing significance becomes incontestable. Indeed, at the conclusion of *Franny and Zooey* the spirit and inspiration of *The Way of a Pilgrim* have become convincing and impelling, and the earlier process of grudging discovery is transformed into an undoubting triumph of affirmation. *The Way of a Pilgrim* is no longer "just something," but the way to redemption and the very beauty and wisdom that Franny desperately and painfully longed for.

It would be best at this point to say a few things about *The Way of a Pilgrim* before going on to appraise its significance in Salinger's work. The complete title of the book is *The Way of a Pilgrim and The Pilgrim Continues His Way*, translated from the Russian by R. M. French. The first translation of *The Way of a Pilgrim* was published in 1930, and its sequel, *The Pilgrim Continues His Way*, was published separately at a later date; in 1941 both were published for the first time as a continuous narrative in one volume. The Pilgrim's story was first discovered in manuscript form at a Greek Orthodox monastery on Mount Athos by a Russian abbot, who copied the manuscript, on the basis of which a book was published in Kazan in 1884. This volume narrates the experiences of a Russian wanderer over the steppes and fields of Russia at some time prior to the liberation of the serfs in 1861. In particular it is the story of the Pilgrim's practicing a way of prayer which arises out of his desire to understand the words "Pray without ceasing," from the first Epistle of Saint Paul to the Thessalonians. In the process of learning the meaning of "unceasing interior prayer," the Pilgrim seeks the advice of a monk (*staretz*) known for his wisdom and spiritual counsel. "Learn first to acquire the power of prayer," he is advised, "and you will easily practise all the other virtues" (8). The monk also tells him that the essence of the prayer is found in the words "Lord Jesus Christ, have mercy on me." Soon the Pilgrim obtains a copy of the *Philokalia*, or *The Love of Spiritual Beauty*, a collection of mystical and ascetic writings by the Fathers of the Eastern Orthodox Church. Compiled in the eighteenth century, the Greek *Philokalia* was first published in Venice in 1782; in the nineteenth century it was translated into Russian (*Dobrotolubiye*), and this translation was to play an important role in Russian religious life and thought.

Often described as "the foremost and best manual of the contemplative spiritual life," the *Philokalia* was to be for the Pilgrim a major guide in his attaining purification and in his comprehending more fully the Jesus Prayer. This achievement was no easy matter, for the Pilgrim was to experience the inevitable assaults of laziness, boredom, and distraction. It was not merely a matter of learning and repeating the Jesus Prayer, but of making it become a "self-acting spiritual prayer." Constant effort and stern self-discipline are necessary for the Pilgrim to purge his soul. In the end, with the understanding and assistance of his *staretz*, the Pilgrim discovers the mystery of prayer. He gradually reaches a state of happiness and innocence, free from evil-thinking and an ego-tainted consciousness. Although he is only thirty-three years of age, the Pilgrim is a widower. He has a withered left arm. His sole worldly possessions are a knapsack containing some dried bread, a Bible, and the *Philokalia*. Nevertheless, in his arduous travels and in his encounters with all kinds of persons, he meets with success; for the Jesus Prayer has become an organic part of his life and purpose, enabling him to see and feel God everywhere.

From all this it should not be inferred that Salinger has adopted Russian mysticism as a kind of religious prop or that he has been experimenting with Eastern Orthodoxy as a means of religious conversion. On the contrary, his approach is entirely nonsectarian: it is mainly a search for religious meaning and for spiritual vision on higher levels of experience. It is expressed in a preeminently modern idiom and context. The fact remains that *Franny and Zooey* is not a "devotional manual," but rather a creative work of art that transcends religious doctrine, creed, and so-called theological dimensions. Its preoccupation is with religious sensibility, with vital emotions, responses, and instincts outside the pale of the rational and the empirical. Any attempt to treat Salinger's work on a religious plane should be detached from the strictly theological and homiletic. Religion, *not* religiosity, is what distinguishes *Franny and Zooey*.

Note

1. J. D. Salinger, *Franny and Zooey* (Boston: Little, Brown, 1961); *The Way of a Pilgrim and The Pilgrim Continues His Way*, trans. R. M. French (New York: Harper, 1954).

Bernice and Sanford Goldstein

While it is true that Zen has become a glittering catchword as connotative as existentialism and at times as meaningless, the fact remains that Zen does exist and that Salinger has shown a definite partiality towards it. Since Zen recognizes that all boundaries are artificial, Salinger's Western experience is not outside the universe Zen encompasses. The importance of the present moment; the long search and struggle in which reason, logic, cleverness, and intellect prove ineffectual; the inadequacy of judgment and criticism which reinforce and stimulate the artificial boundary between self and other; and some degree of enlightenment which results from the non-rational and spontaneous blending of dualities, an enlightenment which permits experience that is complete and unadulterated and makes the moment and, in effect, life non-phoney—all these aspects of Zen can be found in Salinger's world.

First, what is Zen and what is the participant in Zen experience? An explanation of the latter may help clarify the former. The main actor in the typical Zen drama is besieged by doubt and desire. He is not at all certain what enlightenment is, but is convinced it exists, wants it, and is willing to struggle for it. Believing enlightenment is remote from him yet intensely desiring it, he pursues it only to find it continually eludes him. This peculiar dilemma results from the fact that he believes the search he is making with all his heart and mind, with all his being and self and ego, is for something that is *outside* himself. The Zen master, to whom he has gone for guidance towards the Way, grants him formal interviews with an abundance of ceremony which are probably intended to make him fully cognizant and thoroughly frightened, so the seeker fails in the exercise of the spontaneous answer to the irrational question, for example, "What is the sound of one hand clap-

From "Zen and Salinger," *Modern Fiction Studies* 12 (Autumn 1966): 313–16. © 1966 by Purdue Research Foundation, West Lafayette, Indiana. Reprinted by permission.

ping?" When not being questioned by the Zen master, the disciple spends time in the traditional method of sitting, ponders over various *koan* or puzzles like the above, and does various tasks with a minimum of verbal distraction. He is not permitted any of the temporary satisfactions which give his ego an illusion of satisfaction or well-being. These pursuits are not done merely for the sake of subduing or chastising the ego in an attempt to make it deny itself, but rather to expose the ego itself as an artificial entity whose very *searching for enlightenment* is spurious. . . .

Zen's peculiar problem is to bring the self back into a kind of controlled state of infantile non-separation through which it can recognize the arbitrary nature of all the artificial boundaries set up by abstraction and can see the unity in all experience and the existence of ego within that unity. The student seeking enlightenment, therefore, must proceed through his long search and struggle in which reason, logic, cleverness, and intellect prove useless; he must recognize that judgment and criticism reinforce and stimulate the artificial boundary lines of the ego. Finally in the non-rational blending of spurious dualities, he may acquire some degree of enlightenment which will enable him to fully participate in every moment of his day-to-day life. The Zen Master Yasutani-Roshi recites to one of his students the following lines from a famous master: "'When I heard the temple bell ring, suddenly there was no bell and no I, just sound.' In other words, he no longer was aware of a distinction between himself, the bell, the sound, and the universe."[1]

We feel Salinger's main aim is to have his Glass children achieve the liberated moment, that is, experiences fully lived in which there is no separation between self and other. The major conflict in Franny, Zooey, and Buddy concerns the way to achieve this liberated state. Their Zen master is the dead Seymour. The concentrated area in which they will be permitted to act fully, freely, spontaneously, in their chosen métier. . . .

Since Franny, Zooey, and Buddy all desire to reach the state that Seymour had attained, their problem is how to achieve it. What is to be their process toward enlightenment? Salinger, we feel, has in mind a verbal, highly speeded-up version of Zen enlightenment as he conceives it. To take the final step first: the wisdom eventually attained by Franny, Zooey, and Buddy is the wisdom of merging opposites, that is, the cancelling out of supposed opposites, events, objects, ideas, states of feeling, persons, for all dualities are merely arbitrarily drawn lines.

Note

1. Philip Kapleau, *The Three Pillars of Zen* (Tokyo: John Westerhill, 1965), 107.

Chronology

1919   Jerome David Salinger is born 1 January in New York City to Sol and Miriam (formerly Marie Jillich) Salinger.

1932   Attends the McBurney School in Manhattan, where he manages the school fencing team, performs a female part in two plays, and reports for the student newspaper.

1934   Attends Valley Forge Military Academy in Pennsylvania, where he supposedly writes stories by flashlight under covers after lights-out. Serves as literary editor of his class yearbook, *Crossed Sabres*, and is a member of the school's Mask and Spur Dramatic Club.

1936   Graduates from Valley Forge Military Academy.

1937   Enrolls at New York University and travels to Europe in summer.

1938   Attends Ursinus College in Collegeville, Pennsylvania, in fall; for nine weeks writes a column, "The Skipped Diploma," for the *Ursinus Weekly.*

1939   During spring enrolls in Whit Burnett's writing class at Columbia University.

1940   Publishes "The Young Folks" (*Story*); "Go See Eddie" (*University of Kansas City Review*).

1941   "The Hang of It" (*Collier's*); "The Heart of a Broken Story" (*Esquire*). Sells "Slight Rebellion off Madison" to the *New Yorker,* which publishes the story in 1946.

1942   "The Long Debut of Lois Taggett" (*Story*); "Personal Notes on an Infantryman" (*Collier's*). Is drafted into the U.S. Army. "Paula" is sold to *Stag* magazine, but the manuscript is never published.

1943   "The Varioni Brothers" (*Saturday Evening Post*). Is stationed in Nashville, Tennessee, with the rank of staff sergeant; is admitted to the Army Counter Intelligence Corps.

1944 "Both Parties Concerned" (*Saturday Evening Post*); "Soft-Boiled Sergeant" (*Saturday Evening Post*); "Last Day of the Last Furlough" (*Saturday Evening Post*); "Once a Week Won't Kill You" (*Story*). Undergoes counterintelligence training in Devonshire, England; on D day lands on Utah Beach.

1945 "Elaine" (*Story*); "A Boy in France" (*Saturday Evening Post*); "This Sandwich Has No Mayonnaise" (*Esquire*); "The Stranger" (*Collier's*); "I'm Crazy" (*Collier's*). Is discharged from the army.

1946 "Slight Rebellion off Madison" (*New Yorker*). Completes, submits, and withdraws a novella about Holden Caulfield.

1947 "A Young Girl in 1941 with No Waist at All" (*Mademoiselle*); "The Inverted Forest" (*Cosmopolitan*).

1948 "A Perfect Day for Bananafish" (*New Yorker*); "A Girl I Knew" (*Good Housekeeping*); "Uncle Wiggily in Connecticut" (*New Yorker*); "Just before the War with the Eskimos" (*New Yorker*); "Blue Melody" (*Cosmopolitan*).

1949 "The Laughing Man" (*New Yorker*); "Down at the Dinghy" (*Harper's*).

1950 "For Esmé—with Love and Squalor" (*New Yorker*).

1951 "Pretty Mouth and Green My Eyes" (*New Yorker*); *The Catcher in the Rye*.

1952 "De Daumier-Smith's Blue Period" (*World Review*).

1953 "Teddy" (*New Yorker*); *Nine Stories*. Moves to Cornish, New Hampshire.

1955 "Franny" (*New Yorker*); "Raise High the Roof Beam, Carpenters" (*New Yorker*). Marries Claire Douglas on 17 February; a daughter, Margaret Ann, is born on 10 December.

1957 "Zooey" (*New Yorker*).

1959 "Seymour: An Introduction" (*New Yorker*).

1960 A son, Matthew, is born on 13 February.

1961 *Franny and Zooey*.

1963 *Raise High the Roof Beam, Carpenters and Seymour: An Introduction*.

1965 "Hapworth 16, 1924" (*New Yorker*)—most recent published story.

1967 Is divorced from Claire Salinger.

1974 *The Complete Uncollected Stories of J. D. Salinger,* a pirated edition, appears, prompting Salinger to give a telephone interview to the *New York Times* in order to decry this publication.

1975 "Epilogue: A Salute to Whit Burnett, 1899–1972" (*Fiction Writer's Handbook*). The piece was probably written in 1965.

1977 Appearance of an unsigned tale, "For Rupert—with No Promises" (*Esquire*), creates a Salinger-is-back stir but proves to have been written by Gordon Lish, fiction editor of *Esquire*.

1986 Salinger is granted an injunction to halt the publication by Random House of Ian Hamilton's unauthorized biography.

1987 The ruling against Random House and Ian Hamilton is made permanent when the U.S. Supreme Court refuses to review earlier verdicts.

Selected Bibliography

Primary Works

Short Fiction Collections

Franny and Zooey. Boston: Little, Brown, 1961. Both stories first published in the *New Yorker*: "Franny," 29 January 1955, 24–32, 35–43; "Zooey," 4 May 1957, 32–42, 44–139.

Nine Stories. Boston: Little, Brown, 1953. The stories and where they were first published are as follows: "A Perfect Day for Bananafish," *New Yorker*, 31 January 1948, 21–25; "Uncle Wiggily in Connecticut," *New Yorker*, 20 March 1948, 30–36; "Just before the War with the Eskimos," *New Yorker*, 5 June 1948, 37–40, 42, 44, 46; "The Laughing Man," *New Yorker*, 19 March 1949, 27–32; "Down at the Dinghy," *Harper's*, April 1949, 87–91; "For Esmé—with Love and Squalor," *New Yorker*, 8 April 1950, 28–36; "Pretty Mouth and Green My Eyes," *New Yorker*, 14 July 1951, 20–24; "De Daumier-Smith's Blue Period," *World Review* 39 (May 1952): 33–48; "Teddy," *New Yorker*, 31 January 1953, 26–36, 38.

Raise High the Roof Beam, Carpenters and Seymour: An Introduction. Boston: Little, Brown, 1963. Both stories first published in the *New Yorker*: "Raise High the Roof Beam, Carpenters," 19 November 1955, 51–58, 60–116; "Seymour: An Introduction," 6 June 1959, 42–52, 54–111.

Uncollected Stories

"Blue Melody." *Cosmopolitan*, September 1948, 51, 112–19.

"Both Parties Concerned." *Saturday Evening Post*, 26 February 1944, 14, 47–48.

"A Boy in France." *Saturday Evening Post*, 31 March 1945, 21, 92.

"Elaine." *Story* 26 (March–April 1945): 38–47.

"A Girl I Knew." *Good Housekeeping*, February 1948, 37, 186, 188, 191–96.

"Go See Eddie." *University of Kansas City Review* 7 (December 1940): 121–24.

"The Hang of It." *Collier's*, 12 July 1941, 22.

"Hapworth 16, 1924." *New Yorker*, 19 June 1965, 32–113.

"The Heart of a Broken Story." *Esquire*, September 1941, 32, 131, 132, 133.

"I'm Crazy." *Collier's*, 22 December 1945, 36, 48, 51.

166

"The Inverted Forest." *Cosmopolitan*, December 1947, 73–80, 85–86, 88, 90, 92, 95–96, 98, 100, 102, 107, 109.

"Last Day of the Last Furlough." *Saturday Evening Post*, 15 July 1944, 26–27, 61–62, 64.

"The Long Debut of Lois Taggett." *Story* 21 (September–October 1942): 28–34.

"Once a Week Won't Kill You." *Story* 25 (November–December 1944): 23–27.

"Personal Notes on an Infantryman." *Collier's*, 12 December 1942, 96.

"Slight Rebellion off Madison." *New Yorker*, 21 December 1946, 76–79.

"Soft-Boiled Sergeant." *Saturday Evening Post*, 26 February 1944, 18, 82, 84–85.

"The Stranger." *Collier's*, 1 December 1945, 18, 77.

"The Varioni Brothers." *Saturday Evening Post*, 17 July 1943, 12–13, 76–77.

"The Young Folks." *Story* 16 (March–April 1940): 26–30.

"This Sandwich Has No Mayonnaise." *Esquire*, October 1945, 54–64, 147–49.

"A Young Girl in 1941 with No Waist at All." *Mademoiselle*, May 1947, 222–223, 292–302.

Novel

The Catcher in the Rye. Boston: Little, Brown, 1951.

Secondary Works

Books

Alsen, Eberhard. *Salinger's Glass Stories as a Composite Novel.* Troy, N.Y.: Whitston, 1983.

Blotner, Joseph, and Frederick L. Gwynn. *The Fiction of J. D. Salinger.* Pittsburgh: University of Pittsburgh Press, 1958.

French, Warren. *J. D. Salinger.* Boston: Twayne, 1963; rev. ed. 1976.

———. *J. D. Salinger Revisited.* Boston: Twayne, 1988.

Grunwald, Henry Anatole, ed. *Salinger: A Critical and Personal Portrait.* New York: Harper & Row, 1962.

Hamilton, Ian. *In Search of J. D. Salinger.* New York: Random House, 1988.

Lundquist, James. *J. D. Salinger.* New York: Ungar, 1979.

Miller, James E., Jr. *J. D. Salinger.* Minneapolis: University of Minnesota Press, 1965.

Sublette, Jack R. *J. D. Salinger: An Annotated Bibliography, 1938–1981.* New York: Garland, 1984.

Articles and Parts of Books

Ahrne, Marianne. "Experience and Attitude in *The Catcher in the Rye* and *Nine Stories.*" *Moderna Sprak* 61, no. 3 (Fall 1967): 242–63.

Antico, John. "The Parody of J. D. Salinger: Esmé and the Fat Lady Exposed." *Modern Fiction Studies* 12 (Autumn 1966): 325–40.

Barr, Donald. "Saints, Pilgrims, and Artists." In *Salinger: A Critical and Personal Portrait,* edited by Henry Anatole Grunwald, 170–76. New York: Harper & Row, 1962.

Baskett, Sam S. "The Splendid/Squalid World of J. D. Salinger." *Wisconsin Studies in Contemporary Literature* 4 (Winter 1963): 48–61.

Bawer, Bruce. "Salinger's Arrested Development." *New Criterion* 5 (September 1986): 34–47.

Boe, Alfred. "Street Games in J. D. Salinger and Gerald Green." *Modern Fiction Studies* 33, no. 1 (Spring 1987): 65–72.

Bostwick, Sally. "Reality, Compassion, and Mysticism in the World of J. D. Salinger." *Midwest Review* 5 (Summer 1963): 30–43.

Bryan, James E. "J. D. Salinger: The Fat Lady and the Chicken Sandwich." *College English* 23 (December 1961): 226–29.

———. "Salinger's Seymour's Suicide." *College English* 24 (December 1962): 226–29.

———. "The Admiral and Her Sailor in Salinger's 'Down at the Dinghy.'" *Studies in Short Fiction* 17 (Spring 1980): 174–78.

Bufithis, Philip. "J. D. Salinger and the Psychiatrist." *West Virginia University Bulletin: Philological Papers* 21 (December 1974): 67–77.

Burke, Brother Fidelian, F.S.C. "Salinger's 'Esmé': Some Matters of Balance." *Modern Fiction Studies* 12 (Autumn 1966): 341–47.

Cotter, James Finn. "Religious Symbols in Salinger's Shorter Fiction." *Studies in Short Fiction* 15 (Spring 1978): 121–32.

Davis, Tom. "J. D. Salinger: The Identity of Sergeant X." *Western Humanities Review* 16 (Spring 1962): 181–83.

———. "J. D. Salinger: 'The Sound of One Hand Clapping.'" *Wisconsin Studies in Contemporary Literature* 4 (Winter 1963): 41–47.

Davison, Richard Allan. "Salinger Criticism and 'The Laughing Man': A Case of Arrested Development." *Studies in Short Fiction* 18 (Winter 1981): 1–15.

Deer, Irving, and John H. Randall III. "J. D. Salinger and the Reality beyond Words." *Lock Haven Review* 6 (Spring 1964): 14–29.

Elmen, Paul. "Twice-blessed Enamel Flowers: Reality in Contemporary Fiction." In *The Climate of Faith in Modern Literature,* edited by Nathan A. Scott, Jr., 84–101. New York: Seabury Press, 1964.

Fiedler, Leslie A. "The Eye of Innocence: Some Notes on the Role of the

Child in Literature." In his *No! in Thunder: Essays on Myth and Literature*, 251–91. Boston: Beacon Press, 1960.

Finkelstein, Sidney. "Cold War, Religious Revival, and Family Alienation: William Styron, J. D. Salinger, and Edward Albee." In his *Existentialism and Alienation in American Literature*, 219–34. New York: International Publishers, 1965.

Fosburgh, Lacey. "J. D. Salinger Speaks about His Silence." *New York Times*, 3 November 1974: 1, 69.

Galloway, David. "The Love Ethic." In his *The Absurd Hero in his American Fiction: Updike, Styron, Bellow, Salinger*, 204–27. Austin: University of Texas Press, 1966; rev. ed., 1981.

Genthe, Charles V. "Six, Sex, Sick: Seymour, Some Comments." *Twentieth Century Literature* 10 (January 1965): 170–71.

Goldstein, Bernice, and Sanford. "Zen and Salinger." *Modern Fiction Studies* 12 (Autumn 1966): 313–24.

———. "Bunnies and Cobras: Zen Enlightenment in Salinger." *Discourse* 13 (Winter 1970): 98–106.

———. "'Seymour: An Introduction'—Writing as Discovery." *Studies in Short Fiction* 7 (Spring 1970): 248–56.

———. "Zen and *Nine Stories*." *Renascence* 22 (Summer 1970): 171–82.

———. "Some Zen References in Salinger." *Literature East and West* 15, no. 1 (March 1971): 83–95.

———. "Seymour's Poems." *Literature East and West* 17 (June–September–December 1973): 335–48.

Gross, Theodore L. "J. D. Salinger: Suicide and Survival in the Modern World." In his *The Heroic Ideal in American Literature*, 262–71. New York: Free Press, 1971.

Hagopian, John V. "'Pretty Mouth and Green My Eyes': Salinger's Paulo and Francesca in New York." *Modern Fiction Studies* 12 (Autumn 1966): 349–54.

Hamilton, Kenneth. "J. D. Salinger's Happy Family." *Queen's Quarterly* 71 (Summer 1964): 176–87.

———. "One Way to Use the Bible: The Example of J. D. Salinger." *Christian Scholar* 47 (Fall 1964): 243–51.

Harper, Howard M., Jr. "J. D. Salinger—through the Glasses Darkly." In his *Desperate Faith: A Study of Bellow, Salinger, Mailer, Baldwin, and Updike*, 65–95. Chapel Hill: University of North Carolina Press, 1967.

Hassan, Ihab. "The Rare Quixotic Gesture." In *Salinger: A Critical and Personal Portrait*, edited by Henry Anatole Grunwald, 138–63. New York: Harper & Row, 1962.

———. "Almost the Voice of Silence: The Later Novelettes of J. D. Salinger." *Wisconsin Studies in Contemporary Literature* 4 (Winter 1963): 5–20.

Hermann, John. "J. D. Salinger: Hello Hello Hello." *College English* 22 (January 1961): 262–64.

Hicks, Granville. "The Search for Wisdom." In *Salinger: A Critical and Personal Portrait,* edited by Henry Anatole Grunwald, 191–94. New York: Harper & Row, 1962.

Jacobson, Josephine. "The Felicity of J. D. Salinger." *Commonweal,* 26 February 1960, 589–91.

Johannson, Ernest J. "Salinger's Seymour." *Carolina Quarterly* 12 (Winter 1959): 51–59.

Karlstetter, Klaus. "J. D. Salinger, R. W. Emerson, and the Perennial Philosophy." *Moderna Sprak* 63, no. 3 (Fall 1969): 224–36.

Kazin, Alfred. "'Everybody's Favorite.'" In *Salinger: A Critical and Personal Portrait,* edited by Henry Anatole Grunwald, 43–52. New York: Harper & Row, 1962.

Kinney, Arthur. "J. D. Salinger and the Search for Love." *Texas Studies in Literature and Language* 5 (Spring 1963): 111–26.

Kirschner, Paul. "Salinger and His Society." *Literary Half-Yearly* 12 (Fall 1971): 51–60; 14 (Fall 1973): 63–78.

Lane, Gary. "Seymour's Suicide Again: A New Reading of J. D. Salinger's 'A Perfect Day for Bananafish.'" *Studies in Short Fiction* 10 (Winter 1973): 27–33.

Levine, Paul. "J. D. Salinger: The Development of the Misfit Hero." *Twentieth Century Literature* 4 (October 1958): 92–99.

Livingston, James T. "J. D. Salinger: The Artist's Struggle to Stand on Holy Ground." In *Adversity and Grace,* edited by Nathan A. Scott, Jr., 113–32. Chicago: University of Chicago Press, 1968.

Lodge, David. "Postmodern Fiction." In his *The Modes of Modern Writing: Metaphor, Metonymy and the Typology of Modern Literature,* 241–42. Ithaca: Cornell University Press, 1979.

Lyons, John O. "The Romantic Style of Salinger's 'Seymour: An Introduction.'" *Wisconsin Studies in Contemporary Literature* 4 (Winter 1963): 62–69.

Metcalf, Frank. "The Suicide of Salinger's Seymour Glass." *Studies in Short Fiction* 9 (Summer 1972): 243–46.

Mizener, Arthur. "The Love Song of J. D. Salinger." In *Salinger: A Critical and Personal Portrait,* edited by Henry Anatole Grunwald, 23–36. New York: Harper & Row, 1962.

O'Connor, Dennis L. "J. D. Salinger's Religious Pluralism: The Example of *Raise High the Roof Beam, Carpenters." Southern Review* 20, no. 2 (April 1984): 316–32.

Ohmann, Richard. "The Shaping of a Canon: U.S. Fiction, 1960–1975." *Critical Inquiry* 10, no. 1 (September 1983): 199–223.

Panichas, George A. "J. D. Salinger and the Russian Pilgrim." In his *The Rev-*

erent Discipline: Essays in Literary Criticism and Culture, 292–305. Knoxville: University of Tennessee Press, 1974.

Phillips, Paul. "Salinger's *Franny and Zooey*." *Mainstream* 15 (January 1962): 32–39.

Piwinski, David J. "Salinger's 'De Daumier-Smith's Blue Period': Pseudonym as Cryptogram." *Notes on Contemporary Literature* 15, no. 5 (October 1985): 3–4.

Quagliano, Anthony. "'Hapworth 16, 1924': A Problem in Hagiography." *University of Dayton Review* 8 (Fall 1971): 35–43.

Russell, John. "Salinger's Feat." *Modern Fiction Studies* 12 (Autumn 1966): 299–311.

Seitzman, Daniel. "Therapy and Antitherapy in Salinger's 'Zooey.'" *American Imago* 25 (Summer 1968): 140–62.

Simms, L. Moody, Jr. "Seymour Glass: The Salingerian Hero as Vulgarian." *Notes on Contemporary Literature* 5 (November 1975): 6–8.

Skow, John. "Sonny: An Introduction." In *Salinger: A Critical and Personal Portrait*, edited by Henry Anatole Grunwald, 3–18. New York: Harper & Row, 1962.

Slabey, Robert M. "Sergeant X and Seymour Glass." *Western Humanities Review* 16 (Autumn 1962): 376–77.

Slethaug, G. E. "Form in Salinger's Shorter Fiction." *Canadian Review of American Studies* 3 (Spring 1972): 50–59.

Stein, William Bysshe. "Salinger's 'Teddy': *Tat Tvam Asi* or That Thou Art." *Arizona Quarterly* 29 (Autumn 1973): 253–65.

Stone, Edward. "J. D. Salinger." In his *A Certain Morbidness: A View of American Literature*, 121–39. Carbondale: Southern Illinois University Press, 1969.

Tanner, Tony. "Afterword: Wonder and Alienation—the Mystic and the Moviegoer." In his *The Reign of Wonder: Naivety and Reality in American Literature*, 336–61. Cambridge, England: Cambridge University Press, 1965.

Updike, John. "Franny and Zooey." In *Salinger: A Critical and Personal Portrait*, edited by Henry Anatole Grunwald, 53–56. New York: Harper & Row, 1962.

Weinberg, Helen. "J. D. Salinger's Holden and Seymour and the Spiritual Activist Hero." In her *The New Novel in America*, 141–64. Ithaca, N.Y.: Cornell University Press, 1970.

Wenke, John. "Sergeant X, Esmé, and the Meaning of Words." *Studies in Short Fiction* 18 (Summer 1981): 251–59.

Wiebe, Dallas E. "Salinger's 'A Perfect Day for Bananafish.'" *Explicator* 23 (September 1964): item 3.

Wiegand, William. "Seventy-eight Bananas." In *Salinger: A Critical and Personal Portrait*, edited by Henry Anatole Grunwald, 123–36. New York: Harper & Row, 1962.

———. "Salinger and Kierkegaard." *Minnesota Review* 5 (May–July 1965): 1137–56.

Index

Abbott, Lee K., *Strangers in Paradise*, 32–33
Alsen, Eberhard, 36–37, 66, 107, 154
Anderson, Sherwood, *Winesburg, Ohio*, 32

Barth, John, 12; *Lost in the Funhouse*, 32–33
Bawer, Bruce, 5, 122, 133, *146–47*
Blake, William, 21
Blaney, Shirley, 123, 127
Blotner, Joseph, and Frederick L. Gwynn, 5
Bostwick, Sally, 65
Burnett, Whit, 3, 16, 124

Capote, Truman, 124
Caulfield, Holden, 5, 6, 7, 16, *23–30*, 34, 42, 63, 72, 73, 80, 106, 123, 124, 129, 146
Chaplin, Charlie, 17, 124
Chapman, Mark David, 129
Collier's, 5, 9, 13, 14, 15, 124
Cooper, James Fenimore, 147
Cosmopolitan, 5

Davidson, Richard Allan, 45, 46
Death Takes a Holiday, 21
Dedalus, Stephen, 141
Deer, Irving, and John H. Randall, III, 46
Dickens, Charles, *Bleak House*, 75
Dickinson, Emily, 21
Die Zeit Ohne Beispiel, 51, 138
Dostoevski, Fyodor, 51, 70, 138
Dumoulin, Heinrich, *History of Zen Buddhism*, 143
Douglas, Claire [Salinger], 127

Eicho, Toyo, *Zenrin Kushu*, 145
Eliot, T. S., 68, 69; *The Waste Land*, 36
Eppes, Betty, 123
Esquire, 5, 14, 124

Faulkner, William, *Go Down, Moses*, 32
Fiedler, Leslie A., *Love and Death in the American Novel*, 147
Finn, Huck, 23, 24, 147
Fitzgerald, F. Scott, 67, 147
Flaubert, Gustave, 70, 73
Ford, Richard, 3; *Rock Springs*, 32–33
Fosburgh, Lacey, 129
French, Warren, 4, 6, 16, 24, 31, 37, 53, 59, 66, 133, *153–56*
Freud, Sigmund, 70, 152

Ginsberg, Allen, *Howl*, 155–56
Giroux, Robert, 125–26
Glass Family, The, 33, 38, *63–108*
Glass, Seymour, 5, 10, 16, 25, 32, 34–38, 39, 42, 43, 48, 63, 64, 65, 66, 71, 72, 73, 78, 79–89, *90–108*, 134, 136, 147, 161
Goldstein, Bernice and Sanford, 102, 133, *160–62*
Good Housekeeping, 5
Greenberg, John, 128, 129
Gross, Theodore L., 93, 101, 133, *134–35*

Hakuin, 143
Hamilton, Ian, 5, 12, 101, 108, 110n32, 122, 123, 124, 125, 128–29
Harper, Howard M. Jr., 57

Hassan, Ihab, 7, 52, 101, 102
Hawthorne, Nathaniel, 119; *The Scarlet Letter*, 75
Hayward, Susan, 125
Heller, Joseph, *Catch-22*, 15, 124
Hemingway, Ernest, 16, 124, 147; *In Our Time*, 32
Hope, Bob, 52

Jesus Christ, 86, 88, 98, 122
Jesus Prayer, The, *73–75*, 83, 84, 86, 87, 154, 158–59
Jillich, Marie [Miriam Salinger], 122
Joyce, James, *Dubliners*, 32–33; *Portrait of the Artist as a Young Man, A*, 140

Kafka, Franz, 3, 100, 102
Kierkegaard, Soren, 100, 102

Lardner, Ring, 4
Lennon, John, 129
Lundquist, James, 34, 102, *143–46*

Mailer, Norman, 120, 124; *The Naked and the Dead*, 15
Maugham, Somerset, *The Razor's Edge*, 155
Maxwell, William, 126
Melville, Herman, *Billy Budd*, 142, 147; *Typee*, 75
Miller, Daisy, 147
Miller, James E. Jr., 31, 35, 45, 94, 133, *136–42*
Minot, Susan, *Monkeys*, 32–33
Mizener, Arthur, 5
Mitty, Walter, 13
My Foolish Heart, 125

New Yorker, 6, 90, 108, 124, 125, 126, 127, 128, 135, 153, 155–56
New York Times, 126, 127, 128, 129

O'Connor, Dennis L., 92, 100
O'Hara, John, 4
O'Neill, Eugene, 124
O'Neill, Oona, 124

Panichas, George, 133, *157–59*
Philokalia, 158–59
Picasso, Pablo, 57, 151
Pilgrim Continues His Way, The, 73, 81, 85, 154, 158
Preminger, Otto, *The Moon Is Blue*, 155
Prufrock, J. Alfred, 13
Pynchon, Thomas, 12

Quagliano, Anthony, 107

Rieff, Philip, 152
Rilke, Rainer Maria, 35, 37, 151
Rohmer, Eric, *Claire's Knee, My Night at Maud's*, 155
Roth, Philip, 12
Russell, John, 57

St. Francis [of Assisi], 86
Salinger, J. D.: on artist figure, 5, *9–12*, 65, 84, 88, 95, 100–106, 134; biography of, *119–30;* on childhood, 8, 19, 21, 23, 30, 36–37, 39, *43–50*, 61, 63, 79, 122; Eastern thought, 33–34, 60–62, 64, 74, 79–80, 91–92, 98, 99, 101, *101–6*, 127, 140–41, 143–46, 147, 160–62; the lost idyll, 5, 10, 11, 18–19, 32, 39, 55, 63; on phoniness, 4–7, 26–27, 54, 55, *67–71;* on psychoanalysis, 35–37, 82, 93, 95, 98–99, 101, 105–6; the serial story, 18, *43–46*, 63, 66, 81; interest in theater, *3*, 71–72; on war, 15–23, *49–53*, 65

WORKS: NOVEL AND COLLECTIONS
Catcher in the Rye, The, 6, 21, 23, *25–30*, 63, 65, 107, 123, 124, 126, 127, 129, 156; preparation for, *23–30*
Franny and Zooey, 65, 66, 82, 128, 135, 152, *157–59*
Nine Stories, 6, *31–34*, 38, 66, 127, 133, 135, 136, 143, 145–46

Works (*Continued*)
*Raise High the Roof Beam,
Carpenters and Seymour: An
Introduction,* 65, 90, 128

WORKS: STORIES
"Blue Melody," 3, 31, 106
"Both Parties Concerned," 6, 24,
27–28
"Boy in France, A," 18, *19–22*
"Elaine," 6, *7–9*
"De Daumier-Smith's Blue
Period," 31, *56–60*, 62, 127,
139–40, 149–52
"Down at the Dinghy," 31, 32, 33,
46–49, 64, 65, 127, 136–37, 153
"For Esme—with Love and
Squalor," 15, 16, 31, 32, 34, *49–53*, 106,107, 125, 135, 138–39,
146
"Franny," 64, 66, *67–75*, 80–89,
91, 128, 153–56, 161
"Girl I Knew, A," 31
"Go See Eddie," 6, 7
"Hang of It, The," 5, 6, 15, 16
"Hapworth 16, 1924," 25, 65, 67,
74, 76, 90, 91, *107–8*, 128, 134
"Heart of a Broken Story, The," 5,
9, *12–15*, 77
"I'm Crazy," 5, 6, 24, 25, *28–30*,
124
"Inverted Forest, The," 5, 6, 31,
65
"Just Before the War with the
Eskimos," 31, 34, *41–43*, 125,
135, 137
"Last and Best of the Peter Pans,
The," 24
"Last Day of the Last Furlough,"
6, *18–19*, 24, 124
"Laughing Man, The," 31, 32,
43–46, 107, 137
"Long Debut of Lois Taggett,
The," 6, *7–9*, 65
"Ocean Full of Bowling Balls,
The," 25
"Once a Week Won't Kill You," 6

"Perfect Day for Bananafish, A,"
6, 31, 32, 33, *34–38*, 41, 48, 64,
65, 93, 125, 134, 135, 146, 153
"Personal Notes on an
Infantryman," 6, 15, 16
"Pretty Mouth and Green My
Eyes," *53–56*, 135, 137
"Raise High the Roof Beam,
Carpenters," 63, 64, 74, *91–100*,
101, 102, 128, 153, 154, 155
"Sandwich Has No Mayonnaise,
This," 6, *18–23*, 25
"Seymour: An Introduction," 3,
12, 65, 66, 67, 74, 76, 77, 91,
100–106, 107, 128, 134
"Slight Rebellion off Madison," 6,
24–28, 124
"Soft-Boiled Sergeant," 6, *16–18*,
49
"Stranger, The," 18, *22–23*, 24
"Teddy," 32, 34, *60–62*, 64, 65,
79, 135, 136, 139–41, 146, 154
"Uncle Wiggily in Connecticut,"
31, 34, *38–41*, 48, 64, 65, 125,
135, 137, 146
"Varioni Brothers, The," 5, 6, *9–12*, 65
"Young Folks, The," *4–5*, 6, 124
"Zooey," 64, 66, 73, 74, *75–89*,
91, 94, 98, 101, 102, 128, 153,
155, 161

Salinger, Margaret Ann, 127
Salinger, Matthew, 127
Salinger, Sol, 122
Sappho, 97
Saturday Evening Post, 5, 124
Saturday Review, 126
Scow, John, 16
Shakespeare, William, 70, 122;
Hamlet, 100
Slethaug, G. E., 71
Sri Ramakrishna, 127
Stone, Edward, 59, *149–52*
Story, 3, 125
Sublette, Jack R., 24
Suzuki, Dr., 79

Swami Nikhilananda, 127
Synge, John Millington, *The Playboy of the Western World*, 64

Time, 119
Tolstoy, Leo, 70

University of Kansas City Review, 5, 124
Updike, John, 63, 66, 153–54, 155

Way of a Pilgrim, The, 73, 81, 85, 154, *157–59*

Welty, Eudora, *The Golden Apples*, 32
Wenke, Joseph, 119–30
Wiebe, Dallas E., 37

Van Gogh, Vincent, 85, 100
Vonnegut, Kurt, Jr., 12; *Slaughterhouse–Five*, 15

Zanuck, Darryl, 125
Zen Koan, 33–34, 97, 104, *143–46*, 160–61

The Author

John Wenke received his B.A. in English from the University of Notre Dame and his M.A. and Ph.D. in English from the University of Connecticut. He has taught at the University of Connecticut and Marquette University, has served for a semester as visiting associate professor at Trinity College in Hartford, and is currently an associate professor of English at Salisbury State University. He has published articles on Thomas Nash, George Washington Harris, Gelett Burgess, James Joyce, J. D. Salinger. He has also published numerous essays on Herman Melville, the most recent of which have appeared in *A Companion to Melville Studies* (1986), *Texas Studies in Literature and Language,* and *Critical Essays on Melville's Moby-Dick* (1991).

The Editor

Gordon Weaver earned his Ph.D. in English and creative writing at the University of Denver, and is currently professor of English at Oklahoma State University. He is the author of several novels, including *Count a Lonely Cadence, Give Him a Stone, Circling Byzantium,* and most recently *The Eight Corners of the World.* His short stories are collected in *The Entombed Man of Thule, Such Waltzing Was Not Easy, Getting Serious, Morality Play,* and *A World Quite Round.* Recognition of his fiction includes the St. Lawrence Award for Fiction (1973), two National Endowment for the Arts fellowships (1974 and 1989), and the O. Henry First Prize (1979). He edited *The American Short Story, 1945–1980: A Critical History* and is currently editor of the *Cimarron Review.* Married and the father of three daughters, he lives in Stillwater, Oklahoma.